North Carolina Slave Narratives

The **John Hope Franklin Series**

in African American History and Culture

Waldo E. Martin Jr. & Patricia Sullivan, editors

North Carolina Slave Narratives

The Lives of Moses Roper, Lunsford Lane, Moses Grandy, & Thomas H. Jones

WILLIAM L. ANDREWS, *General Editor*

David A. Davis, Tampathia Evans, Ian Frederick Finseth,

and Andreá N. Williams, *Editors*

The University of North Carolina Press CHAPEL HILL & LONDON

This book was published with the assistance of
the H. Eugene and Lillian Youngs Lehman Fund
of the University of North Carolina Press.

Library of Congress
Cataloging-in-Publication Data
North Carolina slave narratives : the lives of Moses
Roper, Lunsford Lane, Moses Grandy, and Thomas H.
Jones / William L. Andrews, general editor ; David A.
Davis . . . [et al.], editors.
    p. cm. — (The John Hope Franklin series in African
American history and culture)
Includes bibliographical references.
ISBN-13: 978-0-8078-2821-2 (cloth: alk. paper)
ISBN-10: 0-8078-2821-1 (cloth: alk. paper)
ISBN-13: 978-0-8078-5658-1 (pbk.: alk. paper)
ISBN-10: 0-8078-5658-4 (pbk.: alk. paper)
1. Slaves — North Carolina — Biography. 2. Slavery —
North Carolina. 3. North Carolina — History — 1775-
1865 — Biography. I. Andrews, William L., 1946-
II. Davis, David A. (David Alexander), 1975- III. Series.
E445.N8 .N67 2003
305.5'67'0922756 — dc21
                    2003009249

cloth: 07 06 05 04 03   5 4 3 2 1
paper: 10 09 08 07 06   6 5 4 3 2

To the memory of Blyden Jackson

CONTENTS

ACKNOWLEDGMENTS

The editors are grateful to Natalia Smith, Digitization Librarian
at the University of North Carolina at Chapel Hill, for her help in
preparing the illustrations for this book. David A. Davis would like
to acknowledge the following individuals and institutions for their
generous assistance in researching *The Experience of Rev. Thomas H.
Jones*: John Ernest, University of New Hampshire; William B. Gould IV,
Stanford University School of Law; Laurie Maffly-Kipp, University of
North Carolina at Chapel Hill; Eli Naeher, Lower Cape Fear Historical
Society; North Carolina Collection, University of North Carolina at
Chapel Hill; and Robert W. Woodruff Library Special Collections,
Emory University.

North Carolina Slave Narratives

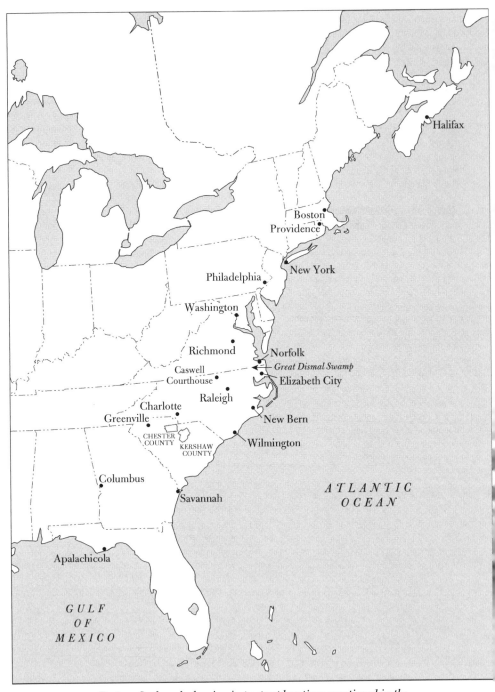

Eastern Seaboard, showing important locations mentioned in the
Roper, Lane, Grandy, and Jones narratives

GENERAL INTRODUCTION
William L. Andrews

In the war of words that presaged the ultimate downfall of slavery in the United States, those affected most by the South's "peculiar institution"—black people themselves—played a central role. The antislavery cause gave most of black America's literary pioneers a ready forum, particularly those who had experienced firsthand the injustice of human bondage. The most popular and lasting African American literary contributions to the abolition movement were the autobiographical narratives of fugitive slaves. Before the close of the eighteenth century, the life stories of African-born slaves, such as James Albert Ukawsaw Gronniosaw and Olaudah Equiano, began to appear in England. In addition to substantial attention and sales in Great Britain, *A Narrative of the Most Remarkable Particulars in the Life of James Albert Ukawsaw Gronniosaw, an African Prince* (1772) and *The Interesting Narrative of the Life of Olaudah Equiano, or Gustavus Vassa, the African* (1789) went through multiple reprint editions in the early United States, indicating a receptive audience for such writing in colonial North America and the early Republic.[1] Not until the 1830s, however, did the antislavery movement in the United States seek purposefully to enlist the talents and energies of black American writers in a national movement to extirpate slavery from the so-called "land of the free." The four North Carolina slave narratives reprinted in this book played key roles in building national, indeed international, indignation against the evils of slavery. The narratives of Moses Roper, Lunsford Lane, Moses Grandy, and Thomas H. Jones also helped lay the groundwork for an African American literary tradition that has inspired some of America's greatest novels, from Harriet Beecher Stowe's *Uncle Tom's Cabin* (1853) to Toni Morrison's *Beloved* (1987) and Charles Johnson's *Middle Passage* (1990).

Before Nat Turner's bloody slave revolt in Southampton, Virginia, in August 1831, most white Americans considered slavery, if a problem at all, as a matter for the South to handle on its own. Four years before the Southampton uprising, the editor of the *Genius of Emancipation*, an early antislavery periodical, estimated that the number of antislavery societies in the South outnumbered those in the North by almost four to one, although the total membership of such societies in the entire United States probably comprised no more than 7,000. Opponents of slavery effected partial measures, such as the abolition of the African slave trade to the United States in 1808, which salved guilty consciences without appreciably affecting the institution, already well established and self-propagating in half the nation by the beginning of the nineteenth century. The majority of those who favored the abolition of slavery espoused a gradualist program of reform or simply opposed the spread of slavery north and west of the Mason-Dixon line. Politicians as different as Thomas Jefferson and Abraham Lincoln thought that the ultimate solution to the problem of slavery was the enforced expatriation of emancipated slaves out of the United States. Meanwhile, the growing minorities of free black residents of northern cities, particularly Philadelphia, New York, and Boston, founded numerous societies for community uplift, sociopolitical debate, and cultural expression during the early decades of the nineteenth century. From 1830 until the end of the Civil War, free African Americans held national conventions in various northern cities, at which antislavery activism was always at the top of the agenda.[2]

Interracial cooperation within the antislavery vanguard was not a high priority among white abolitionists in the early years of the movement. When the American Convention of Abolition Societies met in 1800 to undertake a history of slavery in the United States, no one thought to engage the services of a black author in the writing of this document. African Americans chafed at this indifference on the part of the white friends of freedom and resented the assumption of leadership and spokesmen roles by white converts to antislavery.[3] The first black-run newspaper, *Freedom's Journal*, appeared in New York City on March 16, 1827, editorializing in its initial issue, "We wish to plead our own cause. Too long have others spoken for us." Within two years the Boston agent for *Freedom's Journal*, a black activist named David Walker (c. 1796–1830), published his *Appeal to the Colored Citizens of the World*, now recognized as the most influential African American pamphlet of the antebellum era.[4]

Walker indicted American slavery as nothing less than a monumental and historically unparalleled crime against humanity, for which white Americans would almost certainly atone with their blood. The duty of black people in the South and the North was to prepare themselves, intellectually, psychologically, and economically, for resistance to slavery and racism by any means necessary. "The man who would not fight under our Lord and Master Jesus Christ, in the glorious and heavenly cause of freedom and of God" (14), Walker thundered, had no right to expect deliverance from his chains. But to those who heeded his call Walker promised a renewed sense of manhood, self-respect, and communal and spiritual identity. "Are we MEN!! — I ask you, O my brethren! are we MEN? Did our Creator make us to be slaves to dust and ashes like ourselves? . . . Have we any other Master but Jesus Christ alone?" (18). The implicit answers to these questions infused into antislavery agitation a radical, uncompromising principle that justified a slave's seizing of his freedom as not only his God-given right but his masculine duty to his family and to the enslaved black nation in America. Walker's *Appeal* so alarmed authorities in the South that they were reputed to have put a price on his head while vigorously suppressing his pamphlet wherever it turned up.

Prophet of a militant abolitionism that would eventually defeat American slavery, David Walker was the first important African American writer from North Carolina. A native of Wilmington, he was born free in a seaport city where slaves outnumbered whites two to one. Wilmington and its environs were dependent on slaves' mastery of many skilled trades, including carpentry, masonry, and building design. Slaves also comprised a large proportion of the area's most experienced watermen, who enriched the maritime industries of the Wilmington region but also aided black fugitives heading for freedom in the outlying coves and swamps of the Cape Fear.[5] Perhaps it was the example of the proud and capable slaves of Wilmington that taught David Walker to hate slavery. Perhaps he absorbed the antislavery gospel from the black Methodists with whom he worshiped as a youth. In any case, after arriving in Boston in 1825, the author of the *Appeal* made certain that when he took up his pen, his cry for liberation would be heard in his native state. In August 1830 a Wilmington slave named Jacob Cowan was apprehended and sold to Alabama for circulating hundreds of copies of the *Appeal* to slaves who visited his tavern.[6]

Did one of those contraband pamphlets find its way into the hands of Thomas H. Jones, a local slave dockworker who, like Walker, had contrived to learn to read and write in Wilmington? Was Moses Grandy, enslaved captain of canal boats that ran between the North Carolina coastal ports of Camden and Elizabeth City and Norfolk in southeastern Virginia in the 1820s, spurred on in his quest for freedom by Walker's *Appeal*, which Wilmington police claimed had been widely distributed in North Carolina's ports, particularly New Bern and Elizabeth City?[7] The narratives of Jones and Grandy do not mention Walker, but the spirit of resistance that he championed was rife in the coastal North Carolina slave communities from which Jones and Grandy sprang.

A few months before the appearance of Walker's historic *Appeal*, another black North Carolinian, the enslaved poet George Moses Horton (c. 1797–

c. 1883) of Chatham County, broke onto the national literary scene with the publication of five poems in three different newspapers. On April 4, 1828, the *Lancaster (Mass.) Gazette* printed "Liberty and Slavery," in which the first American slave to use poetry to protest his condition pleaded, "Alas! and am I born for this, / To wear this slavish chain?" The next nine stanzas of controlled, anguished verse testified both to the poet's art and his plangent desire for liberty, "the gift of nature's God!"[8] On July 18, the *Raleigh (N.C.) Register* published a brief sketch of Horton's life along with another poem, "On the Evening and Morning," in which Horton demonstrated his mastery of the heroic couplet. *Freedom's Journal* published "Slavery. By a Carolinian Slave named George Horton" simultaneously with the *Register*'s introduction of Horton to its readers. Three weeks later *Freedom's Journal* took up the cause of Horton's freedom, urging its subscribers to contribute to the poet's purchase price, reputedly $500. In October David Walker made his own donation to his fellow North Carolinian's freedom. A few days later the *Raleigh Register* printed Horton's "On Hearing of the Intention of a Gentleman to Purchase the Poet's Freedom" and announced that the Manumission Society of North Carolina had expressed its own interest in Horton's case.

Despite the efforts of the poet himself to publish his way to freedom, as it were, abetted by serious campaigns within and outside North Carolina to raise the money for his emancipation, George Moses Horton remained a slave until liberated by the invading Union army in April 1865. By that time the self-educated slave was probably North Carolina's most famous living poet. In 1829 he had secured a publisher in Raleigh for his first book, *The Hope of Liberty*, a collection of twenty-one poems, the first book published by an African American in the South. The volume was twice reprinted in the North by abolitionists intent on using Horton's case, as well as his poetic protests against slavery, as support for the antislavery movement. Growing resistance in the South to manumission in the wake of the Nat Turner revolt blocked Horton's attempts to buy his freedom in the 1830s. He persevered, nevertheless, as a poet, publishing in 1845 *The Poetical Works of George M. Horton, the Colored Bard of North-Carolina*, in Hillsborough, just a few miles north of Chapel Hill, where Horton, whose master allowed him to hire his time at the state university, had become something of an institution because of his facility at composing romantic verse for the university's students to send to their sweethearts.[9]

Did Lunsford Lane, a Raleigh slave with yearnings for liberty as intense as Horton's in the late 1820s and early 1830s, find a copy of *The Hope of Liberty* or read about Horton in the *Raleigh Register*? Is it significant that Weston R. Gales, son of the publisher of *The Hope of Liberty* and Horton's business agent, also co-signed a letter of recommendation for Lunsford Lane, which the former slave took with him in the spring of 1841 when he left Raleigh in search of a new home for himself and his family in New York? Nowhere in his narrative does Lane mention Horton, or David Walker for that matter, nor do the narratives of Grandy or Jones indicate that either man had read Horton's work. But two factors — the remarkable publicity given to Horton's case within the popular media of his native state and the ambitions of Lane, Grandy, and Jones to gain their freedom and that of their families through means similar to Horton's, that is, through payment rather than escape — make one wonder whether the example of Horton, if not his writings, along with the notoriety of Walker and his text, helped to inspire in North Carolina slaves such as the four men whose narratives appear in this volume a determination to attain their liberty.

In the late 1830s, as the American antislavery movement became increasingly aggressive in its attacks on slavery as a monstrous evil, the antislavery press began to seek out narratives by fugitive slaves who could document convincingly what they had experienced or witnessed in the South. As Theodore Dwight, secretary of the American Anti-Slavery Society, observed in an 1837 letter, "the north is so blinded it will not *believe* what we [abolitionists] say about slavery," but "facts and testimony as to the actual condition of the Slaves," Dwight asserted, "would thrill the land with Horror."[10] Up to this time the autobiographies of former slaves had been more concerned with the slavery of sin than with the sin of slavery. But as the antislavery press expanded in the late 1830s and antislavery leaders took on the mantle of crusaders rather than mere reformers, the climate was ready for narratives that would sound the depths of slavery's corruption and expose slaveholders for "acting more like devils than accountable men," as David Walker contended (19).

A Narrative of the Adventures and Escape of Moses Roper, from American Slavery (1837) gave the antislavery movement in England and America exactly what it wanted — a hard-hitting tour of slavery as a visitation of hell on earth, conducted by someone who had seen and suffered it all but who had survived to tell his story in a manner likely to evoke both credence and sympathy. The British clergyman who wrote the preface to Roper's narrative solicited curious and prurient readers by promising them a kind of pious pornography: "There is no vice too loathsome — no passion too cruel or remorseless, to be engendered by this horrid system [of slavery]. It brutalizes all who administer it, and seeks to efface the likeness of God, stamped on the brow of its victims. It makes the former class demons, and reduces the latter to the level of brutes." The twenty-two-year-old author of the *Narrative of the Adventures and Escape of Moses Roper* delivered what his white antislavery sponsors desired. The first scene of Roper's *Narrative* details in a shocking but deadpan manner how the author, born in Caswell County, North Carolina, the son of his master and one of his master's slaves, barely escaped death at the hands of his master's enraged wife. Light-skinned and cooperative as a boy, Moses was trained for the comparatively mild duties of a domestic slave. But when he was sold to a South Carolina cotton planter whom Roper identifies only as Mr. Gooch, teenaged Moses was put to work in the fields, where he was subjected to floggings almost daily. Roper's portrait of Gooch as an unmitigated sadist gave American antislavery literature the first example of what would become in Stowe's horrendous creation Simon Legree a distillation of all that black America despised in the arrogant Anglo-Saxon: brutality, violence, hypocrisy, and tyranny.[11]

Portraying himself as a cruelly abused youth whose only offenses were his multiple attempts to escape the torture Gooch fiendishly inflicted on him, Roper offers the irony of a slave much more civilized than his master. In this Roper anticipates a rhetorical reversal discernible in more famous slave narratives of the 1840s, in which fugitive slaves are portrayed as high-minded and heroic while their masters exemplify degeneracy and savagery. In several other respects the *Narrative of the Adventures and Escape of Moses Roper* can be seen as a pioneering text in the slave narrative tradition. Antislavery adherents in the 1830s regularly inveighed against slaveholders for their sexual violations of enslaved women, but Roper was the first slave narrator to explain how a light complexion could be both a curse and a blessing for a slave. As a boy, Roper learned that his light skin could arouse rancor in envious whites; later, as a confirmed escape artist, the resourceful fugitive proved adept at exploiting his color for the purpose of disguise. Recounting his many escape attempts allows Roper to introduce various adventures he had on the back roads and byways of the rural and urban South, which in turn reveal in the fugitive a mix of innocence and wiliness reminiscent of the picaresque hero of European and American literature. What makes Roper unusual in the picaresque tradition is his insistence that his trickery, however brilliant, arose from necessity, not from design. So nervous is Roper about giving the wrong impression to his reader that he apologizes from the outset of his story for certain aspects of his conduct on the road "which I now deeply deplore." "The ignorance in which the poor slaves are kept by their masters, preclude almost the possibility of their being alive to any moral duties," Roper assures his reader. Whether Roper truly regretted his duplicitous behavior while trying to elude his captors, or whether he simply was not sure that his readers would accept the survival ethic and alternate morality of the slave community in the hostile white American South, is unclear. For all he unveiled of human depravity in whites, Roper seems to have been unsure about how much he could celebrate human ingenuity among blacks in the United States.

A Narrative of the Adventures and Escape of Moses Roper, from American Slavery was the prototype for the classic American slave narratives of the 1840s as authored by internationally renowned fugitives such as Frederick Douglass, William Wells Brown, Henry Bibb, and James W. C. Pennington. Less self-revealing and rhetorically contentious than its more famous successors, Roper's *Narrative* set a template, nevertheless, on which its literary descendants could build and capitalize in later years. Although his autobiography did not bestow on Roper the fame in the United States that the narratives of Douglass, Brown, Bibb, and Pennington gave these men a decade later, the publication of Roper's *Narrative* in London in 1837 was by no means a small-gauge event. Within twenty years Roper's story had become one of the hardiest sellers on the antislavery book list, going through ten British and American editions, including a translation into Celtic, by 1856. A veteran antislavery orator in England, where he reckoned he had given 2,000 speeches by 1844,[12] Roper might have become more widely known in the United States had he returned to his homeland after the publication of his *Narrative*. Instead, he remained in England, marrying in 1839, before moving to Canada in 1844. Little is known of his life and work after he arrived in Canada.

In the summer of 1842 the second North Carolina slave narrative appeared in the United States, chronicling a dimension of slavery seldom explored in antislavery writing up to that time: the experience of an urban slave. The horrendous atrocities and punishing daily routine in the cotton fields that Roper reported tore the mask off the dreamy moonlight-and-magnolias image of the southern plantation marketed by early defenders of slavery. *The Narrative of Lunsford Lane* reaffirmed Roper's descriptions of the plight of rural bondmen while showing how even the most favored of slaves — those who lived in urban centers — still longed for freedom. Acknowledging that he was "comparatively happy" during his enslavement and expressing profound thanks to God "that I was not born a plantation slave, nor even a house servant under what is termed a hard and cruel master," Lunsford Lane presents himself as a man with no ax to grind against slavery and as studiedly impartial, particularly about the white men who had claimed him as property. With regard to his portrait of slavery, Lane informs his reader, "I have dwelt as little as possible upon the dark side — have spoken mostly of the bright." Bending over backward to be fair to slavery as he had known it, Lane characterizes himself from the outset of his story as the most tactful and equitable of slave narrators, a man who can be trusted, especially by those who may have found the barbarism recorded by Roper so shocking as to blame the black victim, rather than his white persecutors, for such horrors.

The Narrative of Lunsford Lane is, essentially, a success story, although the successes Lane earned for himself as a slave came at an increasingly higher price as he progressed steadily toward freedom. Lane was born in Raleigh in 1803 to the owner of three large plantations outside the city. Because his mother was a house servant in Raleigh, her son never joined the rank-and-file who worked on his master's plantations. By the time he was a teenager, Lunsford had been installed in the relatively cushy position of driver of his master's carriage. What forestalled complacency, however, was his awareness, itself born of his comparative advantages, of how much more his master's children could expect from life. Lane was all too aware of how quickly what he had might be lost. Having grown up in an intact, though enslaved, family made him all the more anxious about the possibility that somehow he might be sold away from his kin. Lane seems to suggest that the more favored slaves such as himself might be, the more fearful they were about their future. Lane's *Narrative* predicates its story of a slave's unlikely economic rise on a psychology of daily anxiety in a slave whose comparative good fortune had given him hope and purpose, which enslavement rendered all the more precious — and precarious.

Ambitious, industrious, and politic, Lunsford Lane decided as a young man that the only way to protect himself from the vagaries of slavery was to buy his way out. Consistent with his conservative disposition and devotion to the middle-class work ethic, he apparently never considered running away. A shrewd operator who possessed remarkable entrepreneurial skills, Lane describes how he adapted the code of Benjamin Franklin, white America's archetypal man-on-the-make, to his situation as an upwardly mobile city slave intent on freedom:

> Ever after I entertained the first idea of being free, I had endeavored so to conduct myself as not to become obnoxious to the white inhabitants, knowing as I did their power, and their hostility to the colored people.

The two points necessary in such a case I had kept constantly in mind. First, I had made no display of the little property or money I possessed, but in every way I wore as much as possible the aspect of poverty. Second, I had never appeared to be even so intelligent as I really was. This all colored people at the south, free and slaves, find it peculiarly necessary to their own comfort and safety to observe.

Comments such as these indicate that, however accommodating Lane may have appeared while a slave, he had a private agenda too, which, if not in outright opposition to slavery, was subversive of its primary tenet, the absolute superiority of white over black.

Lane's economic strategy proved both a resounding success and a galling failure. His diligence and business acumen enabled him, by the time he was only twenty-two years old, to amass an astonishing sum, $1,000, to pay his mistress for his liberty. But when he set out to use the same methods to purchase his wife and children, he was stymied. His story comes to an eventual happy ending, but only after Lane is divested of his illusions about how conservative behavior, the acquisition of property, and connections among supposedly paternalistic whites would exempt a proper Negro from the rigors and injustices of slavery and racism. Readers of Ralph Ellison's novel *Invisible Man* (1952) will recognize in Lane, before his liberating disillusionment at the end of his *Narrative*, a forerunner of Ellison's naive hero, who also must learn that role-playing to gain an advantage against white supremacy can easily lead to co-optation by the very system one is trying to exploit.

By 1848 the enthusiastic reception of *The Narrative of Lunsford Lane* required three additional reprintings of the book by his Boston publisher. Lane's abiding status in and importance to the antislavery movement are evidenced by the appearance of a full-length, white-authored biography, *Lunsford Lane; or, Another Helper from North Carolina*, in Boston in 1863.[13] The popularity of Lane's narrative may have been a factor in the publication of Moses Grandy's a year after Lane's first came out. Published initially in London in 1843 while Grandy was on an antislavery lecture tour, the *Narrative of the Life of Moses Grandy; Late a Slave in the United States of America* was quickly reprinted three times in 1844 by another Boston antislavery publisher. That Grandy and Lane were both published by antislavery presses in the same city and also claimed Boston as their place of residence when their narratives appeared suggests that these two North Carolina expatriates may well have met each other, perhaps on the antislavery circuit or in

Boston's lively African American community. In any case, their narratives have much in common. Each recounts the life of an industrious, persevering enslaved family man from North Carolina, who attained his freedom in accordance with the laws of the slavocracy, but not before having been subjected to varying degrees of fraud, humiliation, and threat designed to frustrate the aspirations of even the most obliging and accommodating of slaves. The antislavery movement's strategy of publishing narratives by men like Lane and Grandy seems also to have stemmed from a common purpose: to counter the pervasive proslavery image of the slave as incompetent, shiftless, and dependent. Lane and Grandy stand out as exemplars of the white American work ethic, worthy of the admiration and sympathy of northern middle-class America.

Historian David Cecelski has called the *Narrative of the Life of Moses Grandy* "the most comprehensive firsthand account ever written of slavery and African American maritime life in the South."[14] Born in Camden, a small port on the Pasquotank River in northeastern North Carolina about forty miles from the Atlantic Ocean, Grandy worked on the water as a river ferryman and lighter pilot, a sailor on schooners on the Albemarle Sound, and a canal-boat captain in the Dismal Swamp. Grandy's matter-of-fact storytelling does not linger over the hardships of the slave waterman's life, perhaps because whatever trouble the former slave endured following the sea was counterbalanced by the relative freedom that an enslaved waterman enjoyed and by the profit he stood to earn if he hired his time successfully, as Grandy did. Two masters promised the enterprising Grandy his freedom once he paid them off. But in each case, after raising the required sum, he was rebuffed, his masters pocketing his money. One of the most remarkable features of Grandy's narrative is the detailed accounts he gives of the arguments he had with the white men who cheated him. Pausing in his normally terse narration of his life, Grandy dramatizes several scenes in which he refused to submit tamely to his masters' prevarication and double-dealing. These scenes portray a slave in a striking posture: without threatening his master physically, Grandy goes on the verbal offensive, demanding his rights in accordance with a contract, which to his mid-nineteenth-century northern readers, especially those males who believed that a man's word should be his bond, would have been all but sacred. Emboldened perhaps by the independence and self-confidence he had gained from his life on the water, Grandy shows how he converted instances of potential humiliation into opportunities for public shaming of the men who had robbed him. In a southern court of law, Grandy had no voice, of course, but his narrative shows how effectively he appealed to the court of public opinion, even in the South. Because he skillfully mobilized white male peer pressure on his master, the slave ultimately won the verdict he sought—freedom.

The *Narrative of the Life of Moses Grandy* relates slavery's day-to-day inhumanity and its more sensational cruelties in the course of the narrator's reflections on more than forty years in bondage. After gaining his freedom, Grandy moved north, but unlike Lane and indeed most slave narrators of his era, Grandy refused to rhapsodize over life in the so-called Free States. "When I first went to the Northern States, which is about ten years ago, although I was free as to the law, I was made to feel severely the difference between persons of different colours. No black man was admitted to the same seats in churches with the whites, nor to the inside of public conveyances, nor into street coaches or cabs: we had to be content with the decks of steam-boats in all weathers, night and day, —not even our wives or children being allowed to go below, however it might rain, or snow, or freeze; in various other ways, we were treated as though we were of a race of men below the whites." Crediting abolitionists for ameliorating the worst of these practices, Grandy makes a point of stating the continuing threat of proslavery mobs and of legal sanction for the seizure and sale of "any coloured person who is said to be a slave" in the North. The former slave's prescription for combating such repression is characteristically conservative. Applauding the abolitionists for their agitation, he trusts that his fellow blacks will be accepted "on the same footing as our fellow citizens" when northern whites "see we can and do conduct ourselves with propriety." This is exactly what Grandy as narrator does in recounting the story of his life. Anticipating the counsel of Booker T. Washington to aspiring black Americans in the late nineteenth century, Moses Grandy, an early voice of the black bourgeoisie in the United States (as was Lane), closes his narrative with a deferential bow to white America's middle-class mores and profuse thanks to whites near and far, especially "our untiring friends, the abolitionists," who have helped black people get free or advance themselves in freedom. Grandy the slave— self-reliant, tough-minded, and demanding in his dealings with whites— softens and fades into a more ingratiating freeman by the end of the narrative, no doubt to leave a favorable impression on whites from whom Grandy hoped to secure contributions for the purchase of still-enslaved members of his family. Part of what makes Grandy, as well as Lane, intriguing is the question that is often asked of Washington as well: how much of what we see in these men's autobiographies is a mask—the image they wanted their white readers to have of upwardly mobile black men—and how much is real?

A glance at the title of the first edition of Thomas H. Jones's autobiography, *Experience and Personal Narrative of Uncle Tom Jones; Who Was for Forty Years a Slave*, indicates how important image-making was to the publishers of Jones's autobiography when it first appeared in Boston and New York in 1854. The immense readership that kept *Uncle Tom's Cabin* (1852) selling briskly two years after its initial publication is the most obvious reason why Jones's publishers sought to identify him with the pious, self-sacrificial hero of Stowe's novel. Other than similar first names and a strong Christian faith, however, mid-nineteenth-century readers would have found few affinities between Thomas H. Jones, the formerly enslaved stevedore-preacher of Wilmington, North Carolina, and Stowe's idealized Negro. That does not seem to have dampened enthusiasm for subsequent editions of Jones's autobiography. In 1857 a second, somewhat revised version of Jones's story came out in Worcester, Massachusetts, under the title *The Experience of Thomas H. Jones: Who Was a Slave for Forty-three Years*, featuring a likeness of Jones as a well-dressed, dignified freeman. Selling well through the Civil War years, Jones's autobiography remained popular even after slavery was abolished in the United States, as attested by reprintings in 1868, 1871, 1880, and 1885. Few antebellum slave narratives remained in print after the downfall of slavery. That Jones's autobiography continued to thrive makes it one of the most long-lived of all the slave narratives published in the nineteenth century.

A likely reason for the enduring appeal of Jones's narrative is his engrossing account of how he learned to read and write as a boy while working in his Wilmington master's general store. Nine years before Jones's narrative first appeared, the *Narrative of the Life of Frederick Douglass* (1845) had told a similar story of a slave boy who, in defiance of his master's commands, managed to learn his letters on the streets of Baltimore in a plucky and inventive fashion that endeared him to thousands of readers in the United States and abroad. Thus the linkage of freedom to the acquisition of literacy was forged in the slave narrative. Jones followed Douglass in portraying his own dedication, as a slave boy on his own, to an incipient faith that somehow literacy would lead to freedom. Jones's account of learning to read and write, however, is more suspenseful than Douglass's—and more painful and violent. The struggle for knowledge establishes Jones, even in boyhood, as a battler, willing to face down a disdainful white boy and an outraged, accusing master in order to guard his access to learning. Unlike Moses Roper, who apologizes to his reader for lying when his route to freedom was threatened by whites, Jones unabashedly recounts the canny deceptions he used to defend himself against his intimidating master.

Through learning to read, Jones is converted to Christianity, a process that takes on noteworthy political ramifications as the youth reaches his manhood. Several black churchmen, slave and free, encourage and assist Jones in his quest for salvation, while whites provide at best behind-the-scenes support. Jones's master is as passionately opposed to his slave's becoming a Christian as he was to his becoming educated. Although by the early nineteenth century many slaveholders in the urban South had learned to accept their slaves' active participation in evangelical churches, as long as their faith did not undermine the system of slavery, few masters granted their Negroes complete spiritual equality as Christians.[15] Jones's master discerned a challenge to his authority in his young slave's determination to worship where and when his conscience dictated. The conflict between master and slave over Jones's commitment to conscience and to the African American religious community in Wilmington that sustained him through many subsequent trials and tragedies reminds us of the spiritual and psychological resources that black Christianity in the antebellum South accorded believers like Thomas Jones.

Prior to 1885, Jones's autobiographies depict his life in slavery as progressing from the acquisition of literacy through conversion to Christianity to marriage and ultimate freedom. The climax of these versions of Jones's life comes when he escapes from Wilmington in 1849 to join his family, which he had sent ahead of him, in Boston. Only hinted at in the early editions of his life story, Jones's ministry in slavery seemed sufficiently important to him in 1885, when he was probably more than eighty years old, that he added a second part to his autobiography, where, instead of describing his life in freedom, he returns to his young manhood in antebellum North Carolina to give an account of his career as a slave preacher. This decision allowed Jones to preserve one of the most informative firsthand accounts of the religious practices of slaves and of instances of whites' worshiping with blacks in the slaveholding South ever published in the nineteenth century. Because only the final edition of Jones's autobiography contains both the story of his struggle for freedom and his reminiscences of his preaching career in slavery, the 1885 version of *The Experience of Rev. Thomas H. Jones, Who Was a Slave for Forty-three Years* is reprinted in full in this volume.

Although the narratives of Moses Roper, Lunsford Lane, Moses Grandy, and Thomas H. Jones were each well received and widely distributed in their own time, they have not been as well remembered or extensively read today as the last major slave narrative written by a North Carolinian in the slavery era, Harriet Jacobs's *Incidents in the Life of a Slave Girl* (1861). This anonymously authored autobiography by an escapee from Edenton never achieved even a second printing in the nineteenth century, but since its authentication in the early 1980s it has become one of the most celebrated and studied texts in African American literature. Jacobs's compelling reconstruction of her experience in slavery, together with her insights into sexuality, power, and the conflicted relationship of Edenton's interbred white and black communities, makes *Incidents* as important a contribution to North Carolina's distinguished library of slave narratives as the four texts included in this volume. But unlike the work of her four male contemporaries from her home state, Jacobs's autobiography exists today in multiple reprint editions that are so readily available as to obviate the need to reprint *Incidents* in this volume too.[16]

No other southern state can match the contemporary impact or continuing import of black North Carolina's contribution to American literature during the slavery era. None of North Carolina's white writers of the first half of the nineteenth century can claim nearly the audience that black North Carolina writers, from David Walker and George Moses Horton to Harriet Jacobs, have today. Was the extraordinary literary production of black North Carolina before 1865 attributable not solely to the talents and determination of these writers but also to the conditions from which they emerged? Was slavery in North Carolina, as experienced by Moses Roper, Lunsford Lane, Moses Grandy, and Thomas Jones, of a character sufficiently different from the institution as practiced elsewhere in the South that we might consider these four men somehow less disadvantaged by their enslavement and better prepared to seize the opportunities of freedom, including the literary initiative of the slave narrative? The editors of *North Carolina Slave Narratives* hesitate to speculate on this question, since there is no compelling reason to assume that the experiences of Roper, Lane, Grandy, and Jones in slavery can be generalized throughout an entire state. It is difficult to draw general conclusions about slavery as an institution based on accounts of enslavement as varied as those of these four unusual men. We also doubt whether the severity of an individual's experience of slavery would have any necessary correlation to a person's decision to write a narrative about his or her life in bondage. One can find little evidence in the narratives of those who endured slavery that the degree of cruelty exacted by the system materially affected their desire for freedom or, having achieved that, their willingness to denounce the oppressiveness and injustice of slavery. As Rev. James W. C. Pennington, a fugitive from Maryland, wrote in the preface to his autobiography, *The Fugitive Blacksmith* (1849): "The mildest form of slavery, if there be such a form, looking at the chattel principle as the definition of slavery, is comparatively the worst form; for it not only keeps the slave in the most unpleasant apprehension, like a prisoner in chains awaiting his trial; but it actually, in a great majority of cases, where kind masters do exist, trains him under the most favorable circumstances the system admits of, and then plunges him into the worst of which it is capable."[17]

Survivors of slavery in North Carolina published memoirs of their antebellum trials and postbellum triumphs well into the twentieth century. Except for Friday Jones's self-published narrative, *Days of Bondage* (1883), and William Henry Singleton's *Recollections of My Slavery Days* (1922), however, postbellum North Carolina slave narratives still await scholarly attention and a twenty-first-century readership.[18] The oral histories of former slaves from North Carolina, collected during the 1930s when the Federal Writers Project deployed hundreds of interviewers in the South to elicit testimony from African Americans who remembered slavery, make up two substantial volumes in George P. Rawick's *The American Slave: A Composite Autobiography*.[19] John W. Blassingame's *Slave Testimony: Two Centuries of Letters, Speeches, Interviews, and Autobiographies* contains representative samplings of various forms of short life-writing by black people from North Carolina.[20] There is, in short, a much deeper and wider stream of autobiographical writing and witnessing about slavery and freedom by black North Carolinians than can possibly be represented in one book. The aim of *North Carolina Slave Narratives* is simply to offer its readers access to the wellspring of this inexhaustible tradition.

Notes

1. See the Gronniosaw and Equiano narratives in *Pioneers of the Black Atlantic: Five Slave Narratives from the Enlightenment, 1772–1815*, ed. Henry Louis Gates Jr. and William L. Andrews (Washington, D.C.: Civitas, 1998).

2. For further information on pioneering antislavery work by African Americans, see James Oliver Horton and Lois E. Horton, *In Hope of Liberty* (New York: Oxford University Press, 1997), 203–36; Benjamin Quarles, *Black Abolitionists* (New York: Oxford University Press, 1969); and Patrick Rael, *Black Identity and Black Protest in the Antebellum North* (Chapel Hill: University of North Carolina Press, 2002).

3. For race prejudice among early white antislavery leaders, see Gary B. Nash, *Forg-*

ing Freedom (Cambridge, Mass.: Harvard University Press, 1991), and Richard Newman, "The Transformation of American Abolition, 1780s–1830s" (Ph.D. diss., State University of New York, Buffalo, 1998), chaps. 4–5.

4. David Walker, *Walker's Appeal, in Four Articles, Together with a Preamble to the Colored Citizens of the World* (Boston: the Author, 1829). Further quotations from *Walker's Appeal* are taken from this text. For more information on Walker, see Peter Hinks, *To Awaken My Afflicted Brethren: David Walker and the Problem of Antebellum Slave Resistance* (University Park: Pennsylvania State University Press, 1997).

5. See Catherine Bishir, "Black Builders in Antebellum North Carolina," *North Carolina Historical Review* 61 (October 1984): 422–62; Gale Farlow, "Black Craftsmen in North Carolina," *North Carolina Genealogical Society Journal*, pt. 1: 6, no. 1 (Feb. 1985), 2–13; pt. 2: 6, no. 2 (May 1985): 91–103; Lawrence Lee, *The Lower Cape Fear in Colonial Days* (Chapel Hill: University of North Carolina Press, 1965); and David S. Cecelski, *The Waterman's Song: Slavery and Freedom in Maritime North Carolina* (Chapel Hill: University of North Carolina Press, 2001).

6. *Walker's Appeal*, ed. Peter P. Hinks (University Park: Pennsylvania State University Press, 2000), 104.

7. Ibid., 105.

8. All quotations from Horton's verse are from *The Black Bard of North Carolina: George Moses Horton and His Poetry*, ed. Joan R. Sherman (Chapel Hill: University of North Carolina Press, 1997).

9. For biographical information on Horton, see ibid., 1–32, and Richard Walser, *The Black Poet* (New York: Philosophical Books, 1966).

10. Gilbert H. Barnes and Dwight L. Dumond, eds., *Letters of Theodore Dwight Weld, Angelina Grimké Weld and Sarah Grimké, 1822–1844* (New York: Appleton-Century, 1934), 1:390; 2:717.

11. Mia Bay, *The White Image in the Black Mind* (New York: Oxford University Press, 2000), 107–11.

12. C. Peter Ripley, ed., *The Black Abolitionist Papers*, vol. 1, *The British Isles, 1830–1865* (Chapel Hill: University of North Carolina Press, 1985).

13. William G. Hawkins, *Lunsford Lane; or, Another Helper from North Carolina* (Boston: Crosby and Nichols, 1863).

14. Cecelski, *The Waterman's Song*, 27.

15. For a thorough account of the process by which the slaveholding South accommodated itself to the evangelizing of slaves and to their participation in religious life and institutions, see Albert J. Raboteau, *Slave Religion: the "Invisible Institution" in the Antebellum South* (New York: Oxford University Press, 1978), 96–150.

16. Three of the most valuable current editions of *Incidents in the Life of a Slave Girl*

are those edited by Jean Fagan Yellin (Cambridge, Mass.: Harvard University Press, 2000); Nell Irvin Painter (New York: Penguin Putnam, 2000); and Nellie Y. McKay and Frances Smith Foster (New York: Norton, 2001).

17. James W. C. Pennington, *The Fugitive Blacksmith; or, Events in the History of James W. C. Pennington, Pastor of a Presbyterian Church, New York, Formerly a Slave in the State of Maryland, United States* (London: Charles Gilpin, 1849), v.

18. *Days of Bondage: The Autobiography of Friday Jones* was rediscovered and reprinted in 1999 in a facsimile edition, with an introduction by William L. Andrews, by the J. Y. Joyner Library of East Carolina University. Singleton's *Recollections of My Slavery Days*, edited by Katherine Mellen Charron and David S. Cecelski, was published by the North Carolina Department of Cultural Resources in 1999. Among the post–Civil War narratives of slavery and freedom produced by North Carolinians are London Ferebee, *A Brief History of the Slave Life of Rev. L. R. Ferebee, and the Battles of Life, and Four Years of His Ministerial Life* (Raleigh, N.C.: Edwards, Broughton, Printers, 1882); Allen Parker, *Recollections of Slavery Times* (Worcester, Mass.: Chas. W. Burbank, 1895); William Mallory, *Old Plantation Days* ([Hamilton, Ontario]: s.n., [1902?]); Morgan L. Latta, *The History of My Life and Work: Autobiography by Rev. M. L. Latta, A.M., D.D.* (Raleigh, N.C.: the Author, 1903); and William H. Robinson, *From Log Cabin to the Pulpit; or, Fifteen Years in Slavery* (Eau Claire, Wis.: James H. Tifft, 1913). A diary written by William Gould, a fugitive slave from Wilmington, North Carolina, who became a sailor in the U.S. Navy during the Civil War, has been edited by his great-grandson William B. Gould IV under the title *Diary of a Contraband: The Civil War Passage of a Black Sailor* (Stanford: Stanford University Press, 2002).

19. The *North Carolina Narratives* are volumes 14 and 15 in series 2 of *The American Slave: A Composite Autobiography*, 41 vols. (Westport, Conn.: Greenwood, 1972–79). For critical commentary on the oral histories of ex-slaves, see Paul D. Escott, *Slavery Remembered: The Twentieth-Century Slave Narratives* (Chapel Hill: University of North Carolina Press, 1979); and Ira Berlin, Marc Favreau, and Steven F. Miller, eds. *Remembering Slavery* (New York: New Press, 1998).

20. John W. Blassingame, ed. *Slave Testimony* (Baton Rouge: Louisiana State University Press, 1977).

Suggested Reading

Andrews, William L. *To Tell a Free Story: The First Century of Afro-American Autobiography, 1760–1865*. Urbana: University of Illinois Press, 1986.

Ball, Edward. *Slaves in the Family*. New York: Farrar, Straus and Giroux, 1998.

Berlin, Ira. *Many Thousands Gone: The First Two Centuries of Slavery in North America*. Cambridge, Mass.: Belknap Press, 1998.

Bland, Sterling Lecater. *Voices of the Fugitives: Runaway Slave Stories and Their Fictions of Self-Creation.* Westport, Conn.: Greenwood Press, 2000.

Blassingame, John W. *The Slave Community: Plantation Life in the Antebellum South.* New York: Oxford University Press, 1972.

Boles, John B. *Black Southerners, 1619–1869.* Lexington: University Press of Kentucky, 1983.

Bolster, W. Jeffrey. "'To Feel like a Man': Black Seamen in the Northern States, 1800–1860." In *A Question of Manhood: A Reader in U.S. Black Men's History and Masculinity,* edited by Darlene Clark Hine and Earnestine Jenkins, 354–81. Bloomington: Indiana University Press, 1999.

Cecelski, David. *The Waterman's Song: Slavery and Freedom in Maritime North Carolina.* Chapel Hill: University of North Carolina Press, 2001.

Cornelius, Janet Duitsman. *"When I Can Read My Title Clear": Literacy, Slavery, and Religion in the Antebellum South.* Columbia: University of South Carolina Press, 1991.

Crow, Jeffrey J., Paul D. Escott, and Flora J. Hatley. *A History of African Americans in North Carolina.* Raleigh: North Carolina Division of Archives and History, 1992.

Escott, Paul D. *Slavery Remembered: The Twentieth-Century Slave Narratives.* Chapel Hill: University of North Carolina Press, 1979.

Foster, Frances Smith. *Witnessing Slavery: The Development of Ante-bellum Slave Narratives.* 2d ed. Madison: University of Wisconsin Press, 1994.

Franklin, John Hope, and Alfred A. Moss Jr. *From Slavery to Freedom: A History of African Americans.* New York: Knopf, 2000.

Genovese, Eugene D. *Roll, Jordan, Roll: The World the Slaves Made.* New York: Vintage, 1972.

Jacobs, Donald M., ed. *Courage and Conscience: Black and White Abolitionists in Boston.* Bloomington: Indiana University Press, 1993.

Johnson, Guion G. *Ante-bellum North Carolina: A Social History.* Chapel Hill: University of North Carolina Press, 1937.

Miller, Randall M., and John David Smith. *Dictionary of Afro-American Slavery.* Westport, Conn.: Praeger, 1997.

Olney, James. "'I Was Born': Slave Narratives, Their Status as Autobiography and as Literature." In *The Slave's Narrative,* edited by Charles T. Davis and Henry Louis Gates Jr., 148–75. New York: Oxford University Press, 1985.

Ripley, C. Peter, ed. *The Black Abolitionist Papers.* Vol. 1, *The British Isles, 1830–1865.* Chapel Hill: University of North Carolina Press, 1985.

Scarry, Elaine. *The Body in Pain: The Making and Unmaking of the World.* New York: Oxford University Press, 1985.

Starling, Marion Wilson. *The Slave Narrative: Its Place in American History.* 2d ed. Washington, D.C.: Howard University Press, 1988.

Stevenson, Brenda E. *Life in Black and White: Family and Community in the Slave South.* New York: Oxford University Press, 1996.

Thomas, Helen. *Romanticism and Slave Narratives.* Cambridge: Cambridge University Press, 2000.

A Narrative of
the Adventures &
Escape of
Moses Roper

INTRODUCTION

Ian Frederick Finseth

Almost all of the available information about Moses Roper comes from his own account of his life and from a smattering of extant correspondence. Accordingly, we have a reasonably good biographical picture only until he was about the age of twenty-one, when he wrote his autobiography. The historical record trails off a few years later, in the mid-1840s, after Roper withdrew from public view as an antislavery lecturer and moved to Canada with his wife and child.

The known salient facts are these. Moses Roper was born in 1815 in Caswell County, North Carolina, the son of an enslaved woman named Nancy and her legal owner's son-in-law, Henry H. Roper. When the boy was about six, his and his mother's owner—probably a man named John Farley—died, and the slaves were partitioned in the settling of the estate. Though drawn by a "Mr. Fowler," the light-skinned Moses was soon sold to a slave trader in what amounted to an effort to dispose of the living evidence of miscegenation. Thus began a dizzying series of owners and informal masters—no fewer than fifteen, including traders. Most of these figures have been lost to history, but the primary figure was a South Carolina planter named John Gooch, who owned Roper from 1829 to 1832 and inflicted the brutal punishments that helped, ultimately, secure international fame for the memoir of his recalcitrant slave.

After numerous unsuccessful escape attempts, Roper had the good fortune (such as it was) of being sold to a "Mr. Beveridge" of Apalachicola, Florida, who allowed Roper to work as a steward on board one of his steamboats. After Beveridge's bankruptcy, Roper was sold in July 1834 to a "Mr. Register," from whom he soon escaped and then found his way to Savannah, Georgia. In Savannah, Roper managed to ship as a steward aboard the schooner *Fox*, which sailed for New York in August 1834. Determined not to miss a rare opportunity, Roper abandoned the steamboat when it moored at Poughkeepsie, New York, and headed inland. Over the next fifteen months, he worked or sought work in a variety of New England locations, including upstate New York, Vermont, New Hampshire, and Boston (where he signed the constitution of the American Anti-Slavery Society). Having gotten wind of a search being conducted for him, Roper signed up as a steward on the *Napoleon* and sailed for England in November 1835, with a letter of reference from "an eminent American abolitionist."

With the assistance of several British abolitionists and progressive ministers—principally Francis Cox, John Morison, John Scoble, Alexander Fletcher, and Thomas Price—Roper received a formal education at the Hackney and Wallingford boarding schools and then attended University College in London, though he did not take a degree there. Over the next two years, he attended antislavery meetings and delivered numerous speeches (more than 2,000 by his own count) relating his experiences as a slave. Encouraged by his English benefactors, and now well practiced at autobiographical testimony, Roper put his narrative down on paper and published it in 1837. Thanks to brisk sales of the autobiography, Roper's finances became relatively stable, but he was not wealthy enough to fulfill his plan of buying a farm on the Cape of Good Hope. In 1839 he married a Bristol woman named Ann Stephen Price, and in 1844 he moved to Canada with his wife and child. He returned to England at least twice: in 1846 to attend to the publication of another edition of his autobiography and in 1854 to lecture.

The date and circumstances of Roper's death are unknown.

The *Narrative of the Adventures and Escape of Moses Roper* recounts multiple parallel journeys—out of bondage, out of the South, out of darkness, and into a kinder "city of habitation," a state of religious enlightenment and temporal liberty. Along the way, his remarkable geographic odyssey is the physical counterpart of his passage from a childhood of slavery to a promising adulthood as an antislavery lecturer and author. From a historical perspective, moreover, the narrative itself is a transitional text, one that helps us trace important shifts in abolitionist publishing and in the cultural politics of African American resistance to slavery.

In 1838, when the first American edition appeared as a slim eighty-nine-page volume in Philadelphia, slavery was a divisive but not yet consuming issue for the American public. Memories were fading of the contentious debates in 1819 and 1820 over whether Missouri would be admitted as a free or slave state. Although the abolitionist newspaper editor Elijah Lovejoy had been murdered by a proslavery mob in Illinois in 1837, the financial crisis that swept the United States that same year had left many people still preoccupied with their own difficulties. Among mainstream churches, religious opposition to slavery simmered on low heat. Moderately antislavery preachers might lament the institution as an unfortunate "evil" without denouncing slaveholding as an active "sin"—a subtle distinction that downplayed the master's guilt and represented an olive branch of compromise and gradual emancipation. In Philadelphia itself, meanwhile, the year 1838 brought its own distractions: the narrow ratification of the new Pennsylvania Constitution, the great fire at Chestnut Street Wharf, and the local publication of *The Posthumous Papers of the Pickwick Club* by a promising young author named Charles Dickens.

Nonetheless, the printing of Moses Roper's autobiography in the City of Brotherly Love—and its regional distribution by the firm Merrihew and Gunn—reveals a significance beyond the text's immediate purpose. It symbolized a broader trend in the war of words spawned by slavery. Since the eighteenth century, the antislavery movement in England had been publishing or promoting a number of influential slave narratives—most notably those of James Albert Ukawsaw Gronniosaw, Ottobah Cugoano, and Olaudah Equiano[1]—along with major abolitionist texts by such writers as James Ramsay, Thomas Clarkson, and James Stephen.[2] Yet with the abolition of the Atlantic slave trade by 1807, and with the undeniable momentum of British antislavery agitation (Parliament would vote in 1833 to outlaw non-indigenous slavery in the British empire), the primary battleground began to shift toward the United States, where the South found retrenchment more attractive than liberalization. The publication landscape shifted accordingly. The 1820s and 1830s saw more and more abolitionist periodicals springing up in American cities; antislavery societies issued an increasing number of resolutions and declarations; and sympathetic publishers and tract associations began seeking a broader market for the autobiographical testimony of African Americans. Into this charged climate arrived the narrative of Moses Roper, published in London in 1837 and crossing the Atlantic, figuratively, a year later. At that point, few people knew of Frederick Douglass, who would not escape from slavery until September 1838, and the earthquake of *Uncle Tom's Cabin* was more than a decade away—but momentum was building.[3] From our historical vantage point, we can see Roper's autobiography as one of several early slave narratives whose publication history signaled a broadening of the American front in the campaign against human bondage.

In literary terms, the expanding number of published texts chronicling the lives of fugitive or former slaves already constituted, by the 1830s, a recognizable tradition or genre. At times, slave narrators would allude to, draw from, or explicitly reference earlier texts, self-consciously positioning themselves within a community of writers extending through time and space. More fundamentally, the tradition coheres as such by virtue of the common experiences, thematic preoccupations, and figurative language that link together individual narratives. Yet what makes a particular slave narrative interesting—beyond, of course, its intrinsic historical and testimonial value and the harrowing human drama it recounts—is its idiosyncratic relationship to the "slave narrative," the variations it plays on a given theme. Like any other example of a genre, the *Narrative of the Adventures and Escape of Moses Roper* both follows and resists generic convention.

The narrative's relation to the tradition's mainstream can be fairly quickly sketched out. First, Roper's motivation for telling his story differed little, in its essence, from that of other antebellum slave narrators. Above all, he wrote "with the view of exposing the cruel system of slavery." More implicitly, he wanted to demonstrate the worth of an individual African American life (and by extension the collective promise of the African American community) and to make clear that the "degraded" life of slaves brought shame to the masters rather than the oppressed. Along with other narrators, Roper describes a terribly precarious existence, in which a person unshielded by the law is buffeted by ungovernable circumstances and unforeseeable events: the selling of family members, the whims of owners, the paranoid vigilance of a slave society. By dint of perseverance, perhaps the defining trait of slave narrators, Roper manages to escape—and yet his experience of freedom, for all the joy he feels, is characteristically mixed. He discovers that racism and the possibility of legal recapture have followed him northward. He regrets that his family and friends still languish in servitude. He avows his love for his country and its ideals, disclaiming any desire to insult "the land of my birth." He applies himself to his own moral and religious development and serves the antislavery cause by publishing his autobiography. In its own way, each of the texts included in this anthology tells a similar story, a story of freedom shadowed by almost unbelievable hardship.

But would that story find a sympathetic audience? Since many contemporary readers did not automatically accept either the specific claims or the general authority of an African American narrator, Roper and his antislavery patrons made a point of establishing the text's reliability. The authenticating strategies they employed were stock-in-trade for antislavery publishing. Assure the reader of the narrator's personal probity: Roper's letters of reference "bear unequivocal witness to his sobriety, intelligence, and honesty." Assure the reader that the text comes straight from the source: "It is his own production, and carries with it internal evidence of truth." Claim the high ground of reportorial objectivity: "[T]he facts related here do not come before the reader unsubstantiated by collateral evidence, nor highly colored to the disadvantage of cruel taskmasters." More subtly, acknowledge, for the sake of that objectivity, the limits of one's knowledge: "I had no means of ascertaining the truth of" a particular story. Suggest that the text, for the sake of decency, actually withholds information: "Many instances [of cruelty] . . . are too disgusting to appear in this narrative." Refer to the living testimony of the scarred body: "The marks of this [punishment] still remain upon me."

In general, several factors prompted this defensiveness on the part of slave narrators and their allies: a degree of skepticism on the part of a white reading public conditioned by racial prejudice to doubt the truthfulness of black people, a drum-beat of criticism emanating from proslavery and prosouthern quarters, and the publication of fictionalized narratives such as Richard Hildreth's *The Slave; or, Memoirs of Archy Moore* (1836).[4] Modern scholars, however, have established the basic veracity of the vast majority of American slave testimonies, notwithstanding the known or suspected "contributions" of editors (or transcribers). In the case of Roper's narrative, both the core account and most of the details withstand scrutiny, and the text is largely free of the sort of stylistic embellishing that can generate uncertainty about who is really telling the story. Nonetheless, in several places one senses that the hand of someone other than Roper himself has taken the pen. These are passages in which richly efflorescent commentary breaks through the earthy, matter-of-fact tone of the story—where one hears a rhetorical intensification and a heightened emotionalism, specifically as to family relationships and religious faith. For instance: "Should that Divine Being who made of one flesh all the kindreds of the earth, see fit that I should again clasp [my family members] to my breast, and see in them the reality of free men and free women, how shall I, a poor mortal, be enabled to sing a strain of praise sufficiently appropriate to such a boon from heaven?" This is not to deny that Roper could have written such a passage, or to suggest that it is untrue to his experience if he did not write it; the aim here is to call attention to moments of striking contrast between the narrative's generally unassuming style and its sporadic bursts of forceful eloquence.

In a number of central respects, then, the narrative of Moses Roper stands squarely within the slave narrative tradition as it had evolved by the late 1830s. Yet it is undeniably a unique text that reflects the individual experience and worldview of its author. Taking it on these terms enables us to appreciate how the narrative was breaking new ground and heralding important developments in the genre as slave narrators and antislavery publishers responded to the deteriorating crisis between the states.

To begin with, Roper tells a tale of horrific violence. Hardly a page goes by without the description of disciplinary torture or physical deprivation. Roper's very life started in violence, with the presumed rape or sexual coercion of his mother by Henry Roper. On the first page of his account, he tells us that his mother's mistress (Mrs. Roper, the wife of his father) came with a "large club stick and knife" to murder newborn Moses, fruit of the master's infidelity, and is only prevented from doing so by the intervention of Roper's grandmother. As we read through the text, the beatings and the punishments accumulate, and Roper even provides two illustrations as aids to our imagination. Of course, the institution of slavery depended on violence, and its presence in slave narratives should surprise no one. But Roper's text stands out for the frequency and severity of the violence; he seems at times almost to dwell on it, with a calm literalism that might be called graphic understatement. Even his assurance that he wants to spare us the more gruesome episodes simply invites us to imagine something worse. Moreover, the plain style effectively conveys the routine brutality of slaveholding. If a reader wondered whether slavery constituted an "evil" or a "sin," Roper's testimony might help to resolve the question.

The high level of violence in Roper's narrative was part of a developing trend in the literature of American slavery. Increasingly, narrators, authors, and editors wanted to shock readers out of any complacency they might feel. Where narratives of the late eighteenth and early nineteenth century typically gave more attention to the spiritual and social harm caused by the institution, those of the antebellum era represented a turn inward, toward the experience of the individual. The psychological, emotional, and physical suffering of a narrator or protagonist assumed greater importance. For a reading culture nourished on romanticism's exaltation of the individual and on the dramatic emotionalism of sentimental literature, few spectacles excited keener disgust than that of a vulnerable human body subjected to vicious treatment (lustful or violent or both). In the 1850s audiences shuddered at the outrages perpetrated by Harriet Beecher Stowe's Simon Legree; in the late 1840s at the cold-bloodedness of Frederick Douglass's Austin Gore; and in the early 1840s at the sadistic stamina of Roper's Mr. Gooch.[5] In each case, it is the persecution of an individual victim—the physical abuse of a feeling, sentient being—that defines the villain.

We can also identify in the violence of Roper's narrative deeper tides moving within African American literary and social culture. Prior to the late 1820s, the predominant intellectual and rhetorical currents ran toward the relatively nonconfrontational strategies of collective uplift, moral suasion, and social integration. As the South took the path of greater repression, however, more assertive and in some cases even militant attitudes developed in the African American community—attitudes that ultimately contributed to the downfall of slavery by limiting the political maneuverability of white elites in both the North and the South. While it would be misleading to call Roper a militant, his unflinching portrayal of the brutality of slavery captures the era's increasingly charged rhetorical atmosphere and points to the traumatic upheaval it would take to root out the institution. It is perhaps fitting, therefore, that as the narrative winds down Roper reprints a draft notice calling him to military duty. Not only does this document imply Roper's willingness to fight for his country, but by conjuring up the image of an armed African American fugitive it also plays—albeit probably unconsciously—on the fear of servile insurrection that so haunted the southern imagination.

The violence he suffered may have been intended to crush Roper's spirit, but it seems actually to have had the opposite effect: that of steeling his determination to escape. One has to think long and hard to name a slave narrator who did *not* possess such determination. Yet the difference here is that almost the entirety of Roper's narrative consists of a basic structural pattern repeated multiple times: abuse and forced labor, escape and evasion, capture and punishment. As a historical matter, many slaves knew that dismal cycle all too well. The reason Roper can convey it to us so dramatically (indeed, can convey it to us at all) is that he eventually managed to break out of the cycle and then to involve himself in the British antislavery movement. As testimonial literature, the narrative calls our attention insistently to the unflagging perseverance of a young man whose luck proved less typical than his desire for freedom. Indeed, that perseverance makes the narrative. Roper devotes comparatively little space to other possible topics: his conversion experience, his acquisition of literacy, his impressions of England, to name just three. Of course, a life spent fleeing forced labor and physical abuse was evidently what Roper, at the age of twenty-one, knew best. And that knowledge mattered greatly: for readers in the 1830s and 1840s, the narrative provided a powerful example of the indomitability of the human spirit—in the person of someone legally defined as property.

As he attempts one escape after another, Roper refers several times to the assistance of Providence, and at the end of the narrative he expresses his gratitude to his British friends and benefactors. Yet the support of religion and community seems, if not exactly superimposed on the text, then at least less apparent, less implicitly assumed, than Roper's ability to take care of himself. The narrative leaves the impression that, despite the terrible circumstances into which he was born, Roper has become — is becoming — the architect of his own destiny. In some ways it is a very lonely story; with the exception of a brief reunion with his family, the self-sufficient Roper seems isolated, detached. There is not much on the southern slave community and not much on the sustaining human relationships that could develop under even the most repressive slave regimes. Eight years before Frederick Douglass published his autobiography, Moses Roper staked out similar rhetorical ground as an individual man battling his way against long odds, unbowed and undeterred. Although not as personally invested as Douglass in the image of the self-made man, or in the cultural norms regarding masculinity, Roper nonetheless anticipated the more famous writer's public persona. In the process, he gave contemporary readers something vital to the project of African American uplift and, ultimately, emancipation: the image of a strong African American man capable of making it on his own. The implicit message was of the fitness of African Americans for participation in the American experiment.

It is also significant, therefore, that throughout his long campaign to escape, Roper comes across as a quick thinker, clever and savvy about the ways of the world. In one episode, he tells an overseer who has found him sleeping in a barn that is he simply a runaway apprentice "bound" to a cruel master. The ruse, as the young slave well knows, turns on a semantic distinction: "This statement may appear to some to be a direct lie, but as I understood the word *bound*, I considered it to apply to my case, having been sold to [Mr. Gooch], and thereby bound to serve him." Later in the narrative, he twice tricks people into writing a "passport" for him (to ensure his freedom of travel) by pretending to have lost his original. Such trickery associates Roper with the frontier tradition of the resourceful rogue or confidence man — someone we might encounter, for instance, in a novel by Herman Melville or Mark Twain — but he also knows that the social stigma of deceptiveness attaches more tenaciously to him, as a slave narrator, than to his white contemporaries. Although it probably appears perfectly justified to modern readers, Roper's "lying" carried significant moral freight in the 1830s; hence his religiously inflected reassurances to the reader that he *now* abhors the "sin of lying" and the "wicked deception" he practiced. Several imperatives come to bear: the overriding need to escape in the first place, the desire to display his mental agility, and the need to convince the reader of his upright character.

For all his self-reliant autonomy, Roper does have some unusual assistance in his escape. Ironically enough, it is his skin color that helps him to slip the noose of a watchful slave society. We learn of his extraordinarily light complexion on the second page: "My mother being half white, and my father a white man, I was at that time very white." This "whiteness" is instrumental in several respects. First, as a source of embarrassment to his owner's family, it prompts his sale, at the age of six, to an itinerant trader rather than to someone in the vicinity. In the years that follow, it diminishes his appeal on the market, since buyers typically valued light-skinned women more than light-skinned men, who were often deemed troublesome. Somewhat more positively, it improves his chances of working as a domestic slave than as a field hand ("as they generally prefer slaves of my colour for that purpose")— but for that same reason he has difficulty keeping up when Mr. Gooch does put him in the field. Above all, however, Roper's complexion enables him, at several junctures, to convince suspicious whites that he is not a fugitive slave.

Significantly, the narrative does not take the issue of skin color as an opportunity to explore the complexities of racial inheritance, as so many works of the antebellum era did. That is, Roper does not present his racial intermixture as a matter of having inherited different kinds of "blood" and therefore different kinds of racial traits or racial sympathies. Nor does he present himself as a "tragic mulatto," a character type that was just then coming into existence. An instructive contrast is provided by the short story "The Mulatto," written by the American-born free black writer Victor Séjour and published in Paris, in French, in the same year that Roper's narrative was. Where Séjour uses his protagonist's mixed race to explore other internal divisions—of loyalty, of morality, of emotion—Roper simply, or cleverly, treats his light color as a practical asset or resource. In a society whose dominant racial ideology and system of labor depended on the legibility of the "black" body, Roper quickly recognizes the advantages of illegibility. When he writes that it "required great courage to pass through" Savannah, he seems to speak both literally and metaphorically of his treacherous route through the city and of his boldness in "passing" as a white American. Long before the "novel of passing" reached its vogue in African American literature, in the works of such writers as Charles Chesnutt, Nella Larsen, and James Weldon Johnson, Roper had already lived in person what they treated in fiction. The cultural and literary landscape would change substantially in the intervening years, but once again we find Roper charting important territory.

The territorial metaphor is deliberate because Roper's narrative vividly illustrates the importance that geography held for the fates of runaway slaves. For these fugitives, a knowledge of the terrain—of the countryside, of the waterways, of the woods, of the spatial relationships between particular locations—represented nothing less than survival. Since Roper could not take for granted his freedom to travel, he describes his peregrinations in more detail than one might expect, giving us specific information about distances, means of conveyance, exposed or safe locations, and so forth. To take one example, Roper's description of his tortuous final journey to Savannah might seem, at first glance, unnecessarily conscientious in its attention to geographic detail. If we put ourselves in his shoes, however, richer meanings emerge: the exigencies of illegal flight, the dangers of unfamiliar terrain, the tremendous physical exertion required to put sufficient distance between himself and his pursuers. Without the drama of this arduous geographic odyssey, the larger drama of Roper's passage from bondage into freedom would lose a measure of its emotional force.

Fittingly, as the drama of escape unfolds over the course of the narrative, water—as it does in the *Odyssey*—plays a starring role. The creeks and rivers crisscrossing the South represent both barriers and opportunities for the fugitive, their very substance promising life yet threatening death. Describing one dangerous attempt to cross a large river, Roper recalls a moment of fear and indecision, but ultimately of spiritual potency: "[I]f my master was in pursuit of me, my safest place from him was in the water, if I could keep my head above the surface. I was, however, dreadfully frightened, and most earnestly prayed that I might be kept from a watery grave, and resolved that if again I landed, I would spend my life in the service of God." Not only does he manage to keep his head above water during this figurative baptism, but he uses the water itself in a devious fashion to aid in his escape. Soon, the end is in sight. He passes through Savannah, ships for the North aboard a schooner, and eventually crosses the Atlantic for England's free soil. By virtue of his autobiography, Roper has also breasted the waves of history. It is a narrative whose unique qualities and recognizable influences together help us to map some of the currents of antislavery publishing, of the changing slave narrative tradition, and of the racial politics of nineteenth-century American culture. More than that, it remains a powerful testament to the vitality of human willpower in the face of human cruelty.

Note on the Text

The autobiography of Moses Roper was first published in 1837, by the London firm of Darton, Harvey, and Darton, as *A Narrative of Moses Roper's Adventures and Escape from American Slavery; with a Preface by Reverend T. Price*. In 1838, there appeared both a second London edition and the first American edition, printed by Merrihew and Gunn in Philadelphia. Eventually, the narrative went through ten editions, the last published in 1856. The text reproduced here follows the 1838 Philadelphia version because it represents an important reference point in a broader shift in antislavery publication toward an increasingly American readership.

Notes

1. Gronniosaw's *A Narrative of the Most Remarkable Particulars in the Life of James Albert Ukawsaw Gronniosaw, an African Prince, as Related by Himself* was published in Bath, England, in 1772. Both Cugoano's *Thoughts and Sentiments on the Evil and Wicked Traffic of the Slavery and Commerce of the Human Species, Humbly Submitted to the Inhabitants of Great Britain, by Ottobah Cugoano, a Native of Africa* and Equiano's *The Interesting Narrative of the Life of Olaudah Equiano, or Gustavus Vassa, the African, Written by Himself* were published in London in 1787. All three narratives are collected in *Pioneers of the Black Atlantic: Five Slave Narratives from the Enlightenment, 1772–1815*, ed. Henry Louis Gates Jr. and William L. Andrews (Washington, D.C.: Civitas, 1998).

2. Ramsay (1733–89) was a naval surgeon and Anglican clergyman who lived in the West Indies for about twenty years. His *Essay on the Treatment and Conversion of African Slaves in the British Sugar Colonies* (London, 1784) was one of the first and most influential antislavery works by a writer with personal familiarity with the British sugar colonies. Clarkson (1760–1846) spent most of his life traveling and writing in support of the abolitionist cause. His *Essay on the Slavery and Commerce of the Human Species, Particularly the African: Translated from a Latin Dissertation Which Was Honoured with the First Prize in the University of Cambridge, for the Year 1785* was published in London in 1785 (1786 ed.; reprint, Miami, Fla.: Mnemosyne, 1969). In 1808, Clarkson published *The History of the Rise, Progress and Accomplishment of the Abolition of the African Slave-Trade by the British Parliament*, a highly informative, if self-congratulatory, record of early antislavery efforts. Stephen (1758–1832) was a deeply religious, highly intellectual lawyer and antislavery activist who feared that slavery and the slave trade had corrupted Britain and provoked divine wrath. His major works include *The Crisis of the Sugar Colonies; or, An Enquiry into the Objects and Probable Effects of the French Expedition to the West Indies, and Their Connection with*

the Colonial Interests of the British Empire (London, 1802; reprint, New York, Negro Universities Press, 1969), and *The Dangers of the Country* (London, 1807).

3. Douglass published the first version of his autobiography—*Narrative of the Life of Frederick Douglass, an American Slave, Written by Himself*—in 1845, after several years of preaching and lecturing on behalf of the antislavery cause. The book became the most famous and influential slave narrative the nineteenth century had yet seen, and it was followed by two autobiographical sequels: *My Bondage and My Freedom* (1855) and *Life and Times of Frederick Douglass* (1881). Harriet Beecher Stowe published *Uncle Tom's Cabin* in 1852 (following its ten-month serialization in the *National Era*), and the novel quickly became an international bestseller, helping to crystallize antislavery sentiment in the North and contributing to the eventual breakdown of compromise between North and South.

4. A reprint of the 1856 edition, *Archy Moore, the White Slave; or, Memoirs of a Fugitive*, was published by Negro Universities Press (New York, 1969). An electronic reprint of the 1852 edition, *The White Slave, or, Memoirs of a Fugitive*, is available through the Academic Affairs Library at the University of North Carolina at Chapel Hill, <http://docsouth.unc.edu/neh/hildreth/menu.html>.

5. Simon Legree is the degenerate landowner in *Uncle Tom's Cabin* who buys Tom and, threatened by the slave's spiritual self-possession, ends up beating him to death. In his 1845 *Narrative*, Douglass relates the story of the cruel overseer Austin Gore, who shoots a slave named Demby in the face for nonviolent disobedience.

A NARRATIVE

OF THE

ADVENTURES AND ESCAPE

OF

MOSES ROPER,

FROM

AMERICAN SLAVERY;

WITH A PREFACE

BY THE REV. T. PRICE, D.D.

"Slaves cannot breathe in England; if their lungs
Receive our air, that moment they are free:
They touch our country, and their shackles fall.
That's noble! and bespeaks a nation proud
And jealous of the blessing. Spread it then,
And let it circulate through every vein."

PHILADELPHIA:

MERRIHEW & GUNN, PRINTERS.

1838.

Moses Roper. From The Black Abolitionist Papers, *vol. 1,* The British Isles, 1830–1865, *edited by C. Peter Ripley; copyright 1985 by The University of North Carolina Press; used by permission of the publisher.*

PREFACE.

THE following narrative was to have appeared under the auspices of the Rev. Dr. Morison, of Chelsea,[1] whose generous exertions on behalf of Moses Roper have entitled him to the admiration and gratitude of every philanthropist. But the illness of the doctor having prevented him from reading the manuscript, I have been requested to supply his lack of service. To this request I assent reluctantly, as the narrative would have derived a fuller sanction and wider currency, had circumstances permitted the original purpose to be carried out. Moses Roper was introduced to Dr. Morison by an eminent American abolitionist, in a letter, dated November 9th, 1835, in which honorable testimony is borne to his general character, and the soundness of his religious profession. "He has spent about ten days in my house," says Dr. Morison's correspondent; "I have watched him attentively, and have no doubt that he is an excellent young man, that he possesses uncommon intelligence, sincere piety, and a strong desire to preach the gospel. He can tell you his own story better than any one else; and I believe that if he should receive an education, he would be able to counteract the false and wicked misrepresentations of American slavery, which are made in your country by our Priests and Levites who visit you."

Dr. Morison, as might have been anticipated from his well-known character, heartily responded to the appeal of his American correspondent. He sent his letter to the Patriot newspaper, remarking in his own communication to the editor, "I have seen Moses Roper, the fugitive slave. He comes to this country, as you will perceive, well authenticated as to character and religious standing; and my anxiety is, that the means may forthwith be supplied by some of your generous readers, for placing him in some appropriate seminary, for the improvement of his mind, that he may be trained for future usefulness in the church. His thirst for knowledge is great; and he may yet become a most important agent in liberating his country from the curse of slavery."

Moses Roper brought with him to this country several other testimonies, from persons residing in different parts of the States; but it is unnecessary to extend this preface by quoting them. They all speak the same language, and bear unequivocal witness to his sobriety, intelligence, and honesty.

He is now in the land of freedom, and is earnestly desirous of availing

himself of the advantages of his position. His great ambition is to be qualified for usefulness amongst his own people; and the progress he has already
made justifies the belief that if the means of education can be secured for a
short time longer, he will be eminently qualified to instruct the children of
Africa in the truths of the gospel of Christ. He has drawn up the following
narrative, partly with the hope of being assisted in this legitimate object,
and partly to engage the sympathies of our countrymen on behalf of his oppressed brethren. I trust that he will not be disappointed in either of these
expectations, but that all the friends of humanity and religion among us will
cheerfully render him their aid, by promoting the circulation of his volume.
Should this be done to the extent that is quite possible, the difficulties now
lying in his way will be removed.

Of the narrative itself, it is not necessary that I should say much. It is
his own production, and carries with it internal evidence of truth. Some
of its statements will probably startle those readers who are unacquainted
with the details of the slave system; but no such feeling will be produced in
any who are conversant with the practice of slavery, whether in America or
our own colonies. There is no vice too loathsome—no passion too cruel or
remorseless, to be engendered by this horrid system. It brutalizes all who
administer it; and seeks to efface the likeness of God, stamped on the brow
of its victims. It makes the former class demons, and reduces the latter to
the level of brutes.

I could easily adduce from the records of our own slave system, as well
as from those of America, several instances of equal atrocity to any which
Moses Roper has recorded. But this is unnecessary; and I shall therefore
merely add the unqualified expression of my own confidence in the truth of
his narrative, and my strong recommendation of it to the patronage of the
British public.

THOMAS PRICE.[2]

HACKNEY,[3] July 22d.

INTRODUCTION.

THE determination of laying this little narrative before the public did not arise from any desire to make myself conspicuous, but with the view of exposing the cruel system of slavery, as will here be laid before my readers; from the urgent calls of nearly all the friends to whom I had related any part of the story, and also from the recommendation of anti-slavery meetings, which I have attended, through the suggestion of many warm friends of the cause of the oppressed.

The general narrative, I am aware, may seem to many of my readers, and especially to those who have not been before put in possession of the actual features of this accursed system, somewhat at variance with the dictates of humanity. But the facts related here do not come before the reader unsubstantiated by collateral evidence, nor highly colored to the disadvantage of cruel taskmasters.

My readers may be put in possession of facts respecting this system which equal in cruelty my own narrative, on an authority which may be investigated with the greatest satisfaction. Besides which, this little book will not be confined to a small circle of my own friends in London, or even in England. The slave-holder, the colonizationist, and even Mr. Gooch himself, will be able to obtain this document, and be at liberty to draw from it whatever they are honestly able, in order to set me down as the tool of a party. Yea, even friend Breckenridge, a gentleman known at Glasgow, will be able to possess this, and to draw from it all the forcible arguments on his own side, which in his wisdom, honesty, and candor he may be able to adduce.

The earnest wish to lay this narrative before my friends as an impartial statement of facts, has led me to develope some part of my conduct which I now deeply deplore. The ignorance in which the poor slaves are kept by their masters, precludes almost the possibility of their being alive to any moral duties.

With these remarks, I leave the statement before the public. May this little volume be the instrument of opening the eyes of the ignorant to this system; of convincing the wicked, cruel, and hardened slave-holder; and of befriending generally the cause of oppressed humanity.

MOSES ROPER.

LONDON, June 28, 1837.

ESCAPE, &c.

I was born in North Carolina, in Caswell county,[4] I am not able to tell in what year or month. What I shall now relate is, what was told me by my mother and grandmother. A few months before I was born, my father married my mother's young mistress.[5] As soon as my father's wife heard of my birth, she sent one of my mother's sisters to see whether I was white or black, and when my aunt had seen me, she returned back as soon as she could, and told her mistress that I was white, and resembled Mr. Roper very much. Mr. R.'s wife being not pleased with this report, she got a large club stick and knife, and hastened to the place in which my mother was confined. She went into my mother's room with full intention to murder me with her knife and club, but as she was going to stick the knife into me, my grandmother happening to come in, caught the knife and saved my life. But as well as I can recollect from what my mother told me, my father sold her and myself soon after her confinement. I cannot recollect any thing that is worth notice till I was six or seven years old. My mother being half white, and my father a white man, I was at that time very white. Soon after I was six or seven years of age, my mother's old master died, that is, my father's wife's father. All his slaves had to be divided among the children.* I have mentioned before of my father disposing of me; I am not sure whether he exchanged me and my mother for another slave or not, but think it very likely he did exchange me with one of his wife's brothers or sisters, because I remember when my mother's old master died, I was living with my father's wife's brother-in-law, whose name was Mr. Durham. My mother was drawn with the other slaves.

The way they divide their slaves is this: they write the names of different slaves on a small piece of paper, and put it into a box, and let them all draw. I think that Mr. Durham drew my mother, and Mr. Fowler drew me, so we were separated a considerable distance, I cannot say how far. My resembling my father so very much, and being whiter than the other slaves, caused me to be soon sold to what they call a negro trader who took me to the southern states of America, several hundred miles from my mother. As well as I

---

*Slaves are usually a part of the marriage portion, but lent rather than given, to be returned to the estate at the decease of the father, in order that they may be divided equally among his children.

can recollect, I was then about six years old. The trader, Mr. Michael, after travelling several hundred miles and selling a good many of his slaves, found he could not sell me very well, (as I was so much whiter than the other slaves were,) for he had been trying several months—left me with a Mr. Sneed,[6] who kept a large boarding-house, who took me to wait at table, and sell me if he could. I think I stayed with Mr. Sneed about a year, but he could not sell me. When Mr. Michael had sold his slaves, he went to the north and bought up another drove, and returned to the south with them, and sent his son-in-law into Washington, in Georgia, after me; so he came and took me from Mr. Sneed and met his father-in-law with me, in a town called Lancaster, with his drove of slaves. We stayed in Lancaster a week, because it was court week, and there were a great many people there, and it was a good opportunity for selling the slaves, and there he was enabled to sell me to a gentleman, Dr. Jones, who was both a doctor and a cotton planter. He took me into his shop to beat up and to mix medicines, which was not a very hard employment, but I did not keep it long, as the doctor soon sent me to his cotton plantation, that I might be burnt darker by the sun. He sent for me to be with a tailor to learn the trade, but all the journeymen being white men, Mr. Bryant, the tailor, did not let me work in the shop; I cannot say whether it was the prejudice of his journeymen in not wanting me to sit in the shop with them, or whether Mr. Bryant wanted to keep me about the house to do the domestic work instead of teaching me the trade. After several months my master came to know how I got on with the trade; I am not able to tell Mr. Bryant's answer, but it was either that I could not learn, or that his journeymen were not willing that I should sit in the shop with them. I was only once in the shop all the time I was there, and then only for an hour or two, before his wife called me out to do some other work. So my master took me home, and as he was going to send a load of cotton to Camden, about forty miles distance, he sent me with the bales of cotton to be sold with it, where I was soon sold to a gentleman named Allen, but Mr. Allen soon exchanged me for a female slave to please his wife. The traders who bought me were named Cooper and Linsey, who took me for sale, but could not sell me, people objecting to my being rather white. They then took me to the city of Fayetteville, North Carolina, where he swopt me for a boy that was blacker than me, to Mr. Smith, who lived several miles off.

I was with Mr. Smith nearly a year. I arrived at the first knowledge of my age when I lived with him. I was then between twelve and thirteen years old, it was when President Jackson was elected the first time, and he has been president eight years, so I must be nearly twenty-one years of age. At this time I was quite a small boy, and was sold to Mr. Hodge, a negro trader. Here I began to enter into hardships. After travelling several hundred miles, Mr. Hodge sold me to Mr. Gooch, the cotton planter, Cashaw county, South Carolina; he purchased me at a town called Liberty Hill, about three miles from his home.[7] As soon as he got home, he immediately put me on his cotton plantation to work, and put me under overseers, gave me allowance of meat and bread with the other slaves, which was not half enough for me to live upon, and very laborious work. Here my heart was almost broke with grief at leaving my fellow slaves. Mr. Gooch did not mind my grief, for he flogged me nearly every day, and very severely. Mr. Gooch bought me for his son-in-law, Mr. Hammans, about five miles from his residence.[8] This man had but two slaves besides myself; he treated me very kindly for a week or two, but in summer, when cotton was ready to hoe, he gave me task work connected with this department, which I could not get done, not having worked on cotton farms before. When I failed in my task, he commenced flogging me, and set me to work without any shirt in the cotton field, in a very hot sun, in the month of July. In August, Mr. Condell, his overseer, gave me a task at pulling fodder. Having finished my task before night, I left the field; the rain came on, which soaked the fodder. On discovering this, he threatened to flog me for not getting in the fodder before the rain came. This was the first time I attempted to run away, knowing that I should get a flogging. I was then between thirteen and fourteen years of age. I ran away to the woods half naked; I was caught by a slave-holder, who put me in Lancaster jail. When they put slaves in jail, they advertise for their masters to own them; but if the master does not claim his slave in six months from the time of imprisonment, the slave is sold for jail fees. When the slave runs away, the master always adopts a more rigorous system of flogging; this was the case in the present instance. After this, having determined from my youth to gain my freedom, I made several attempts, was caught and got a severe flogging of one hundred lashes each time. Mr. Hammans was a very severe and cruel master, and his wife still worse; she used to tie me up and flog me while naked.

After Mr. Hammans saw that I was determined to die in the woods, and not live with him, he tried to obtain a piece of land from his father-in-law, Mr. Gooch; not having the means of purchasing it, he exchanged me for the land.

As soon as Mr. Gooch had possession of me again, knowing that I was averse to going back to him, he chained me by the neck to his chaise. In this manner he took me to his home at MacDaniel's Ferry, in the county of

Chester, a distance of fifteen miles. After which, he put me into a swamp, to cut trees, the heaviest work which men of twenty-five or thirty years of age have to do, I being but sixteen. Here I was on very short allowance of food, and having heavy work, was too weak to fulfil my tasks. For this I got many severe floggings; and after I had got my irons off, I made another attempt at running away. He took my irons off in the full anticipation that I could never get across the Catarba River, even when at liberty. On this I procured a small Indian canoe, which was tied to a tree, and ultimately got across the river in it. I then wandered through the wilderness for several days without any food, and but a drop of water to allay my thirst, till I became so starved, that I was obliged to go to a house to beg for something to eat, when I was captured, and again imprisoned.

Mr. Gooch, having heard of me through an advertisement, sent his son after me; he tied me up, and took me back to his father. Mr. Gooch then obtained the assistance of another slave-holder, and tied me up in his black-smith's shop, and gave me fifty lashes with a cow-hide. He then put a long chain, weighing twenty-five pounds, round my neck, and sent me into a field, into which he followed me with the cow-hide, intending to set his slaves to flog me again. Knowing this, and dreading to suffer again in this way, I gave him the slip, and got out of his sight, he having stopped to speak with the other slave-holder.

I got to a canal on the Catarba River, on the banks of which, and near to a lock, I procured a stone and a piece of iron, with which I forced the ring off my chain, and got it off, and then crossed the river, and walked about twenty miles, when I fell in with a slave-holder named Ballad, who had married the sister of Mr. Hammans. I knew that he was not so cruel as Mr. Gooch, and, therefore, begged of him to buy me. Mr. Ballad, who was one of the best planters in the neighbourhood, said, that he was not able to buy me, and stated, that he was obliged to take me back to my master, on account of the heavy fine attaching to a man harbouring a slave. Mr. Ballad proceeded to take me back. As we came in sight of Mr. Gooch's, all the treatment that I had met with there came forcibly upon my mind, the powerful influence of which is beyond description. On my knees, with tears in my eyes, with terror in my countenance, and fervency in all my features, I implored Mr. Ballad to buy me, but he again refused, and I was taken back to my dreaded and cruel master. Having reached Mr. Gooch's, he proceeded to punish me. This he did by first tying my wrists together, and placing them over the knees; he then put a stick through, under my knees and over my arms, and having thus secured my arms, he proceeded to flog me, and gave me five hundred lashes on my bare back. This may appear incredible, but the marks which they left at present remain on my body, a standing testimony to the truth of this statement of his severity. He then chained me down in a log-pen with a 40 lb. chain, and made me lie on the damp earth all night. In the morning after his breakfast he came to me, and without giving me any breakfast, tied me to a large heavy barrow, which is usually drawn by a horse, and made me drag it to the cotton field for the horse to use in the field. Thus, the reader will see, that it was of no possible use to my master to make me drag it to the field, and not through it; his cruelty went so far as actually to make me the slave of his horse, and thus to degrade me. He then flogged me again, and set me to work in the corn field the whole of that day, and at night chained me down in the log-pen as before. The next morning he took me to the cotton field, and gave me a third flogging, and set me to hoe cotton. At this time I was dreadfully sore and weak with the repeated floggings and harsh treatment I had endured. He put me under a black man with orders, that if I did not keep my row up in hoeing with this man, he was to flog me. The reader must recollect here, that not being used to this kind of work, having been a domestic slave, it was quite impossible for me to keep up with him, and, therefore, I was repeatedly flogged during the day.

Mr. Gooch had a female slave about eighteen years old, who also had been a domestic slave, and through not being able to fulfil her task, had run away; which slave he was at this time punishing for that offence. On the third day, he chained me to this female slave, with a large chain of 40 lbs. weight round the neck. It was most harrowing to my feelings thus to be chained to a young female slave, for whom I would rather have suffered a hundred lashes than she should have been thus treated. He kept me chained to her during the week, and repeatedly flogged us both while thus chained together, and forced us to keep up with the other slaves, although retarded by the heavy weight of the log-chain.

Here again words are insufficient to describe the misery which possessed both body and mind whilst under this treatment, and which was most dreadfully increased by the sympathy which I felt for my poor degraded fellow sufferer. On the Friday morning, I entreated my master to set me free from my chains, and promised him to do the task which was given me, and more if possible, if he would desist from flogging me. This he refused to do until Saturday night, when he did set me free. This must rather be ascribed to his own interest in preserving me from death, as it was very evident I could no longer have survived under such treatment.

After this, though still determined in my own mind to escape, I stayed with him several months, during which he frequently flogged me, but not so severely as before related. During this time I had opportunity for recovering my health, and using means to heal my wounds. My master's cruelty was not confined to me, it was his general conduct to all his slaves. I might relate many instances to substantiate this, but will confine myself to one or two. Mr. Gooch, it is proper to observe, was a member of a Baptist church, called Black Jack Meeting-House, in Cashaw county, which church I attended for several years, but was never inside. This is accounted for by the fact, that the coloured population are not permitted to mix with the white population. Mr. Gooch had a slave named Phil,* who was a member of a Methodist church. This man was between seventy and eighty years of age; he was so feeble that he could not accomplish his tasks, for which his master used to chain him round the neck, and run him down a steep hill; this treatment he never relinquished to the time of his death. Another case was that of a slave named Peter, who, for not doing his task, he flogged nearly to death, and afterwards pulled out his pistol to shoot him, but his (Mr. Gooch's) daughter snatched the pistol from his hand. Another mode of punishment which this man adopted was, that of using iron horns, with bells, attached to the back of the slave's neck.

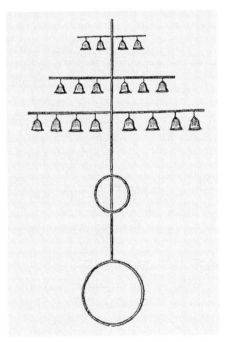

*This is an abbreviation of Philip.

This instrument he used to prevent the negroes running away, being a very ponderous machine, seven feet in height, and the cross pieces being two feet four, and six feet in length. This custom is generally adopted among the slave-holders in South Carolina, and some other slave states. One morning, about an hour before daybreak, I was going on an errand for my master. Having proceeded about a quarter of a mile, I came up to a man named King, (Mr. Sumlin's overseer,) who had caught a young girl that had run away with the above-described machine on her. She had proceeded four miles from her station, with the intention of getting into the hands of a more humane master. She came up with this overseer nearly dead, and could get no farther. He immediately secured her, and took her back to her master, a Mr. Johnston.

Having been in the habit of going over many slave states with my master, I had good opportunities of witnessing the harsh treatment which was adopted by masters towards their slaves. As I have never read or heard of any thing connected with slavery so cruel as what I have myself witnessed, it will be well to mention a case or two.

A large farmer, Colonel M'Quiller, in Cashaw county, South Carolina, was in the habit of driving nails into a hogshead so as to leave the point of the nail just protruding in the inside of the cask. Into this he used to put his slaves for punishment, and roll them down a very long and steep hill. I have heard from several slaves, (though I had no means of ascertaining the truth of the statement,) that in this way he killed six or seven of his slaves. This plan was first adopted by a Mr. Perry, who lived on the Catarba River, and has since been adopted by several planters. Another was that of a young lad, who had been hired by Mr. Bell, a member of a Methodist church, to hoe three quarters of an acre of cotton per day. Having been brought up as a domestic slave, he was not able to accomplish the task assigned to him. On the Saturday night, he left three or four rows to do on the Sunday; on the same night it rained very hard, by which the master could tell that he had done some of the rows on Sunday. On Monday his master took and tied him up to a tree in the field, and kept him there the whole of that day, and flogged him at intervals. At night, when he was taken down, he was so weak that he could not get home, having a mile to go. Two white men, who were employed by Mr. Bell, put him on a horse, took him home, and threw him down on the kitchen floor, while they proceeded to their supper. In a little time they heard some deep groans proceeding from the kitchen; they went to see him die; he had groaned his last. Thus, Mr. Bell flogged this poor boy even to death; for what? for breaking the Sabbath, when he (his master) had set him a task on Saturday which it was not possible for him to do, and which, if he did not do, no mercy would be extended towards him. So much for the regard of this Methodist for the observance of the Sabbath. The general custom in this respect is, that if a man kills his own slave, no notice is taken of it by the civil functionaries; but if a man kills a slave belonging to another master, he is compelled to pay the worth of the slave. In this case, a jury met, returned a verdict of "Wilful murder" against this man, and ordered him to pay the value. Mr. Bell was unable to do this, but a Mr. Cunningham paid the debt, and took this Mr. Bell, with this recommendation for cruelty, to be his overseer.

It will be observed, that most of the cases here cited are those in respect to males. Many instances, however, in respect to females might be mentioned, but are too disgusting to appear in this narrative. The cases here brought forward are not rare, but the continued feature of slavery. But I must now follow up the narrative as regards myself in particular. I stayed with this master for several months, during which time we went on very well in general. In August, 1831, (this was my first acquaintance with any date,) I happened to hear a man mention this date, and, as it excited my curiosity, I asked what it meant; they told me it was the number of the year from the birth of Christ. On this date, August, 1831, some cows broke into a crib where the corn is kept, and ate a great deal. For this his slaves were tied up and received several floggings; but myself and another man, hearing the groans of those who were being flogged, stayed back in the field, and would not come up. Upon this I thought to escape punishment. On the Monday morning, however, I heard my master flogging the other man who was in the field. He could not see me, it being a field of Indian corn, which grows to a great height. Being afraid that he would catch me, and dreading a flogging more than many others, I determined to run for it, and after travelling forty miles I arrived at the estate of Mr. Crawford, in North Carolina, Mecklinburgh county. Having formerly heard people talk about the free states, I determined upon going thither, and if possible, in my way, to find out my poor mother, who was in slavery several hundred miles from Chester; but the hope of doing the latter was very faint, and, even if I did, it was not likely that she would know me, having been separated from her when between five and six years old.

The first night I slept in a barn upon Mr. Crawford's estate, and, having overslept myself, was awoke by Mr. Crawford's overseer, upon which I was dreadfully frightened. He asked me what I was doing there? I made no reply to him then, and he making sure that he had secured a runaway slave, did not press me for an answer. On my way to his house, however, I made up the following story, which I told him in the presence of his wife: — I said, that I had been bound to a very cruel master when I was a little boy, and that having been treated very badly, I wanted to get home to see my mother. This statement may appear to some to be a direct lie, but as I understood the word *bound*, I considered it to apply to my case, having been sold to him, and thereby bound to serve him; though still, I rather hope that he would understand it, that I was bound, when a boy, till twenty-one years of age. Though I was white at the time, he would not believe my story, on account of my hair being curly and woolly, which led him to conclude I was possessed of enslaved blood. The overseer's wife, however, who seemed much interested in me, said she did not think I was of African origin, and that she had seen white men still darker than me. Her persuasion prevailed; and, after the overseer had given me as much buttermilk as I could drink, and something to eat, which was very acceptable, having had nothing for two days, I set off for Charlotte in North Carolina, the largest town in the county. I went on very quickly the whole of that day, fearful of being pursued. The trees were very thick on each side of the road, and only a few houses at the distance of two or three miles apart. As I proceeded, I turned round in all directions to see if I was pursued, and if I caught a glimpse of any one coming along the road, I immediately rushed into the thickest part of the wood, to elude the grasp of what I was afraid might be my master. I went on in this way the whole day; at night I came up with two wagons: they had been to market. The regular road wagons do not generally put up at inns, but encamp in the roads and fields. When I came to them, I told them the same story I had told Mr. Crawford's overseer, with the assurance that the statement would meet the same success. After they had heard me, they gave me something to eat, and also a lodging in the camp with them.

I then went on with them about five miles, and they agreed to take me with them as far as they went, if I would assist them. This I promised to do. In the morning, however, I was much frightened by one of the men putting several questions to me; we were then about three miles from Charlotte. When within a mile of that town, we stopped at a brook to water the horses. While stopping here, I saw the men whispering, and fancying I overheard them say they would put me in Charlotte jail when they got there, I made my escape into the woods, pretending to be looking after something till I got out of their sight. I then ran on as fast as I could, but did not go through the town of Charlotte, as had been my intention; being a large town, I was fearful it might prove fatal to my escape. Here I was at a loss how to get on, as houses were not very distant from each other for nearly two hundred miles.

While thinking what I should do, I observed some wagons before me, which I determined to keep behind, and never go nearer to them than a quarter of a mile; in this way I travelled till I got to Salisbury. If I happened to meet any person on the road, I was afraid they would take me up; I asked them how far the wagons had got on before me, to make them suppose I belonged to the wagons. At night I slept on the ground in the woods, some little distance from the wagons, but not near enough to be seen by the men belonging to them. All this time I had but little food, principally fruit, which I found on the road. On Thursday night, I got into Salisbury, having left Chester on the Monday morning preceding. After this, being afraid my master was in pursuit of me, I left the usual line of road, and took another direction, through Huntoville and Salem, principally through fields and woods. On my way to Caswell Courthouse, a distance of nearly two hundred miles from Salisbury, I was stopped by a white man, to whom I told my old story, and again succeeded in my escape. I also came up with a small cart, driven by a poor man who had been moving into some of the western territories, and was going back to Virginia to move some more of his luggage. On this, I told him I was going the same way to Hilton, thirteen miles from Caswell Courthouse. He took me up in his cart, and we went to the Red House, two miles from Hilton, the place where Mr. Mitchell[9] took me from when six years old, to go to the southern states. This was a very providential circumstance, for it happened that at the time I had to pass through Caswell Court-house, a fair or election was going on, which caused the place to be much crowded with people, and rendered it more dangerous for me to pass through.

At the Red House I left the cart and wandered about a long time, not knowing which way to go to find my mother. After some time, I took the road leading over to Ikeo Creek. I shortly came up with a little girl about six years old, and asked her where she was going; she said to her mother's, pointing to a house on a hill about half a mile off. She had been to the overseer's house, and was returning to her mother. I then felt some emotions arising in my breast which I cannot describe, but will be fully explained in the sequel. I told her that I was very thirsty, and would go with her to get something to drink. On our way, I asked her several questions, such as her name, that of her mother: she said hers was Maria, and her mother's Nancy. I inquired if her mother had any more children? She said five besides herself, and that they had been told that one had been sold when a little boy. I then asked the name of this child? She said, it was Moses. These answers, as we approached the house, led me nearer and nearer to the finding out the object of my pursuit, and of recognising in the little girl the person of my own sister.

At last I got to my mother's house! My mother was at home; I asked her if she knew me? She said, No. Her master was having a house built just by, and the men were digging a well; she supposed that I was one of the diggers. I told her I knew her very well, and thought that if she looked at me a little she would know me; but this had no effect. I then asked her if she had any sons? She said, Yes; but none so large as me. I then waited a few minutes, and narrated some circumstances to her attending my being sold into slavery, and how she grieved at my loss. Here the mother's feelings on that dire occasion, and which a mother only can know, rushed to her mind; she saw her own son before her, for whom she had so often wept; and in an instant we were clasped in each other's arms, amidst the ardent interchange of caresses and tears of joy. Ten years had elapsed since I had seen my dear mother. My own feelings, and the circumstances attending my coming home, have often brought to mind since, on a perusal of the 42d, 43d, 44th, and 45th chapters of Genesis. What could picture my feelings so well, as I once more beheld the mother who had brought me into the world and had nourished me, not with the anticipation of my being torn from her maternal care when only six years old, to become the prey of a mercenary and blood-stained slave-holder, — I say, what picture so vivid in description of this part of my tale, as the 7th and 8th verses of the 42d chapter of Genesis, "And Joseph saw his brethren and he knew them, but made himself strange unto them. And Joseph knew his brethren, but they knew not him." After the first emotion of the mother on recognising her first-born had somewhat subsided, could the reader not fancy the little one, my sister, as she told her simple tale of meeting with me to her mother, how she would say, while the parent listened with intense interest, "The man asked me straitly of our state and of our kindred, saying, Is your father yet alive, and have ye another brother?" Or, when at last, I could no longer refrain from making myself known, I say I was ready to burst into a frenzy of joy. How applicable the 1st, 2d, and 3d verses of the 45th chapter, "Then Joseph could not refrain himself before all them that stood by him; and he wept aloud, and said unto his brethren, I am Joseph; doth my father still live?" Then when the mother knew her son, when the brothers and sisters owned their brother; "He kissed all his brethren and wept over them, and after that his brethren talked with him." 15th verse. At night, my mother's husband, a blacksmith, belonging to Mr. Jefferson, at the Red House, came home. He was surprised to see me with the family, not knowing who I was. He had been married to my mother when I was a babe, and had always been very fond of me. After the same tale had been told him, and the same emotions filled his soul, he again kissed the object of his early affection. The next morning I wanted to go on my journey, in order to make sure of my escape to the free states. But, as might be expected, my mother, father, brothers, and sisters, could ill part with their long lost one, and persuaded me to go into the woods in the daytime, and at night come home and sleep there. This I did for about a week. On the next Sunday night, I laid me down to sleep between my two brothers, on a pallet which my mother had prepared for me. About twelve o'clock I was suddenly awoke, and found my bed surrounded by twelve slave-holders with pistols in hand, who took me away (not allowing me to bid farewell to those I loved so dearly) to the Red House, where they confined me in a room the rest of the night, and in the morning lodged me in the jail of Caswell Courthouse.

What was the scene at home, what sorrow possessed their hearts, I am unable to describe, as I never after saw any of them more. I heard, however, that my mother, who was in the family-way when I went home, was soon after confined, and was very long before she recovered the effects of this disaster. I was told afterwards that some of those men who took me were professing Christians, but to me they did not seem to live up to what they professed. They did not seem, by their practices, at least, to recognise that God as their God, who hath said, "Thou shalt not deliver unto his master, the servant which is escaped from his master unto thee; he shall dwell with thee, even among you, in that place which he shall choose, in one of thy gates, where it liketh him best; thou shalt not oppress him." Deut. xxiii. 15, 16.

I was confined here in a dungeon under ground, the grating of which looked to the door of the jailer's house. His wife had a great antipathy to me. She was Mr. Roper's wife's cousin. My grandmother used to come to me nearly every day, and bring me something to eat, besides the regular jail allowance, by which my sufferings were somewhat decreased. Whenever the jailer went out, which he often did, his wife used to come to my dungeon and shut the wooden door over the grating, by which I was nearly suffocated, the place being very damp and noisome. My master did not hear of my being in jail for thirty-one days after I had been placed there. He immediately sent his son and son-in-law, Mr. Anderson, after me. They came in a horse and chaise, took me from the jail to a blacksmith's shop, and got an iron collar fitted round my neck, with a heavy chain attached, then tied up my hands, and fastened the other end of the chain on another horse, and put me on its back. Just before we started, my grandmother came to bid me farewell; I gave her my hand as well as I could, and she having given me two or three presents, we parted. I had felt enough, far too much, for the weak state I was in; but how shall I describe my feelings upon parting with the *last* relative that I *ever saw?* The reader must judge by what would be his own feelings under similar circumstances. We then went on for fifty miles; I was very weak, and could hardly sit on the horse. Having been in prison so long, I had lost the southern tan; and, as the people could not see my hair, having my hat on, they thought I was a white man, a criminal, and asked what crime I had committed. We arrived late at night at the house of Mr. Britton. I shall never forget the journey that night. The thunder was one continued roar, and the lightning blazing all around. I expected every minute that my iron collar would attract it, and I should be knocked off the horse and dragged along the ground. This gentleman, a year or two before, had liberated his slaves, and sent them into Ohio, having joined the society of Friends, which society does not allow the holding of slaves. I was, therefore, treated very well there, and they gave me a hearty supper, which did me much good in my weak state.

They secured me in the night by locking me to the post of the bed on which they slept. The next morning we went on to Salisbury. At that place we stopped to water the horses; they chained me to a tree in the yard, by the side of their chaise. On my horse they had put the saddle bags which contained the provisions. As I was in the yard, a black man came and asked me what I had been doing; I told him I had run away from my master; after which he told me several tales about the slaves, and among them, he mentioned the case of a Quaker, who was then in prison, waiting to be hung, for giving a free pass to a slave. I had been considering all the way how I could escape from my horse, and once had an idea of cutting his head off, but thought it too cruel, and at last thought of trying to get a rasp and cut the chain by which I was fastened to the horse. As they often let me get on nearly a quarter of a mile before them, I thought I should have a good opportunity of doing this without being seen. The black man procured me a rasp, and I put it into the saddle-bags which contained the provisions. We then went on our journey, and one of the sons asked me if I wanted any thing to eat; I answered, No, though very hungry at the time, as I was afraid of their going to the bags and discovering the rasp. However, they had not had their own meal at the inn, as I supposed, and went to the bags to supply themselves, where they discovered the rasp. Upon this, they fastened my horse beside the horse in their chaise, and kept a stricter watch over me. Nothing remarkable occurred, till we got within eight miles of Mr. Gooch's, where we stopped a short time; and, taking advantage of their absence, I broke a switch from some boughs above my head, lashed my horse, and set off at full speed. I had got about a quarter of a mile before they could get their horse loose from the chaise; one then rode the horse, and the other ran as fast as he could after me. When I caught sight of them, I turned off the main road into the woods, hoping to escape their sight; their horse, however, being much swifter than mine, they soon got within a short distance of me. I then came to a rail fence, which I found it very difficult to get over, but breaking several rails away, I effected my object. They then called upon me to stop, more than three times, and I not doing so, they fired after me, but the pistol only snapped. This is according to law; after three calls they may shoot a runaway slave. Soon after the one on the horse came up with me, and catching hold of the bridle of my horse, pushed the pistol to my side; the other soon came up, and breaking off several stout branches from the trees, they gave me about a hundred blows. They did this very near to a planter's house; the gentleman was not at home, but his wife came out, and begged them not to *kill* me *so near the house*: they took no notice of this, but kept on beating me. They then fastened me to the axle-tree of their chaise, one of them got into the chaise, the other took my horse, and they run me all the eight miles as fast as they could, the one on my horse going behind to guard me. In this way we came to my old master, Mr. Gooch. The first person I saw was himself; he unchained me from the chaise, and at first seemed to treat me very gently, asking me where I had been, &c. The first thing the sons did, was to show the rasp which I had got to cut my chain. My master gave me a hearty dinner, the best he ever did give me, but it was to keep me from dying before he had given me all the flogging he intended. After dinner he took me to a log-house, stripped me quite naked, fastened a rail up very high, tied my hands to the rail, fastened my feet together, put a rail between my feet, and stood on one end of it to hold it down; the two sons then gave me fifty lashes each, the eldest another fifty, and Mr. Gooch himself fifty more. While doing this, his wife came out and begged him not to kill me, the first act of sympathy I ever noticed in her. When I called for water, they brought a pail-full and threw it over my back, ploughed up by the lashes. After this, they took me to the blacksmith's shop, got two large bars of iron, which they bent round my feet, each bar weighing twenty pounds, and put a heavy log-chain on my neck. This was on Saturday. On the Monday, he chained me to the same female slave as before. As he had to go out that day, he did not give me the punishment which he intended to give me every day, but at night when he came home, he made us walk round his estate, and by all the houses of the slaves, for them to taunt us. When we came home, he told us we must be up very early in the morning, and go to the fields before the other slaves. We were up at daybreak, but we could not get on fast, on account of the heavy irons on my feet. We walked about a mile in two hours, but knowing the punishment he was going to inflict on us, we made up our minds to escape into the woods, and secrete ourselves. This we did, and he not being able to find us, sent all his slaves, about forty, and his sons, to find us, which they could not do; and about twelve o'clock, when we thought they would give up looking for us at that time, we went on, and came to the banks of the Catauba. Here I got a stone, and prized the ring of the chain on her neck, and got it off; and as the chain round my neck was only passed through a ring, as soon as I had got hers off, I slipped the chain through my ring and got it off my own neck. We then went on by the banks of the river for some distance, and found a little canoe about two feet wide. I managed to get in, although the irons on my feet made it very dangerous, for if I had upset the canoe I could not swim. The female got in after me, and gave me the paddles, by which we got some distance down the river. The current being very strong, it drove us against a small island; we paddled round the island to the other side, and then made towards the opposite bank. Here again we were stopped by the current, and made up to a large rock in the river, between the island and the opposite shore. As the weather was very rough, we landed on the rock and secured the canoe, as it was not possible to get back to the island. It was a very dark night and rained tremendously, and as the water was rising rapidly towards the top of the rock, we gave all up for lost, and sometimes hoped, and sometimes feared to hope, that we should never see the morning. But Providence was moving in our favour; the rain ceased, the water reached the edge of the rock, then receded, and we were out of danger from this cause. We remained all night upon the rock, and in the morning reached the opposite shore, and then made our way through the woods, till we came to a field of Indian corn, where we plucked some of the green ears and eat them, having had nothing for two days and nights. We came to the estate of ——, where we met with a colored man who knew me, and having run away himself from a bad master, he gave us some food, and told us we might sleep in the barn that night. Being very fatigued, we overslept ourselves; the proprietor came to the barn, but as I was in one corner under some Indian corn tops, and she in another, he did not perceive us, and we did not leave the barn before night, (Wednesday.) We then went out, got something to eat, and stayed about the estate till Sunday. On that day, I met with some men, one of whom had had irons on his feet the same as me; he told me, that his master was going out to see his friends, and that he would try and get my feet loose. For this purpose I parted with this female, fearing, that if she were caught with me, she would be forced to tell who took my irons off. The man tried some time without effect; he then gave me a file and I tried myself, but was disappointed, on account of their thickness.

On the Monday, I went on towards Lancaster, and got within three miles of it that night, and went towards the plantation of Mr. Crockett, as I knew some of his slaves, and hoped to get some food given me. When I got there, however, the dogs smelt me out and barked; upon which Mr. Crockett came out, followed me with his rifle, and came up with me. He put me on a horse's back, which put me to extreme pain, from the great weight hanging from my feet. We reached Lancaster jail that night, and he lodged me there. I was placed in the next dungeon to a man who was going to be hung. I shall never forget his cries and groans, as he prayed all night for the mercy of God. Mr. Gooch did not hear of me for several weeks; when he did, he sent his son-in-law, Mr. Anderson, after me. Mr. Gooch himself came within a mile of Lancaster, and waited until Mr. Anderson brought me. At this time I had but one of the irons on my feet, having got so thin round my ankles that I had slipped one off while in jail. His son-in-law tied my hands, and made me walk along till we came to Mr. Gooch. As soon as we arrived at M'Daniel's Ford, two miles above the ferry, on the Catauba River, they made me wade across, themselves going on horseback. The water was very deep, and having irons on one foot and round my neck, I could not keep a footing. They dragged me along by my chain, floating on the top of the water. It was as much as they could do to hold me by the chain, the current being very strong. They then took me home, flogged me, put extra irons on my neck and feet, and put me under the driver, with more work than ever I had before. He did not flog me so severely as before, but continued it every day. Among the instruments of torture employed, I here describe one:

This is a machine used for packing and pressing cotton. By it he hung me up by the hands at letter *a*, a horse moving round the screw *e*, and carrying it up and down, and pressing the block *c* into the box *d*, into which the cotton is put. At this time he hung me up for a quarter of an hour. I was carried up ten feet from the ground, when Mr. Gooch asked me if I was tired. He then let me rest for five minutes, then carried me round again, after which he let me down and put me into the box *d*, and shut me down in it for about ten minutes. After this torture, I stayed with him several months, and did my work very well. It was about the beginning of 1832 when he took off my irons, and being in dread of him, he having threatened me with more punishment, I attempted again to escape from him. At this time I got into North Carolina; but a reward having been offered for me, a Mr. Robinson caught me, and chained me to a chair, upon which he sat up with me all night, and next day proceeded home with me. This was Saturday, Mr. Gooch had gone to church, several miles from his house. When he came back, the first thing he did was to pour some tar on my head, then rubbed it all over my face, took a torch, with pitch on, and set it on fire. He put it out before it did me very great injury, but the pain which I endured was most excruciating, nearly all my hair having been burnt off. On Monday he put irons on me again, weighing nearly fifty pounds. He threatened me again on the Sunday with another flogging; and on the Monday morning, before daybreak, I got away again, with my irons on, and was about three hours going a distance of two miles. I had gone a good distance, when I met with a colored man, who got some wedges and took my irons off. However, I was caught again, and put into prison in Charlotte, where Mr. Gooch came, and took me back to Chester. He asked me how I got my irons off? They having been got off by a slave, I would not answer his question, for fear of getting the man punished. Upon this, he put the fingers of my left hand into a vice, and squeezed all my nails off. He then had my feet put on an anvil, and ordered a man to beat my toes, till he smashed some of my nails off. The marks of this treatment still remain upon me, my nails never having grown perfect since. He inflicted this punishment, in order to get out of me how I got my irons off, but never succeeded. After this he hardly knew what to do with me, the whole stock of his cruelties seemed to be exhausted. He chained me down in the log-house. Soon after this, he sent a female slave to see if I was safe. Mr. Gooch had not secured me as he thought, but had only run my chain through the ring, without locking it. This I observed; and while the slave was coming, I was employed in loosening the chain with the hand that was not wounded. As soon as I observed her coming, I drew the chain up tight, and she observing that I seemed fast, went away and told her master who was in the field ordering the slaves. When she was gone, I drew the chain through the ring, escaped under the flooring of the log-house, and went on under his house, till I came out at the other side, and ran on; but being sore and weak, I had not got a mile before I was caught, and again carried back. He tied me up to a tree in the woods at night and made his slaves flog me. I cannot say how many lashes I received, but it was the worst flogging I ever had, and the last which Mr. Gooch ever gave me.

There are several circumstances which occurred on this estate while I was there, relative to other slaves, which it may be interesting to mention. Hardly a day ever passed without some one being flogged. To one of his female slaves he had given a dose of castor oil and salts together, as much as she could take; he then got a box, about six feet by two and a half, and one and a half feet deep; he put this slave under the box, and made the men fetch as many stones as they could get, and put them on the top of it; under this she was made to stay all night. I believe, that if he had given this slave one, he had given her three thousand lashes. Mr. Gooch was a member of a Baptist church. His slaves, thinking him a very bad sample of what a professing Christian ought to be, would not join the connexion he belonged to, thinking they must be a very bad set of people; there were many of them members of the Methodist church. On Sunday, the slaves can only go to church at the will of their master, when he gives them a pass for the time they are to be out. If they are found by the patrole after the time to which their pass extends, they are severely flogged.

On Sunday nights, a slave, named Allen, used to come to Mr. Gooch's estate for the purpose of exhorting and praying with his brother slaves, by whose instrumentality many of them had been converted. One evening Mr. Gooch caught them all in a room, turned Allen out, and threatened his slaves with a hundred lashes each, if they ever brought him there again. At one time Mr. Gooch was ill and confined to his room; if any of the slaves had done any thing which he thought deserving a flogging, he would have them brought into his bed-room and flogged before his eyes.

With respect to food, he used to allow us one peck of Indian meal each, per week, which, after being sifted and the bran taken from it, would not be much more than half a peck. Meat we did not get for sometimes several weeks together; however, he was proverbial for giving his slaves more food than any other slave-holder. I stayed with Mr. Gooch a year and a half. During that time the scenes of cruelty I witnessed and experienced, are not at all fitted for these pages. There is much to excite disgust in what has been narrated, but hundreds of other cases might be mentioned. After this, Mr. Gooch, seeing that I was determined to get away from him, chained me, and sent me with another female slave, whom he had treated very cruelly, to Mr. Britton, son of the before-mentioned, a slave-dealer. We were to have gone to Georgia to be sold, but a bargain was struck before we arrived there. Mr. Britton had put chains on me to please Mr. Gooch; but having gone some little distance, we came up with a white man, who begged Mr. Britton to unchain me; he then took off my hand-cuffs. We then went on to Union Courthouse, where we met a drove of slaves; the driver came to me, and ultimately bought me, and sent me to his drove; the girl was sold to a planter in the neighbourhood, as bad as Mr. Gooch. In court week, the negro traders and slaves encamp a little way out of the town. The traders here will often sleep with the best-looking female slaves among them, and they will often have many children in the year, which are said to be slave-holder's children, by which means, through his villany, he will make an immense profit of this intercourse, by selling the babe with its mother. They often keep an immense stock of slaves on hand. Many of them will be with the trader a year or more before they are sold. Mr. Marcus Rowland, the drover who bought me, then returned with his slaves to his brother's house, (Mr. John Rowland,) where he kept his drove, on his way to Virginia. He kept me as a kind of servant. I had to grease the faces of the blacks every morning with sweet oil, to make them shine before they are put up to sell. After he had been round several weeks and sold many slaves, he left me and some more at his brother's house, while he went on to Washington, about six hundred miles, to buy some more slaves, the drove having got very small. We were treated very well while there, having plenty to eat, and little work to do, in order to make us fat. I was brought up more as a domestic slave, as they generally prefer slaves of my colour for that purpose. When Mr. Rowland came back, having been absent about five months, he found all the slaves well, except one female, who had been grieving very much at being parted from her parents, and at last died of grief. He dressed us very nicely, and went on again. I travelled with him for a year, and had to look over the slaves, and see that they were dressed well, had plenty of food, and to oil their faces. During this time, we stopped once at White House Church, a Baptist association; a protracted camp meeting was holding there, on the plan of the revival meetings in this country. We got there at the time of the meeting, and sold two female slaves on the Sunday morning, at the time the meeting broke up, to a gentleman who had been attending the meeting the whole of the week. While I was with Mr. Rowland we were at many such meetings, and the members of the churches are by

this means so well influenced towards their fellow creatures, at these meetings for the worship of God, that it becomes a fruitful season for the drover,
who carries on immense traffic with the attendants at these places. This is
common to Baptists and Methodists. At the end of the year he exchanged
me to a farmer, Mr. David Goodley, for a female slave, in Greenville, about
fourteen miles from Greenville Courthouse. The gentleman was going to
Missouri to settle, and on his way had to pass through Ohio, a free state. But
having learnt, after he bought me, that I had before tried to get away to the
free states, he was afraid to take me with him, and I was again exchanged to
a Mr. Marvel Louis. He was in the habit of travelling a great deal, and took
me as a domestic slave to wait on him. Mr. Louis boarded at the house of
Mr. Clevelin, a very rich planter at Greenville, South Carolina. Mr. L. was
paying his addresses to the daughter of this gentleman, but was surprised
and routed in his approaches, by a Colonel Dorkin, of Union Court-house,
who ultimately carried her off in triumph. After this Mr. Louis took to drinking, to drown his recollection of disappointed love. One day he went to
Pendleton races, and I waited on the road for him; returning intoxicated, he
was thrown from his horse into a brook, and was picked up by a gentleman
and taken to an inn, and I went there to take care of him. Next day he went on
to Punkintown with Mr. Warren R. Davis, a member of Congress;[10] I went
with him. This was at the time of the agitation of the Union and Nullifying
party, which was expected to end in a general war.[11] The Nullifying party
had a grand dinner on the occasion, after which they gave their slaves all the
refuse, for the purpose of bribing them to fight on the side of their party.
The scene on this occasion was most humorous, all the slaves scrambling
after bare bones and crumbs, as if they had had nothing for months. When
Mr. Louis had got over this fit of drunkenness, we returned to Greenville,
where I had little to do, except in the warehouse. There was preaching in the
Courthouse on the Sunday, but scarcely had the sweet savour of the worship of God passed away, when, on Monday, a public auction was held for
the sale of slaves, cattle, sugar, iron, &c., by Z. Davis, the high constable,
and others.

On these days, I was generally very busy in handing out the different
articles for inspection, and was employed in this way for several months.
After which, Mr. Louis left this place for Pendleton; but his health getting
worse, and fast approaching consumption, he determined to travel. I went
with him over Georgia to the Indian springs, and from there to Columbus;
here he left me with Lawyer Kemp, a member of the State Assembly, to
take care of his horses and carriage till he came back from Cuba, where he

went for the benefit of his health. I travelled round with Mr. Kemp, waiting until my master came back. I soon after heard that Mr. Louis had died at Appalachicola, and had been buried at Tennessee Bluff. I was very much attached to the neighbourhood of Pendleton and Greenville, and feared, from Mr. Louis's death, I should not get back there.

As soon as this information arrived, Mr. Kemp put me, the carriage and horses, a gold watch, and cigars, up to auction, on which I was much frightened, knowing there would be some very cruel masters at the sale, and fearing I should again be disappointed in my attempt to escape from bondage. Mr. Beveridge, a Scotchman, from Appalachicola, bought me, the horses, and cigars. He was not a cruel master; he had been in America eighteen years, and, I believe, I was the first slave he ever bought. Mr. Kemp had no right to sell me, which he did, before he had written to Mr. Louis's brother.[12]

Shortly after this, Mr. Kemp, having some altercation with General Woodfork, it ended in a duel, in which Mr. W. was killed. A few weeks after, as Mr. Kemp was passing down a street, he was suddenly shot dead by Mr. Milton, a rival lawyer. When I heard this, I considered it a visitation of God on Mr. Kemp for having sold me unjustly, as I did not belong to him. This was soon discovered by me, Mr. Louis's brother having called at Mackintosh Hotel, Columbus, to claim me, but which he could not effect. After this, I travelled with Mr. Beveridge, through Georgia to the warm springs, and then came back to Columbus, going on to Marianna, his summer house, in Florida.

Here I met with better treatment than I had ever experienced before; we travelled on the whole summer; at the fall, Mr. Beveridge went to Appalachicola on business. Mr. Beveridge was contractor for the mail from Columbus to Appalachicola, and owner of three steamboats, the Versailles, Andrew Jackson, and Van Buren. He made me steward on board the Versailles, the whole winter. The river then got so low that the boats could not run. At this time Mr. Beveridge went to Mount Vernon. On our way we had to pass through the Indian nation. We arrived at Columbus, where I was taken dangerously ill of a fever. After I got well, Mr. Beveridge returned to Marianna, through the Indian nation. Having gone about twelve miles, he was taken very ill. I took him out of the carriage to a brook, and washed his hands and feet until he got better, when I got him into the carriage again, and drove off till we came to General Irving's, where he stopped several days on account of his health. While there, I observed on the floor of the kitchen several children, one about three months old, without anybody to take care of her; I asked where her mother was, and was told that Mrs. Irving had given her a very hard task to do at washing in a brook about a quarter of a mile distant. We heard after, that not being able to get it done, she had got some cords, tied them round her neck, climbed up a tree, swung off, and hung herself. Being missed, persons were sent after her, who observed several buzzards flying about a particular spot, to which they directed their steps, and found the poor woman nearly eaten up.

After this, we travelled several months without any thing remarkable taking place.

In the year 1834, Mr. Beveridge, who was now residing in Appalachicola, a town in West Florida, became a bankrupt, when all his property was sold, and I fell into the hands of a very cruel master, Mr. Register, a planter in the same state, of whom, knowing his savage character, I always had a dread. Previously to his purchasing me, he had frequently taunted me, by saying, "You have been a gentleman long enough, and, whatever may be the consequences, I intend to buy you." To which I remarked, that I would on no account live with him if I could help it. Nevertheless, intent upon his purpose, in the month of July, 1834, he bought me, after which, I was so exasperated that I cared not whether I lived or died; in fact, whilst I was on my passage from Appalachicola, I procured a quart bottle of whiskey, for the purpose of so intoxicating myself, that I might be able, either to plunge myself into the river, or so to enrage my master, that he should despatch me forthwith. I was, however, by a kind Providence, prevented from committing this horrid deed by an old slave on board, who, knowing my intention, secretly took the bottle from me; after which my hands were tied, and I was led into the town of Ochesa, to a warehouse, where my master was asked, by the proprietor of the place, the reason for his confining my hands; in answer to which, Mr. Register said, that he had purchased me. The proprietor, however, persuaded him to untie me; after which my master being excessively drunk, asked for a cow-hide, intending to flog me, from which the proprietor dissuaded him, saying, that he had known me for some time, and he was sure that I did not require to be flogged. From this place, we proceeded about mid-day on our way, he placing me on the bare back of a half starved old horse, which he had purchased, and upon which sharp *surface* he kindly intended I should ride about eighty miles, the distance we were then from his home. In this unpleasant situation, I could not help reflecting upon the prospects before me, not forgetting that I had heard that my new master had been in the habit of stealing cattle and other property, and among other things, a slave woman, and that I had said, as it afterwards turned out, in the hearing of some one who communicated the saying to my master, that I had been accustomed to live with a gentleman, and not with a rogue; and, finding that he had been informed of this, I had the additional dread of a few hundred lashes for it, on my arrival at my destination.

About two hours after we started, it began to rain very heavily, and continued to do so until we arrived at Marianna, about twelve at night, where we were to rest till morning. My master here questioned me, as to whether I intended to run away or not; and I not then knowing the sin of lying, at once told him that I would not. He then gave me his clothes to dry; I took them to the kitchen for that purpose, and he retired to bed, taking a bag of clothes belonging to me with him, as a kind of security, I presume, for my safety. In an hour or two afterwards I took his clothes to him dried, and found him fast asleep. I placed them by his side, and said, that I would then take my own to dry too, taking care to speak loud enough to ascertain whether he was asleep or not, knowing that he had a dirk and a pistol by his side, which he would not have hesitated using against me, if I had attempted secretly to have procured them. I was glad to find, that the effects of his drinking the day before had caused his sleeping very soundly, and I immediately resolved on making my escape; and without loss of time, started with my few clothes into the woods, which were in the immediate neighbourhood; and, after running many miles, I came to the river Chapoli, which is very deep, and so beset with alligators, that I dared not attempt to swim across. I paced up and down this river, with the hope of finding a conveyance across, for a whole day, the succeeding night, and till noon the following day, which was Saturday. About twelve o'clock on that day I discovered an Indian canoe, which had not, from all appearance, been used for some time; this, of course, I used to convey myself across, and after being obliged to go a little way down the river, by means of a piece of wood I providentially found in the boat, I landed on the opposite side. Here I found myself surrounded by planters looking for me, in consequence of which I hid myself in the bushes until night, when I again travelled several miles, to the farm of a Mr. Robinson, a large sugar-planter, where I rested till morning in a field. Afterwards I set out, working my way through the woods about twenty miles towards the east; this I knew by my knowledge of the position of the sun at its rising. Having reached the Chattahoochee River, which divides Florida from Georgia, I was again puzzled to know how to cross. It was three o'clock in the day, when a number of persons were fishing; having walked for some hours along the banks, I at last, after dark, procured a ferry-boat, which not being able, from the swiftness of the river, to steer direct across, I was carried many miles down the river, landing on the Georgian side, from whence I proceeded on through the woods two or three miles, and came to a little farm-house about twelve at night; at a short distance from the house, I found an old slave hut, into which I went, and informed the old man, who appeared seventy or eighty years old, that I had had a very bad master, from whom I had run away; and asked him, if he could give me something to eat, having had no suitable food for three or four days; he told me, he had nothing but a piece of dry Indian bread, which he cheerfully gave me; having eaten it, I went on a short distance from the hut, and laid down in the wood to rest for an hour or two. All the following day, (Monday,) I continued travelling through the woods, was greatly distressed for want of water to quench my thirst, it being a very dry country, till I came to Spring Creek, which is a wide, deep stream, and with some of which I gladly quenched my thirst. I then proceeded to cross the same by a bridge close by, and continued my way till dusk. I came to a gentleman's house in the woods, where I inquired how far it was to the next house, taking care to watch an opportunity to ask some individual whom I could master, and get away from, if any interruption to my progress was attempted. I went on for some time, it being a very fine moonlight night, and was presently alarmed by the howling of a wolf very near me, which I concluded was calling other wolves to join him in attacking me, having understood that they always assemble in numbers for such a purpose. The howling increased, and I was still pursued, and the numbers were evidently increasing fast; but I was happily rescued from my dreadful fright, by coming to some cattle, which attracted the wolves, and saved my life; for I could not get up the trees for safety, they being very tall pines, the lowest branches of which were at least forty or fifty feet from the ground, and the trunks very large and smooth.

About two o'clock I came to the house of a Mr. Cherry, on the borders of the Flint River; I went up to the house, and called them up to beg something to eat; but having nothing cooked, they kindly allowed me to lie down in the porch, where they made me a bed. In conversation with this Mr. Cherry, I discovered that I had known him before, having been in a steamboat, the Versailles, some months previous, which sunk very near his house, but which I did not at first discern to be the same. I then thought that it would not be prudent for me to stop there, and therefore told them I was in a hurry to get on, and must start very early again, he having no idea who I was; and I gave his son six cents to take me across the river, which he did when the sun was about half an hour high, and unfortunately landed me where there was a man building a boat, who knew me very well, and my former master too; he calling me by name, asked me where I was going.

I was very much frightened at being discovered, but summoned up courage, and said, that my master had gone on to Tallyhassa by the coach, and that there was not room for me, and I had to walk round to meet him. I then asked the man to put me into the best road to get there, which, however, I knew as well as he did, having travelled there before; he directed me the best way, but I of course took the contrary direction, wanting to get on to Savannah. By this hasty and wicked deception I saved myself from going to Bainbridge prison, which was close by, and to which I should surely have been taken had it been known that I was making my escape.

Leaving Bainbridge, I proceeded about forty miles, travelling all day under a scorching sun through the woods, in which I saw many deer and serpents, until I reached Thomas Town in the evening. I there inquired the way to Augusta of a man whom I met, and also asked where I could obtain lodgings, and was told that there was a poor minister about a mile from the place who would give me lodgings. I accordingly went and found them in a little log-house, where, having awakened the family, I found them all lying on the bare boards, where I joined them for the remainder of the night.

In the morning the old gentleman prayed for me that I might be preserved on my journey; he had previously asked me where I was going, and I knowing, that if I told him the right place, any that inquired of him for me would be able to find me, asked the way to Augusta instead of Savannah, my real destination. I also told him that I was partly Indian and partly white, but I am also partly African; but this I omitted to tell him, knowing if I did I should be apprehended. After I had left this hut, I again inquired for Augusta, for the purpose of misleading my pursuers, but I afterwards took my course through the woods, and came into a road, called the Coffee road, which General Jackson cut down for his troops, at the time of the war between the Americans and Spaniards, in Florida;[13] in which road there are but few houses, and which I preferred for the purpose of avoiding detection.

After several days I left this road, and took a more direct way to Savannah, where I had to wade through two rivers before I came to the Alatamah, which I crossed in a ferry-boat, about a mile below the place where the rivers Oconee and Ocmulgee run together into one river, called the Alatamah. I here met with some cattle drovers, who were collecting cattle to drive to Savannah. On walking on before them, I began to consider in what way I could obtain a passport for Savannah, and determined on the following plan:—

I called at a cottage, and after I had talked some time with the wife, who began to feel greatly for me, in consequence of my telling her a little of my history, (her husband being out hunting,) I pretended to show her my passport, feeling for it everywhere about my coat and hat, and not finding it, I went back a little way pretending to look for it, but came back saying I was very sorry, but I did not know where it was. At last the man came home, carrying a deer upon his shoulders, which he brought into the yard and began to dress it. The wife then went out to tell him my situation, and after long persuasion he said he could not write, but that if I could tell his son what was in my passport he should write me one; and knowing that I should not be able to pass Savannah without one, and having heard several free colored men read theirs, I thought I could tell the lad what to write. The lad sat down and wrote what I told him, nearly filling a large sheet of paper for the passport, and another sheet with recommendations. These being completed, I was invited to partake of some of the fresh venison, which the woman of the house had prepared for dinner, and having done so, and feeling grateful for their kindness, I proceeded on my way. Going along I took my papers out of my pocket, and looking at them, although I could not read a word, I perceived that the boy's writing was very unlike other writing that I had seen, and was greatly blotted besides; consequently I was afraid that these documents would not answer my purpose, and began to consider what other plan I could pursue to obtain another pass.

I had now to wade through another river to which I came, and which I had great difficulty in crossing in consequence of the water overflowing the banks of several rivers to the extent of upwards of twenty miles. In the midst of the water I passed one night upon a small island, and the next day I went through the remainder of the water. On many occasions I was obliged to walk upon my toes, and consequently found the advantage of being six feet two inches high, and at other times was obliged to swim. In the middle of this extremity I felt it would be imprudent for me to return; for if my master was in pursuit of me, my safest place from him was in the water, if I could keep my head above the surface. I was, however, dreadfully frightened, and most earnestly prayed that I might be kept from a watery grave, and resolved that if again I landed, I would spend my life in the service of God.

Having through mercy again started on my journey, I met with the drovers, and having, whilst in the water, taken the pass out of my hat, and so dipped it in the water as to spoil it, I showed it to the men, and asked them where I could get another. They told me, that in the neighbourhood there lived a rich cotton merchant, who would write me one. They took me to him, and gave their word, that they saw the passport before it was wet, (for I had previously showed it to them,) upon which the cotton planter wrote a free pass and a recommendation, to which the cow-drovers affixed their marks.

The recommendation was as follows:

"John Roper, a very interesting young lad, whom I have seen and travelled with for eighty or ninety miles on his road from Florida, is a free man, descended from Indian and white. I trust, he will be allowed to pass on without interruption, being convinced from what I have seen that he is free, and though dark, is not an African. I had seen his papers before they were wetted."

These cow-drovers, who procured me the passport and recommendation from the cotton planter, could not read; and they were intoxicated when they went with me to him. I am part African, as well as Indian and white, my father being a white man, Henry Roper, Esq., Caswell county, North Carolina, U.S., a very wealthy slave-holder, who sold me when quite a child, for the strong resemblance I bore to him. My mother is part Indian, part African; but I dared not disclose that, or I should have been taken up. I then had eleven miles to go to Savannah, one of the greatest slave-holding cities in America, and where they are always looking out for runaway slaves. When at this city, I had travelled about five hundred miles.* It required great courage to pass through this place. I went through the main street with apparent confidence, though much alarmed; did not stop at any house in the city, but went down immediately to the dock, and inquired for a berth, as a steward to a vessel to New York. I had been in this capacity before on the Appalachicola River. The person whom I asked to procure me a berth was steward of one of the New York packets; he knew Captain Deckay, of the schooner Fox, and got me a situation on board that vessel, in five minutes after I had been at the docks. The schooner Fox was a very old vessel, twenty-seven years old, laden with lumber and cattle for New York; she was rotten and could not be insured. The sailors were afraid of her; but I ventured on board, and five minutes after we dropped from the docks into the river. My spirits then began to revive, and I thought I should get to a free country directly. We cast anchor in the stream, to keep the sailors on, as they were so dissatisfied with the vessel, and lay there four days; during which time I had to go into the city several times, which exposed me to great danger, as my master was after me, and I dreaded meeting with him in the city.

Fearing the Fox would not sail before I should be seized, I deserted her,

---

*The distance between these two places is much less than five hundred miles; but I was obliged to travel round about, in order to avoid being caught.

and went on board a brig sailing to Providence, that was towed out by a steamboat, and got thirty miles from Savannah. During this time I endeavoured to persuade the steward to take me as an assistant, and hoped to have accomplished my purpose; but the captain had observed me attentively, and thought I was a slave; he therefore ordered me, when the steamboat was sent back, to go on board her to Savannah, as the fine for taking a slave from that city to any of the free states is five hundred dollars. I reluctantly went back to Savannah, among slave-holders and slaves. My mind was in a sad state, and I was under strong temptation to throw myself into the river. I had deserted the schooner Fox, and knew that the captain might put me into prison till the vessel was ready to sail; if this had happened, and my master had come to the jail in search of me, I must have gone back to slavery. But when I reached the docks at Savannah, the first person I met was the captain of the Fox, looking for another steward in my place. He was a very kind man, belonging to the free states, and inquired if I would go back to his vessel. This usage was very different to what I expected, and I gladly accepted his offer. This captain did not know that I was a slave. In about two days we sailed from Savannah for New York.

I am (August, 1834) unable to express the joy I now felt. I never was at sea before, and, after I had been out about an hour, was taken with sea-sickness, which continued five days. I was scarcely able to stand up, and one of the sailors was obliged to take my place. The captain was very kind to me all this time; but even after I recovered, I was not sufficiently well to do my duty properly, and could not give satisfaction to the sailors, who swore at me, and asked me why I shipped, as I was not used to the sea. We had a very quick passage, and in six days after leaving Savannah, we were in the harbour at Staten Island, where the vessel was quarantined for two days, six miles from New York. The captain went to the city, but left me aboard with the sailors, who had most of them been brought up in the slave-holding states, and were very cruel men. One of the sailors was particularly angry with me because he had to perform the duties of my place; and while the captain was in the city, the sailors called me to the fore-hatch, where they said they would treat me. I went, and while I was talking, they threw a rope round my neck and nearly choked me. The blood streamed from my nose profusely. They also took up ropes with large knots, and knocked me over the head. They said I was a negro; they despised me; and I expected they would have thrown me into the water. When we arrived at the city, these men, who had so ill-treated me, ran away, that they might escape the punishment which would otherwise have been inflicted on them. When I arrived in the city of New

York, I thought I was free; but learned I was not, and could be taken there.[14] I went out into the country several miles, and tried to get employment, but failed, as I had no recommendation. I then returned to New York, but finding the same difficulty there to get work as in the country, I went back to the vessel, which was to sail eighty miles up the Hudson River, to Poughkeepsie. When I arrived, I obtained employment at an inn, and after I had been there about two days, was seized with the cholera, which was at that place. The complaint was, without doubt, brought on by my having subsisted on fruit only for several days, while I was in the slave states. The landlord of the inn came to me when I was in bed, suffering violently from cholera, and told me he knew I had that complaint, and as it had never been in his house, I could not stop there any longer. No one would enter my room, except a young lady, who appeared very pious and amiable, and had visited persons with the cholera. She immediately procured me some medicine at her own expense, and administered it herself; and whilst I was groaning with agony, the landlord came up and ordered me out of the house directly. Most of the persons in Poughkeepsie had retired for the night, and I lay under a shed on some cotton bales. The medicine relieved me, having been given so promptly, and next morning I went from the shed, and laid on the banks of the river below the city. Towards evening I felt much better, and went on in a steamboat to the city of Albany, about eighty miles. When I reached there, I went into the country, and tried for three or four days to procure employment, but failed.

At that time I had scarcely any money, and lived upon fruit; so I returned to Albany, where I could get no work, as I could not show the recommendations I possessed, which were only from slave states, and I did not wish any one to know I came from them. After a time, I went up the western canal as steward in one of the boats. When I had gone about 350 miles up the canal, I found I was going too much towards the slave states, in consequence of which I returned to Albany, and went up the northern canal into one of the New England states, Vermont. The distance I had travelled, including the 350 miles I had to return from the west, and the 100 to Vermont, was 2300 miles. When I reached Vermont, I found the people very hospitable and kind; they seemed opposed to slavery, so I told them I was a runaway slave. I hired myself to a firm in Sudbury.* After I had been in Sudbury some time,

* During my stay in this town, I thought of the vow I made in the water, (page 72 [of the 1838 Philadelphia edition; see page 66 in this edition],) and I became more thoughtful about the salvation of my soul. I attended the Methodist chapel, where a Mr. Benton

the neighboring farmers told me that I had hired myself for much less money than I ought. I mentioned it to my employers, who were very angry about it; I was advised to leave by some of the people round, who thought the gentlemen I was with would write to my former master, informing him where I was, and obtain the reward fixed upon me. Fearing I should be taken, I immediately left and went into the town of Ludlow, where I met with a kind friend Mr. ——,* who sent me to school for several weeks. At this time I was advertised in the papers, and was obliged to leave; I went a little way out of Ludlow to a retired place, and lived two weeks with a Mr. ——, deacon of a church at Ludlow; at this place I could have obtained education, had it been safe to have remained.* From there I went to New Hampshire, where I was not safe, so went to Boston, Massachusetts, with the hope of returning to Ludlow, to which place I was much attached. At Boston I met with a friend, who kept a shop, and took me to assist him for several weeks. Here I did not consider myself safe, as persons from all parts of the country were continually coming to the shop, and I feared some might come who knew me. I now had my head shaved and bought a wig, and engaged myself to a Mr. Perkins of Brookline, three miles from Boston, where I remained about a month. Some of the family discovered that I wore a wig, and said that I was a runaway slave, but the neighbors all round thought I was a white, to prove which, I have a document in my possession to call me to military duty. The law is, that no slave or colored person performs this, but every other person in America of the age of twenty-one is called upon to perform military duty, once or twice in the year, or pay a fine.

---

preached, and there I began to feel that I was a great sinner. During the latter part of my stay here, I became more anxious about salvation, and I entertained the absurd notion that religion would come to me in some extraordinary way. With this impression, I used to go into the woods two hours before daylight to pray, and expected something would take place, and I should become religious.

*It would not be proper to mention any names, as a person in any of the states of America found harboring a slave, would have to pay a heavy fine.

*While in this neighborhood, I attended the Baptist meeting, and trust the preaching of the gospel was much blessed to my soul. As this was the first time I was ever favored with any education, I was very intent upon learning to read the Bible, and in a few weeks I was able, from my own reading, to repeat by heart the whole of the last chapter of Matthew. I also attended the prayer and inquiry meetings, where the attendants used to relate their experience, and I was requested to do the same. I found these meetings a great blessing, and they were the means, under God, of communicating to my mind a more clear and distinct knowledge of the way of salvation by Jesus Christ.

COPY OF THE DOCUMENT.

"Mr. Moses Roper,

"You being duly enrolled as a soldier in the company, under the command of Captain Benjamin Bradley, are hereby notified and ordered to appear at the Town House in Brookline, on Friday 28th instant, at 3 o'clock, P. M., for the purpose of filling the vacancy in said company occasioned by the promotion of Lieut. Nathaniel M. Weeks, and of filling any other vacancy which may then and there occur in said company, and there wait further orders.

"By order of the captain,

"F. P. WENTWORTH, clerk.

"*Brookline, August 14th, 1835.*"*

I then returned to the city of Boston, to the shop where I was before.* Several weeks after I had returned to my situation two colored men informed me that a gentleman had been inquiring for a person whom, from the description, I knew to be myself, and offered them a considerable sum if they would disclose my place of abode; but they being much opposed to slavery, came and told me, upon which information I secreted myself till I could get off. I went into the Green Mountains for several weeks, from thence to the city of New York, and remained in secret several days, till I heard of a ship, the Napoleon, sailing to England, and on the 11th of November, 1835, I sailed, taking with me letters of recommendation to the Rev. Drs. Morison and Raffles, and the Rev. Alex. Fletcher.[15] The time I first started from slavery was in July, 1834, so that I was nearly sixteen months in making my escape.

On the 29th of November, 1835, I reached Liverpool, and my feelings when I first touched the shores of Britain were indescribable, and can only be properly understood by those who have escaped from the cruel bondage of slavery.

*During the first part of my abode in this city, I attended at the colored church in Bellnap street; and I hope I found both profit and pleasure in attending the means of divine grace. I now saw the wicked part I had taken in using so much deception in making my escape. After a time, I found slave-owners were in the habit of going to this colored chapel to look for runaway slaves. I became alarmed and afterwards attended the preaching of the Rev. Dr. Sharp. I waited upon the doctor to request he would baptize me, and admit me a member of his church; and after hearing my experience, he wished me to call again. This I did, but he was gone into the country, and I saw him no more.

*Being very tall, I was taken to be twenty-one, but my correct age, as far as I can tell, is stated in page 13 [of the 1838 Philadelphia edition; see page 42 of this edition].

"'Tis liberty alone that gives the flower of fleeting life its lustre and
    perfume;
And we are weeds without it."
"Slaves cannot breathe in England;
If their lungs receive our air, that moment they are free;
They touch our country and their shackles fall." — *Cowper*.[16]

When I reached Liverpool, I proceeded to Dr. Raffles, and handed my
letters of recommendation to him. He received me very kindly, and introduced me to a member of his church, with whom I stayed the night. Here I
met with the greatest attention and kindness. The next day, I went on to Man-
chester, where I met with many kind friends, among others Mr. Adshead,
a hosier of that town, to whom I desire through this medium, to return my
most sincere thanks for the many great services which he rendered me, adding both to my spiritual and temporal comfort. I would not, however, forget
to remember here, Mr. Leese, Mr. Childs, Mr. Crewdson, and Mr. Clare,
the latter of whom gave me a letter to Mr. Scoble, the secretary of the Antislavery Society.[17] I remained here several days, and then proceeded to London, December 12th, 1835, and immediately called on Mr. Scoble, to whom
I delivered my letter; this gentleman procured me a lodging. I then lost no
time in delivering my letters to Dr. Morison and the Rev. Alexander Fletcher,
who received me with the greatest kindness, and shortly after this Dr. Morison sent my letter from New York, with another from himself, to the *Patriot*
newspaper, in which he kindly implored the sympathy of the public in my
behalf. The appeal was read by Mr. Christopherson, a member of Dr. Morison's church, of which gentleman I express but little of my feelings and
gratitude, when I say, that throughout he has been towards me a parent, and
for whose tenderness and sympathy, I desire ever to feel that attachment
which I do not know how to express.

I stayed at his house several weeks, being treated as one of the family.
The appeal in the *Patriot*, referred to getting a suitable academy for me,
which the Rev. Dr. Cox[18] recommended at Hackney, where I remained half
a year, going through the rudiments of an English education. At this time I
attended the ministry of Dr. Cox, which I enjoyed very much, and to which
I ascribe the attainment of clearer views of divine grace than I had before. I
had attended here several months, when I expressed my wish to Dr. Cox to
become a member of his church; I was proposed, and after stating my experience was admitted, March 31st, 1836. Here I feel it a duty to present my
tribute of thankfulness, however feebly expressed, to the affectionate and

devoted attention of the Rev. Doctor, from whom, under God, I received very much indeed of spiritual advice and consolation, as well as a plentiful administration to my temporal necessities. I would not forget also to mention the kindness of his church generally, by whom I was received with Christian love and charity. Never, I trust, will be effaced from my memory, the parental care of the Rev. Dr. Morison, from whom I can strictly say, I received the greatest kindness I ever met with, and to whom, as long as God gives me lips to utter, or mind to reflect, I desire to attribute the comfort which I have experienced since I set my foot upon the happy shores of England.

Here it is necessary that I should draw this narrative to a close, not that my materials are exhausted, but that I am unwilling to extend it to a size which might preclude many well-wishers from the possession of it.

But I must remark, that my feelings of happiness at having escaped from cruel bondage, are not unmixed with sorrow of a very touching kind. "*The land of the Free*" still contains the mother, the brothers, and the sisters of Moses Roper, not enjoying liberty, not the possessors of like feelings with me, not having even a distant glimpse of advancing towards freedom, but still slaves! This is a weight which hangs heavy on me. As circumstances at present stand, there is not much prospect of ever again seeing those dear ones—that dear mother, from whom, on the Sunday night, I was torn away by armed slave-holders, and carried into cruel bondage.* And, nothing would contribute so much to my entire happiness, if the kindness of a gracious Providence should ever place me in such favorable circumstances as to be able to purchase the freedom of so beloved a parent. But I desire to express my entire resignation to the will of God. Should that Divine Being who made of one flesh all the kindreds of the earth, see fit that I should again clasp them to my breast, and see in them the reality of free men and free women, how shall I, a poor mortal, be enabled to sing a strain of praise sufficiently appropriate to such a boon from heaven?

But if the all-wise Disposer of all things should see fit to keep them still in suffering and bondage, it is a mercy to know that he orders all things well, that he is still the Judge of all the earth, and that under such dispensations of his Providence, he is working out that which shall be most for the advantage of his creatures.

Whatever I may have experienced in America, at the hands of cruel task-masters, yet I am unwilling to speak in any but respectful terms of the land of my birth. It is far from my wish to attempt to degrade America in the eyes

*See page 36 [of the 1838 Philadelphia edition; see page 52 of this edition].

of Britons. I love her institutions in the free states, her zeal for Christ; I bear no enmity even to the slave-holders, but regret their delusions; many I am aware are deeply sensible of the fault, but some I regret to say are not, and I could wish to open their eyes to their sin; may the period come when God shall wipe off this deep stain from her constitution, and may America soon be *indeed* the land of the free.

In conclusion, I thank my dear friends in England for their affectionate attentions, and may God help me to show by my future walk in life, that I am not wanting in my acknowledgments of their kindness. But above all, to the God of all grace, I desire here before his people, to acknowledge that all the way in which he has led me, has been the right way; and as in his mercy and wisdom, he has led me to this country, where I am allowed to go free, may all my actions tend to lead me on, through the mercy of God in Christ, in the right way, to a city of habitation.

THE END.

Notes

The epigraph on the title page is from "The Task" (1785), by William Cowper (1731–1800), book 2 ("The Timepiece"), lines 40–45. The sentence of lines 44–45 actually continues in lines 46–47: "Of all your empire; that where Britain's power / Is felt, mankind may feel her mercy too."

1. John Morison, D.D. (1791–1859), a Congregationalist minister in Chelsea, educated at the University of Glasgow, who authored numerous minor works and discourses on religious topics.

2. Reverend Thomas Price, D.D. (dates not known). Within a couple of years after publication, Price became angered that Roper intended to continue his antislavery lecturing, instead of traveling to Africa as a missionary, and requested that his preface be removed from later editions of the narrative.

3. A boarding school in London. Roper received some education here after sailing to England in 1835.

4. Caswell County is located about halfway across the state of North Carolina, immediately south of Virginia. The county was founded in 1777 and named after Richard Caswell, the first governor of North Carolina following American independence. Its antebellum economy was primarily agricultural.

5. Moses Roper's father was Henry H. Roper, a planter in Caswell County, North Carolina. The year of his birth has been variously reported as 1784 and as 1788. Henry Roper probably died in 1845, as Caswell County estate records indicate that his will was probated in July of that year. He was the son of William Roper (c. 1766–?) and Keziah Yates (c. 1766–?), an unmarried couple. Caswell County marriage records indicate that

Henry Roper married Rachel Farley (c. 1792–c. 1831) on October 4, 1810, and Polly Elmore on November 9, 1832. Rachel Farley's father was probably John Farley, since there is no marriage record for the other Farley (Stephen) in Caswell County. Federal census records for Caswell County indicate that Henry Roper's household included six slaves in 1820 and six slaves in 1830.

6. This person is probably connected to the Caswell County Gooch line (see note 7). William Gooch's daughter Mary Gooch married a John Sneed in 1765 and their descendants, including John Gooch Sneed, moved to South Carolina and Georgia.

7. John Gooch (c. 1793–1840), son of William Gosling Gooch (?–1803). The South Carolina Gooch line had connections to Caswell County, North Carolina. In 1775, William Gosling Gooch bought land in Bute County (now Franklin and Warren Counties), North Carolina; in 1778, he witnessed a land deed for William and Frances Gooch of Caswell County (relationship unclear); he later bought land himself in Caswell County before settling in Kershaw County around 1800. The Caswell-Kershaw link, however, is probably coincidental to Roper's sale to Gooch, given the number of intervening exchanges between his departure from Caswell County and his arrival in Kershaw County. Kershaw County is located in north-central South Carolina. The area was settled by the British in the early 1730s, and the county takes its name from Joseph Kershaw (1727–91). Its most famous resident is probably Mary Boykin Chesnut (1823–86), the diarist and chronicler of the Civil War.

8. Leroy Hammond (1801?–81), a resident of Kershaw County, was evidently the son of Samuel Burford Hammond (1782–1857) and Nancy Twitty. He is reported to have married John Gooch's daughter Nancy (or Nancey) Robinson Gooch in 1822.

9. Roper evidently means the same person as the "Mr. Michael" who is mentioned in the second paragraph of the narrative.

10. Warren Ransom Davis (1793–1835), an attorney from Pendleton, South Carolina, who served in the U.S. House of Representatives from 1827 to 1835, first as a Jacksonian and then as a Nullifier.

11. In 1832 and 1833, a dispute erupted between South Carolina and the U.S. government over the federal tariffs of 1828 and 1832, which reduced the value of exports and thus posed a threat to South Carolina's agricultural economy. Led by John C. Calhoun, the South Carolina legislature in November 1832 passed the "South Carolina Ordinance of Nullfication," which declared the tariffs void within the state and included measures for military preparations and even secession. In the face of President Andrew Jackson's determination to crush this defiance, the South Carolina legislature repealed the nullification ordinance in March 1833.

12. At this point, Roper was still legally part of the estate of "Mr. Louis."

13. The Coffee Road, running east-west across southern Georgia, was built on land ceded by the Lower Creek Indians to the United States in 1814, as part of a treaty nego-

tiated by Andrew Jackson. Its completion in 1824 facilitated white settlement in the distant Southeast. The road was named after General John Coffee, Jackson's cavalry commander in the War of 1812, who supervised its construction.

14. The U.S. Constitution (art. 4, sec. 2), provided for the return of "fugitives from service." This text was the basis for the Fugitive Slave Acts passed by Congress in 1793 and 1850.

15. Probably Alexander Fletcher, D.D. (1787–1860), a Presbyterian divine, educated at the University of Glasgow, who went on to become an enormously popular minister in London.

16. From Cowper's "The Task" (1785); see the note concerning the epigraph. The first excerpt is from book 5 ("The Winter Morning Walk"), lines 446–48. The second is from book 2 ("The Timepiece"), lines 40–42.

17. John Scoble (1799–c. 1867), a Congregational minister and antislavery activist who in 1831 was appointed lecturer of the Agency Committee, an organization founded by the Anti-Slavery Society for purposes of public agitation. Scoble helped found the British and Foreign Anti-Slavery Society in 1839 and was appointed its secretary in 1842. He assumed managerial control of the black settlement at Dawn, in Canada West, in 1852, and served in the Canadian parliament from 1863 to 1867.

18. Francis Augustus Cox, D.D. (1783–1853), the Baptist pastor at Hackney from 1811 to 1853. He played a generous role in financing Roper's education in London. Cox's reputation in antislavery circles was mixed, however, because he saw himself more as a churchman than as an activist.

The Narrative of

Lunsford Lane

INTRODUCTION
Tampathia Evans

Once the Raleigh, North Carolina, police apprehended the former slave Lunsford Lane shortly after his return to that city in late April 1842, the local authorities questioned him repeatedly in an impromptu "call court" about his recent activities while traveling in the North. Having spent the last year soliciting donations in New York and Boston for the purchase of his enslaved family, Lane found himself accused of *"delivering abolition lectures,"* a subversive and dangerous activity for any North Carolinian, particularly a former slave, in 1842. Lane acknowledged that he had associated with known abolitionists while in Boston, but he testified that he "did not know whether I had given abolition lectures or not." Lane claimed he simply "went out from house to house, from place of business to place of business, and from church to church, relating, where I could gain an ear, the same heart-rending and soul-trying story." Throughout his interrogation, the former slave maintained that his only interest in going north had been to raise the money needed to free his wife and seven children. In response to the charge of consorting with abolitionists, Lane shrewdly argued that he could not afford to be partial to any particular faction in achieving his goal: "In pursuing that course, the people, first one and then another contributed, until I had succeeded in raising the amount alluded to, namely, thirteen hundred and eighty dollars. I may have had contributions from abolitionists, but I did not stop to ask those who assisted me whether they were anti-slavery or pro-slavery, for I considered that the money coming from either, would accomplish the object I had in view."

Lane's testimony, which quickly drew a large crowd of white towns-people, suggested that his priority while in the North had been his family's welfare, not politics. Lane's interrogators, however, sensed in the very existence of this resourceful black man and self-emancipated slave a threat to antebellum southern society, founded as it was on the myth that black men were fitted for enslavement and were naturally dependent on their masters. Lane, on the other hand, even while a slave had developed a series of successful business ventures in his hometown of Raleigh, which had enabled him to purchase his own home and garner the respect and patronage of some of the most influential white men in the entire state of North Carolina.

Thwarted in their hopes of finding evidence of subversive activity on the part of Lane and perhaps apprehensive about drawing the ire of his wealthy patrons, Lane's interrogators, many of them well-respected men of the city, released him. Yet Lane's trials had only begun. While attempting to make his way to the home of a white friend, he was abducted again, this time by the "rabble" of the town, a mob of mostly working-class whites, who carted Lane off toward the town gallows for a second round of questioning. Unconvinced by the ex-slave's earlier alibi, the mob demanded of Lane "the truth about those abolition lectures you have been giving at the North." Expecting to be put to death at any moment, Lane replied that he had already told the truth and that he had no intention of passing "into the other world with a lie upon my lips." Ingeniously, he managed to deflect his accusers' suspicions and threats by forcing the white men to accept his version of his activities in the North or contradict their own firmly held prejudices about abolitionists. "I replied that the people of Raleigh had always said the abolitionists did not believe in buying slaves, but contended that their masters ought to free them without pay. I had been laboring to buy my family; and how then could they suppose me to be in league with the abolitionists?"

Frustrated in their attempt to intimidate the former slave and perhaps unnerved by Lane's familiarity with some members of the mob, the white men reassured Lane that they had no intention of killing him. Instead, the mob settled on a relatively mild version of punishment — tarring and feathering — before releasing their victim. "They all expressed great interest in my welfare," Lane writes in his autobiography; they "told me to stay in the place as long as I wished, and with other such words of consolation they bid me good night." Later in 1842, when Lunsford Lane related this disturbing experience at a meeting of the American Anti-Slavery Society in New York, he added a rather telling amendment. Asked by an audience member "how he escaped from his tormenters," after being tarred and feathered, Lane replied: "I was set at liberty by the people, who said, 'Now we have done what we wished to do. Now go home, and be not afraid. You may do what business you please, and you shall not be hurt. We merely wished to let the aristocracy know that they should not have their own way.'"[1]

Lane's allusion to the "aristocracy" calls attention to one of the central themes addressed in his autobiography, *The Narrative of Lunsford Lane, Formerly of Raleigh, N.C., Embracing an Account of His Early Life, the Redemption by Purchase of Himself and Family from Slavery, and His Banishment from the Place of His Birth for the Crime of Wearing a Colored Skin.* Self-published in July 1842, a few months after he and his family reach their new home of Boston, Massachusetts, Lane's narrative reveals the complex social and economic dynamics that informed race relations in the antebellum South. His position within the urban community of Raleigh, initially as a house servant for a prominent Raleigh family and later as a self-employed businessman and entrepreneur, allowed Lane an unusual perspective on the class divisions between well-to-do and working-class whites as well as the social stratifications that developed between rural and urban slaves. Lane's relations with the poor whites of Raleigh serve to foreground his "friendship" with the aristocracy, "the first people of the place," while he depicts his "town slave" status as a blessing from heaven, granting him privileges seldom afforded rural plantation slaves. Charting the social and economic means by which he became a successful slave entrepreneur who purchased himself and, ultimately, his family, Lane portrays himself in his autobiography as the personification of the Protestant work ethic, at one point managing five different business ventures simultaneously. This construction of Lane's self-image as the quintessential self-made man, a "Franklinesque role player," serves not only to ally him ideologically with the majority of his targeted audience—white middle-class northerners—but also provides an answer to proslavery concerns regarding the American slave's preparation for freedom and his ability to achieve economic self-sufficiency.[2]

What Lane chooses not to include in his narrative is also significant in shaping his rhetorical strategy. Although the "heart-rending and soul-trying story" that he recounts for us details at length his legal and financial tribulations in purchasing himself and his family from slavery, it contains few of the physically violent and emotionally scarring atrocities associated with slave life frequently reported by slave narrators. Absent are the bloodthirsty whippings, the sexual exploitation of black women, and the occasional dispassionate killing of an enslaved person. Nor does Lane draw on the black militancy espoused by contemporary revolutionaries like Nat Turner, whose 1831 rebellion took place in the neighboring state of Virginia as the twenty-eight-year-old Lunsford was working his way toward manumission, or the protest rhetoric of David Walker, a fellow North Carolinian whose radical *Appeal*, initially published in 1829, advocated aggressive resistance against slavery. "I have not, in this publication attempted or desired to argue anything," Lane tells us in his preface. Regardless of whether we take him entirely at his word, the most pronounced thesis of Lane's narrative testifies to his determination, as a slave, to work *within* the system imposed by whites in the South—and to manipulate and exploit it as much as possible. Emphasizing his financial and social successes rather than the psychological costs of his accommodations to slavery, Lane delivers on the promise of his preface: to highlight the "bright," rather than the dark, side of slavery.

In its initial publication, Lunsford Lane's narrative had a twofold purpose. Written primarily to raise money for the support of his family by its sale to abolitionist sympathizers, his life story, he hoped, would also "produce an impression favorable to my countrymen in bondage." Clearly, Lane was sensitive to the possibilities that his achievements symbolized for the approximately 2.5 million blacks enslaved in the United States in 1842.[3] If the slave Lunsford Lane, self-educated and with few resources, could start several businesses (and create a relatively significant amount of wealth) in one of the strongholds of the southern slavocracy, and thus transform himself into the freeman Lunsford Lane, what potential did that accomplishment hold out for other blacks in his position? The social implication of the outcome of Lane's narrative highlights the dilemma for upwardly mobile slaves. The presence of a Lunsford Lane in the South threatened the fragile accord that existed between the white upper class, which benefited the most from slavery, and the white working class, which often found itself in competition against enterprising slaves and free blacks like Lane.

Lunsford Lane was born on May 30, 1803, the only child of Edward and Clarissa Lane, slaves on neighboring plantations in Raleigh, North Carolina. Lunsford's mother served as cook and house servant to the family of Sherwood Haywood, "a man of considerable respectability, a planter and the cashier of a bank," who owned several plantations in and around the city of Raleigh. Like many slave children raised alongside the white children of their masters, Lane was at first unaware of his status as property, writing, "I knew no difference between myself and the white children; nor did they seem to know any in turn." Lane alludes to the depth of his relationship to his white peers when he later visits the adult children of his ex-master in preparation for his departure to the North. He writes that they all wept, recalling how they "had been children together, playing in the same yard. . . . And in those infant years there were pencillings made upon the heart, which time and opposite fortunes could not all efface."

Yet these heartfelt feelings shared by members of the benevolent Haywood household did not preclude the inevitable. Eventually, the Haywood children began to order young Lunsford about. "I found too," he writes, "that they had learned to read, while I was not permitted to have a book in my hand." Nevertheless, by his own admission, Lane's "condition as a slave was comparatively a happy, indeed a highly favored one."

This status as a "favored" slave in his master's household provided a partial foundation from which Lane began his push toward self-reliance and economic independence. As was the case with many slaves living in towns and urban areas, Lane's everyday circumstances afforded him a greater measure of personal autonomy than his rural counterparts would have experienced on the plantation. His proximity to his master and his family as a "house servant" allowed him certain privileges (better food and clothing, less physically strenuous work) and a degree of personal and familial security that most slaves did not typically receive. Lane concedes, "If for any thing this side of the invisible world, I bless heaven, it is that I was not born a plantation slave."

In his 1863 biography of Lane, *Lunsford Lane; or, Another Helper from North Carolina*, the abolitionist minister Rev. William G. Hawkins expounds on the contrast between the relatively comfortable environment that Lane enjoyed and what potentially could have been his fate on one of his master's outlying plantations: "The wretched condition of the slaves on this plantation [in Tarboro, North Carolina] was owing, in a great measure, to his master's residence in Raleigh, and his inability, from other engagements, to supervise matters personally. Their improvidence led to much sickness and to frequent deaths. The house-servants of Mr. Haywood dreaded nothing so much as the threat of being transferred to this plantation."[4]

Lane's enslaved contemporaries would have agreed that living in town was clearly a more advantageous existence than being transferred to the plantation, which was tantamount to severe punishment. When Harriet Jacobs, the Edenton, North Carolina, author of *Incidents in the Life of a Slave Girl* (1861), refused the sexual advances of her master, he banished her temporarily to his plantation outside of town as retribution.[5] Frederick Douglass recalls in *My Bondage and My Freedom* (1855) that when Thomas Auld, his Eastern Shore master, judged the teenaged Douglass's attitude "unsuitable" because of the "very pernicious effect" of his growing up in Baltimore, Auld dispatched his slave to the rural plantation of a slave-breaker, Edward Covey, "to be broken."[6]

For Lane however, who learns to get along by going along, such a punishment never seems to be a real danger. Although as a boy he is genuinely concerned about being sold away, "conveyed to the far South," Lane's fears of being separated from his family and friends never materialize. Even as an adult, when the death of his master forces his widow to sell off several slave children from their parents and slave husbands from their wives, Lane's family remains intact. However, his remarks on the subject reveal that he is conscious of the disparities generated by the inequitable living conditions within the slave community that contribute to the development of class divisions among people of color:

> [A]ltogether I fared quite differently from many poor fellows whom it makes my blood run chill to think of, confined to the plantation, with not enough food and that little of the coarsest kind, to satisfy the gnawings of hunger, — compelled oftentimes, to hie away in the night-time, when worn down with work, and *steal*, (if it be stealing,) and privately devour such things as they can lay their hands upon, — made to feel the rigors of bondage with no cessation, — torn away sometimes from the few friends they love, friends doubly dear because they are few, and transported to a climate where in a few hard years they die, — or at best conducted heavily and sadly to their resting place under the sod, upon their old master's plantation, — sometimes, perhaps, enlivening the air with merriment, but a forced merriment, that comes from a stagnant or stupefied heart. Such as this is the fate of the plantation slaves generally, but such was not my lot. My way was comparatively light, and what is better, it conducted to freedom.

As a result of his family's "favored status," Lane has access to both his mother and father apparently throughout his entire adolescence, an unusual blessing for a child in the slave-trading economy of the South, where few slave children were raised with both biological parents in close proximity. As Richard Wade notes in *Slavery in the Cities*, "urban proximity permitted wider opportunity for the choice of a mate," but the "greater instability of slavery in the towns meant that attachments were seldom permanent."[7] Thus the significance and influence of an intact family unit cannot be underestimated when considering the resources Lane drew on for his unlikely entrepreneurial career. Lane's parents provided a stable familial model that he later emulated in caring for his own family.

While we learn of Lunsford's love for his mother, Clarissa, and his concern for her well-being as he prepares to go north, we are told little about his relationship to her. Rather, it is his father, Edward, who makes the greatest impact on Lane's life, perhaps more so than any other individual. It is Edward Lane who gives young Lunsford the means to make his first income, providing the key to the economic independence Lunsford faithfully believes will open the door to freedom. "One day . . . my father gave me a small basket of peaches. I sold them for thirty cents, which was the first money I ever had in my life." With this paternal encouragement, Lane's entrepreneurial endeavors began.

The relative stability of Lane's slave life coupled with his burgeoning economic independence had a paradoxical effect on the successful slave. Rather than making him feel more secure and confident in his future, his socioeconomic rise actually intensified his self-awareness as a slave. What Lane had to lose made him increasingly conscious of his true situation. For this intelligent and capable young man, the idea that throughout the rest of his life he would "be entirely under the control of another," while achieving real economic success as a result of his own enterprise and hard work, was too much to bear. As he tells us, "Indeed all things now made me *feel*, what I had before known only in words, that *I was a slave.*" Inevitably, Lane started to "plan in my mind from day to day, and from night to night, how I might be free."

In Lane's case, such a self-conscious state of mind inevitably led to an obsession with freedom, as it did for many slaves. Even while their living conditions became more temperate, for some in bondage the more knowledge gained regarding the differences between the enslaved and the enslaver, the stronger the desire for freedom. As Frederick Douglass relates after attaining literacy and garnering a measure of physical comfort, the aspiration toward greater independence filled his every thought and ultimately triggered his flight to freedom: "Liberty! the inestimable birthright of every man, had, for me, converted every object into an asserter of this great right. It was heard in every sound, and beheld in every object. It was ever present, to torment me with a sense of my wretched condition. The more beautiful and charming were the smiles of nature, the more horrible and desolate was my condition. I saw nothing without seeing it, and I heard nothing without hearing it. I do not exaggerate, when I say, that it looked from every star, smiled in every calm, breathed in every wind, and moved in every storm" (Douglass, 160).

Unlike Douglass however, Lane says that he never considered running away as an option. Historians of slavery have noted that because the bonds of marriage and children often lessened the likelihood of a slave's absconding, many slave owners encouraged domestic relations among their slaves to curb desires for freedom. Yet Lane gives no indication in his narrative that even before he married at the age of twenty-five, he considered deserting his home, although he could have easily plied his trades elsewhere. Apparently, Lane's family ties, first to his mother and father, then to his wife and children, along with his privileged position within the "favored class" of house servants and in the Raleigh business community, not to mention his relatively benevolent master, constituted strong incentives for Lane to stay put. In contrast, the young bondsman Frederick Douglass could not lay claim to the kind of supportive long-term familial and communal relationships that Lunsford Lane had cultivated. Douglass resented the controls his Baltimore master placed on his enterprise as a self-employed ship's caulker. With the aid of his freeborn fiancée Douglass could make his escape to the North without having to worry about the disruptive effect his departure would have on his family, from which he had been separated by time and distance. Moreover, Lane, like other privileged slaves, may have considered running away shameful and humiliating, a concession to racist myths that branded African Americans as unreliable, shifty, deceitful, and unappreciative of good treatment. After escaping to freedom and acknowledging his own runaway condition, Frederick Douglass expressed the effect that the public status of being a runaway had on many fugitive slaves: "Up to that time, a colored man was deemed a fool who confessed himself a runaway slave, not only because of the danger to which he exposed himself of being retaken, but because it was a confession of a very *low* origin! Some of my colored friends in New Bedford thought very badly of my wisdom for thus exposing and degrading myself" (Douglass, 361).

Furthermore, Lane's narrative suggests that he expected his privileged status and friendly connections with influential whites to afford him special treatment within the paternalistic, class-conscious community of Raleigh that he had so successfully learned to negotiate. Indeed, until he was forced to leave Raleigh, Lane's course of action as a slave gives us reason to wonder if, even as he stretched and sometimes broke through the bonds of enslavement during his remarkable socioeconomic rise, he also became psychologically co-opted by the very system he was trying to bend to his own ambitions. He seems to have counted on his influential white friends, most of them slave owners, to protect his interests and allow him to achieve his goals in exchange for his tacit acceptance of the status quo, in which slavery was never outwardly challenged and the aristocracy's right to rule never directly questioned.

Given his disinclination to run away, Lane's entrepreneurial interests became his primary focus as a young man. As he tells us, his "plans for money-making took the principal possession of my thoughts." Ever alert to ways of making money, whether by accepting gratuities from houseguests of the Haywoods or stealing away during the night to "get a load of wood to cut for twenty-five cents," Lane is obsessed with the idea that at some point in the future he may purchase his freedom through sheer determination and hard work. Thus his economic, social, and political ambitions merge early on in his life.

Lane is not unprepared to meet the challenge of accruing enough money to buy himself out of slavery. Although not formally educated, he has secretly acquired the rudiments of literacy. In his preface he acknowledges, "While in the South I succeeded by stealth in learning to read and write a little, and since I have been in the North I have learned more." Lane served at various times as the Haywoods' carriage driver, house steward, and headwaiter at many of the family's exclusive dinners, while also working as a general laborer on the estate. These experiences afforded him the opportunity to hone his communication skills and develop a certain level of autonomy. We learn from his biographer that Lane's responsibilities extended even to the oversight of the household economy, as he was "intrusted with the purchase of almost every article needed for [the Haywoods'] daily food" (Hawkins, 23). Lane was an astute bargainer, "attentive . . . and careful in the expenditure of funds placed in his keeping . . . rising early to meet the poor farmers long before sunrise, at their places in the market, and make his purchases" (Hawkins, 23). In addition, the enterprising slave used whatever free time he could glean from his duties to the Haywoods to work odd jobs, one of which found him "industriously at various stores in town arranging their goods upon the sidewalk, and in certain labors that could be performed in the morning or evening without consuming much time" (Hawkins, 24).

Lane was not alone among slaves, especially in towns and cities, who worked after hours and late at night to earn extra money. What distinguishes him is that as a slave he became the owner of his own independent business. It was Edward Lane's idea, his son writes in his autobiography, to devise "a mode of preparing smoking tobacco, different from any then or since employed." The father and son team up to create a product that has the "double advantage of giving the tobacco a peculiarly pleasant flavor" while being cheap to manufacture "out of very indifferent material." Soon Lunsford develops a specialized pipe that maintains their tobacco's "peculiarly grateful flavor." "In the early part of the night I would sell my tobacco and pipes, and manufacture them in the latter part. As the Legislature sit in Raleigh every year, I sold these articles considerably to the members, so that I became known not only in the city, but in many parts of the State, as a *tobacconist.*"

It was not coincidental that Lane solicited customers among the North Carolina state legislators. A slave who had the twin ambitions of purchasing his own freedom and building up his own business undoubtedly realized the advantageousness of knowing men in high places. Lane used his talents as a waiter to further ingratiate himself with the most powerful men in Raleigh. Hawkins writes: "Being famous as a waiter, he was often called upon to attend evening parties, and for his valuable services on such occasions he was liberally compensated. At the season of the year when the Legislature was in session was his greatest harvest. Members having their private rooms at hotels or boarding-houses, were generally waited upon by servants of the wealthy in town who knew how to attend to their wants. Lunsford soon found himself a great favorite; and he knew well how to make the best use of his time and talents" (Hawkins, 23). Lane tells his biographer that the "intemperance among the members was fearful to contemplate," and he frequently found himself helping the intoxicated lawmakers safely to bed (Hawkins, 24).

Lane's business prospered, allowing him to save enough money to contemplate taking a wife. But marriage to Martha Curtis in May 1828 thrust Lane into a new and much more complex relationship to the institution of slavery. Slavery had done little to hinder his resolute economic individualism, but once he married and became responsible for the welfare of a wife and children, the slave husband found himself increasingly thwarted by the power of slavery to dictate his actions and prospects as a family man. Lane recounts how he nevertheless submitted to every demand placed on him, dutifully following the rules of the slavocracy. For instance, when his wife's master, Benjamin Smith, "a merchant, a member and class-leader in the Methodist church, and in much repute for his deep piety and devotion to religion," refused to support his slave (or her offspring) after she married, though Smith was obliged by law and custom to do so, Lane shouldered the burden without complaint, even though it eventually cost him his entire savings. Fortunately, in 1829 or 1830 Lane's widowed mistress, Mrs. Haywood, granted him the right to hire his time (in exchange for giving her a regular monthly payment) and go into the tobacco business full time, which let him accumulate by 1835 the $1,000 he needed to purchase himself. But when Lane decides to buy the freedom of his entire family, he runs into a series of seemingly endless frustrations compounded by legal red tape as well as outright persecution, evidently leveled at him because he is a black man laboring successfully to raise an enormous sum for the purpose of liberating his enslaved family. In the face of all these aggravations, Lane persists in believing that patience, deference to the law, and the intercession of his influential white patrons will secure for him the one boon he asks of the slave system — the chance to remain in North Carolina long enough to earn the money required of him to purchase his family before taking them all out of the state, as North Carolina state law required. In the end, however, all of Lane's attempts to work within the system fail. Despite his connections, his unoffending respectability, and the public support of the private secretary of the governor of North Carolina, in November 1840 the legislature refuses his petition to remain in the state solely for the purpose of earning the money to buy his family.

In recounting this intensely humiliating indignity, Lane permits himself a rare expression of genuine exasperation as though to register his ultimate disillusionment with his own conservatism born of his long-standing reliance on the paternalism of highly placed whites to ensure that he would be fairly treated.

And why must I be banished? Ever after I entertained the first idea of being free, I had endeavored so to conduct myself as not to become obnoxious to the white inhabitants, knowing as I did their power, and their hostility to the colored people. The two points necessary in such a case I had kept constantly in mind. First, I had made no display of the little property or money I possessed, but in every way I wore as much as possible the aspect of poverty. Second, I had never appeared to be even so intelligent as I really was. This all the colored people at the south, free and slaves, find it peculiarly necessary to their own comfort and safety to preserve.

Here as nowhere else in *The Narrative of Lunsford Lane* is Lane's acknowledgment that like Benjamin Franklin he had not only striven to follow the traditional middle-class work ethic to the letter in all his economic relations; he had also taken great care to maintain the most conservative *appearances* to ensure that no one would be offended by his success. In these lines, Lane admits that wearing a mask of black respectability—what many whites would have called "knowing his place"—was as much a factor in his upward mobility in a white supremacist society as his business acumen and hard work. Perhaps it was Lane's disgust with having played this self-degrading social role for so long and with such meager payoff in the end that convinced him to seek more reliable friendship and support in the North among those whom his erstwhile patrons in Raleigh labeled as "abolitionists."

Lane's reception in Raleigh after his return from a fund-raising mission in April 1842 confirmed his earlier realization that no matter how conservative his economic behavior or how politic his social bearing, a black man, free or enslaved, in slaveholding North Carolina had no future unless he was willing to dispense with his self-respect. The purpose of his second interrogation at the hands of those Lane called "the mob" (to differentiate them from "the first men and the more wealthy" who "were my friends") may be interpreted as a pointed reminder by Raleigh's lower-class whites that regardless of how much he might rise above them economically, Lane was still black and, though nominally free, still subject to whatever indignities white men wished to mete out. Thus the final "outrage" Lane had to endure in Raleigh seems to have liberated him from any lingering illusions he may have had about the willingness or the ability of his highly placed patrons in white society to protect his rights, and even his person, in the face of class as well as caste resentment of his successes. In this sense *The Narrative of Lunsford Lane* ends with its protagonist doubly freed. However much he may have once thought that class could trump caste in his case, Lane's last visit to the South disabuses him of any such notion.

For the antislavery movement, Lane's example readily served as a compelling testament to one black man's self-determination, economically, socially, and ultimately psychologically, in the midst of slavery. Lane's story of middle-class success eloquently contradicted the myth of the incompetent slave in perpetual need of a master to ensure his well-being. To those who claimed that chattel slavery, however harshly instituted in law, was mitigated by the benevolent paternalism of white masters, especially the so-called aristocrats of the South, *The Narrative of Lunsford Lane* argued that the institution ignored the individual, whether black or white, whether patron or the object of patronage. Thus even as Lane paid tribute to a number of white North Carolinians who sympathized with him and tried to help him, his story demonstrated that ultimately they had little more control over the system than he had. This evident conclusion to be drawn from Lane's case may help to account for the fact that there is very little documentation regarding Lunsford Lane's ordeal in the annals of North Carolina history. Perhaps, as the historian John Spencer Bassett noted, there was a decided effort on the part of those involved in Lane's case to suppress the record. "As for the main facts of the narrative, I have no reason to reject them," wrote Bassett in 1898. "Information about the case is hard to obtain in Raleigh," Bassett discovered, "but from an old resident I obtained a corroboration of the account of the mobbing of Lane. . . . Still I have not found any mention of the occurence in the Raleigh papers of that day. One of these papers was edited by Thomas Loring who was the Mayor before whom Lunsford was tried, yet it is silent. It is likely that the matter was not published for fear of the effect it would have when copied in Northern papers."[8]

We are not without some knowledge of Lane's activities after he and his family reached what he called the "cradle of Liberty," where "the stern, cruel, hated hand of slavery could never reach us." From his biographer, William Hawkins, we learn a good deal about Lane's life after he and his family settled in Massachusetts. In Boston, Lane almost immediately became involved in the American Anti-Slavery Society, going out on the lecture circuit to relate his extraordinary story. In the meantime he continued his entrepreneurial endeavors, developing a dietary supplement and raising money for local churches and organizations. The last information currently available about the fate of Lunsford Lane appears in Hawkins's account, which in its final pages states that Lane was employed as head steward in a Worcester, Massachusetts, hospital dedicated to serving Civil War patients.

Note on the Text

The text of *The Narrative of Lunsford Lane, Formerly of Raleigh, N.C., Embracing an Account of His Early Life, the Redemption By Purchase of Himself and Family from Slavery, and His Banishment from the Place of His Birth for the Crime of Wearing a Colored Skin* follows the first edition self-published by Lane in Boston in July 1842. *The Slave Mother's Address to Her Infant Child*, an eighty-eight-verse poem by Joshua Pollard Blanchard (1782–1868), is included with the original text. The three subsequent editions omit the poem's first twenty-four lines, perhaps due to a printing error. Also in the second, third, and fourth editions there are minor variations to the preface, but the narrative itself remains unchanged.

Notes

1. John Blassingame, ed., *Slave Testimony: Two Centuries of Letters, Speeches, Interviews, and Autobiographies* (Baton Rouge: Louisiana State University Press, 1977), 149.

2. William L. Andrews, *To Tell a Free Story: The First Century of Afro-American Autobiography* (Urbana: University of Illinois Press, 1986), 116.

3. Ira Berlin. *Slaves without Masters: The Free Negro in the Antebellum South* (New York: Vintage Books, 1974), 397.

4. William G. Hawkins, *Lunsford Lane; or, Another Helper from North Carolina* (Boston: Crosby and Nichols, 1863), 173.

5. Harriet Ann Jacobs, *Incidents in the Life of a Slave Girl, Written by Herself* (Boston: Published for the Author, 1861), 128–29.

6. Frederick Douglass, *My Bondage and My Freedom* (New York: Miller, Orton and Mulligan, 1855), 202–3.

7. Richard C. Wade, *Slavery in the Cities: The South, 1820–1860* (New York: Oxford University Press, 1964), 117.

8. John Spencer Bassett, *Anti-slavery Leaders of North Carolina* (Baltimore: John Hopkins Press, 1898), 61.

THE

NARRATIVE

OF

LUNSFORD LANE,

FORMERLY OF

RALEIGH, N. C.

Embracing an account of his early life, the redemption by purchase
of himself and family from slavery,
And his banishment from the place of his birth for the crime
of wearing a colored skin.

PUBLISHED BY HIMSELF.

SECOND EDITION.

BOSTON :
PRINTED FOR THE PUBLISHER :
J. G. TORREY, PRINTER.

1842.

LUNSFORD LANE.

THE SLAVE MOTHER'S ADDRESS
TO HER INFANT CHILD.

I cannot tell how much I love
To look on thee my child;
Nor how that looking rocks my soul
As on a tempest wild;
For I have borne thee to the world,
And bid thee breathe its air,
But soon to see around thee drawn
The curtains of despair.

Now thou art happy, child I know,
As little babe can be;
Thou dost not fancy in thy dreams
But thou art all as free
As birds upon the mountain winds,
(If thou hast thought of bird,)
Or anything thou thinkest of,
Or thy young ear has heard.

What are thy little thoughts about?
I cannot certain know,
Only there's not a wing of them
Upon a breath of woe,
For not a shadow's on thy face,
Nor billow heaves thy breast,—
All clear as the summer's lake
With not a zephyr press'd.

But thou art born a slave, my child;
Those little hands must toil,
That brow must sweat, that bosom ache
Upon another's soil;
And if perchance some tender joy
Should bloom upon thy heart,
Another's hand may enter there,
And tear it soon apart.

Thou art a little joy to me,
But soon thou may'st be sold,
Oh! lovelier to thy mother far
Than any weight of gold;
Or I may see thee scourg'd and driv'n
Hard on the cotton-field,
To fill a cruel master's store,
With what thy blood may yield.

Should some fair maiden win thy heart,
And thou should'st call her thine;
Should little ones around thee stand,
Or round thy bosom twine,
Thou wilt not know how soon away
These loves may all be riv'n,
Nor what a darkened troop of woe
Through thy lone breast be driv'n.

Thy master may be kind, and give
Thy every wish to thee,
Only deny that greatest wish,
That longing to be free:
Still it will seem a comfort small
That thou hast sweeter bread,
A better hut than other slaves,
Or pillow for thy head.

What joys soe'er may gather round,
What other comforts flow, —
That, like a mountain in the sea,
O'ertops each wave below,
That ever-upward, firm desire
To break the chains, and be
Free as the ocean is, or like
The ocean-winds, be free.

Oh, child! thou art a little slave;
And all of thee that grows,
Will be another's weight of flesh, —
But thine the weight of woes.
Thou art a little slave, my child,

And much I grieve and mourn
That to so dark a destiny
A lovely babe I've borne.

And gladly would I lay thee down
To sleep beneath the sod,
And give thy gentle spirit back,
Unmarr'd with grief, to God:
The tears I shed upon that turf
Should whisper peace to me,
And tell me in the spirit land
My lovely babe was free.

I then should know thy peace was sure,
And only long to go
The road which thou had'st gone, and wipe
Away these tears that flow.
Death to the slave has double power;
It breaks the earthly clod,
And breaks the tyrant's sway, that he
May worship only God.

J.P.B.[1]

TO THE READER.

I HAVE been solicited by very many friends, to give my narrative to the public. Whatever my own judgment might be, I should yield to theirs. In compliance, therefore, with this general request, and in the hope that these pages may produce an impression favorable to my countrymen in bondage also that I may realize something from the sale of my work towards the support of a numerous family, I have committed this publication to press. It might have been made two or three, or even six times larger, without diminishing from the interest of any one of its pages — *indeed with an increased interest* — but the want of the pecuniary means, and other considerations, have induced me to present it as here seen.

I have not, in this publication attempted or desired to argue anything. It is only a simple narration of such facts connected with my own case, as I thought would be most interesting and instructive to readers generally. The facts will, I think, cast some light upon the policy of a slaveholding community, and the effect on the minds of the more enlightened, the more humane, and the *Christian* portion of the southern people, of holding and trading in the bodies and souls of men.

I have said in the following pages, that my condition as a slave was comparatively a happy, indeed a highly favored one and to this circumstance is it owing that I have been able to come up from bondage and relate the story to the public and that my wife, my mother, and my seven children, are here with me this day. If for any thing this side of the invisible world, I bless heaven, it is that I was not born a plantation slave, nor even a house servant under what is termed a hard and cruel master.

It has not been any part of my object to describe slavery generally, and in the narration of my own case I have dwelt as little as possible upon the dark side — have spoken mostly of the bright. In whatever I have been obliged to say unfavorable to others, I have endeavored not to overstate, but have chosen rather to come short of giving the full picture — omitting much which it did not seem important to my object to relate. And yet I would not venture to say that this publication does not contain a single period which might be twisted to convey an idea more than should be expressed.

Those of whom I have had occasion to speak, are regarded, where they are known, as among the most kind men to their slaves. Mr. Smith, some of whose conduct will doubtless seem strange to the reader, is sometimes taunted with being an abolitionist, in consequence of the interest he manifests towards the colored people. If to any his character appear like a riddle, they should remember that men, like other things, have "two sides," and often a top and a bottom in addition.

While in the South I succeeded by stealth in learning to read and write a little, and since I have been in the North I have learned more. But I need not say that I have been obliged to employ the services of a friend, in bringing this Narrative into shape for the public eye. And it should perhaps be said on the part of the writer, that it has been hastily compiled, with little regard to style, only to express the ideas accurately and in a manner to be understood.

LUNSFORD LANE,
Boston, July 4, 1842.

NARRATIVE.

THE small city of Raleigh, North Carolina, it is known, is the capital of the State, situated in the interior, and containing about thirty-six hundred inhabitants. Here lived Mr. SHERWOOD HAYWOOD,[2] a man of considerable respectability, a planter, and the cashier of a bank. He owned three plantations, at the distances respectively of seventy-five, thirty, and three miles from his residence in Raleigh. He owned in all about two hundred and fifty slaves, among the rest my mother,[3] who was a house servant to her master, and of course a resident in the city. My father[4] was a slave to a near neighbor. The apartment where I was born and where I spent my childhood and youth was called "the kitchen," situated some fifteen or twenty rods[5] from the "great house." Here the house servants lodged and lived, and here the meals were prepared for the people in the mansion. The "field hands," of course, reside upon the plantation.

On the 30th of May, 1803, I was ushered into the world but I did not begin to see the rising of its dark clouds, nor fancy how they might be broken and dispersed, until some time afterwards. My infancy was spent upon the floor, in a rough cradle, or sometimes in my mother's arms. My early boyhood in playing with the other boys and girls, colored and white, in the yard, and occasionally doing such little matters of labor as one of so young years could. I knew no difference between myself and the white children; nor did they seem to know any in turn. Sometimes my master would come out and give a biscuit to me, and another to one of his own white boys but I did not perceive the difference between us. I had no brothers or sisters, but there were other colored families living in the same kitchen, and the children playing in the same yard, with me and my mother.

When I was ten or eleven years old, my master set me regularly to cutting wood, in the yard in the winter, and working in the garden in the summer. And when I was fifteen years of age, he gave me the care of the pleasure horses, and made me his carriage driver; but this did not exempt me from other labor, especially in the summer. Early in the morning I used to take his three horses to the plantation, and turn them into the pasture to graze, and myself into the cotton or cornfield, with a hoe in my hand, to work through the day; and after sunset I would take these horses back to the city, a distance of three miles, feed them, and then attend to any other business my master or any of his family had for me to do, until bed time, when with my blanket in my hand, I would go into the dining room to rest through the night. The next day the same round of labor would be repeated, unless some of the family wished to ride out, in which case I must be on hand with the horses to wait upon them, and in the meantime to work about the yard. On Sunday I had to drive to Church twice, which with other things necessary to be done, took the whole day. So my life went wearily on from day to day, from night to night, and from week to week.

When I began to work, I discovered the difference between myself and my master's white children. They began to order me about, and were told to do so by my master and mistress. I found, too, that they had learned to read, while I was not permitted to have a book in my hand. To be in the possession of anything written or printed, was regarded as an offence. And then there was the fear that I might be sold away from those who were dear to me, and conveyed to the far South. I had learned that being a slave I was subject to this worst (to us) of all calamities and I knew of others in similar situations to myself, thus sold away. My friends were not numerous but in proportion as they were few they were dear and the thought that I might be separated from them forever, was like that of having the heart torn from its socket; while the idea of being conveyed to the far South, seemed infinitely worse than the terrors of death. To know, also, that I was never to consult my own will, but was, while I lived, to be entirely under the control of another, was another state of mind hard for me to bear. Indeed all things now made me *feel*, what I had before known only in words, that *I was a slave*. Deep was this feeling, and it preyed upon my heart like a never-dying worm. I saw no prospect that my condition would ever be changed. Yet I used to plan in my mind from day to day, and from night to night, how I might be free.

One day, while I was in this state of mind, my father gave me a small basket of peaches. I sold them for thirty cents, which was the first money I ever had in my life. Afterwards I won some marbles, and sold them for sixty cents, and some weeks after Mr. Hog from Fayetteville,[6] came to visit my master, and on leaving gave me one dollar. After that Mr. Bennahan from Orange county,[7] gave me a dollar, and a son of my master fifty cents. These sums, and the hope that then entered my mind of purchasing at some future time my freedom, made me long for money; and plans for money-making took the principal possession of my thoughts. At night I would steal away with my axe, get a load of wood to cut for twenty-five cents, and the next morning hardly escape a whipping for the offence. But I persevered until I had obtained twenty dollars. Now I began to think seriously of becoming able to buy myself; and cheered by this hope, I went on from one thing to another, laboring "at dead of night," after the long weary day's toil for my master was over, till I found I had collected one hundred dollars. This sum I kept hid, first in one place and then in another, as I dare not put it out, for fear I should lose it.

After this I lit upon a plan which proved of great advantage to me. My father suggested a mode of preparing smoking tobacco, different from any then or since employed. It had the double advantage of giving the tobacco a peculiarly pleasant flavor, and of enabling me to manufacture a good article out of a very indifferent material. I improved somewhat upon his suggestion, and commenced the manufacture, doing as I have before said, all my work in the night. The tobacco I put up in papers of about a quarter of a pound each, and sold them at fifteen cents.[8] But the tobacco could not be smoked without a pipe, and as I had given the former a flavor peculiarly grateful, it occurred to me that I might so construct a pipe as to cool the smoke in passing through it, and thus meet the wishes of those who are more fond of smoke than heat. This I effected by means of a reed, which grows plentifully in that region; I made a passage through the reed with a hot wire, polished it, and attached a clay pipe to the end, so that the smoke should be cooled in flowing through the stem like whiskey or rum in passing from the boiler through the worm of the still. These pipes I sold at ten cents apiece. In the early part of the night I would sell my tobacco and pipes, and manufacture them in the latter part. As the Legislature sit in Raleigh every year, I sold these articles considerably to the members, so that I became known not only in the city, but in many parts of the State, as a *tobacconist*.[9]

Perceiving that I was getting along so well, I began, slave as I was, to think about taking a wife. So I fixed my mind upon Miss Lucy Williams, a slave of Thomas Devereaux, Esq.,[10] an eminent lawyer in the place; but failed in my undertaking. Then I thought I never would marry; but at the end of two or three years my resolution began to slide away, till finding I could not keep it longer I set out once more in pursuit of a wife. So I fell in with her to whom I am now united, Miss MARTHA CURTIS, and the bargain between *us* was completed. I next went to her master, Mr. Boylan,[11] and asked him, according to the custom, if I might "marry his woman." His reply was, "Yes, if you will behave yourself." I told him I would. "And make her behave herself?" To this I also assented; and then proceeded to ask the approbation of my master, which was granted. So in May, 1828, I was bound as fast in wedlock as a slave can be. God may at any time sunder that band in a freeman; either master may do the same at pleasure in a slave. The bond is not recognized in law. But in my case it has never been broken; and now it cannot be, except by a higher power.

When we had been married nine months and one day, we were blessed with a son, and two years afterwards with a daughter. My wife also passed from the hands of Mr. Boylan, into those of Mr. BENJAMIN B. SMITH, a merchant, a member and class-leader in the Methodist church, and in much repute for his deep piety and devotion to religion. But grace (of course) had not wrought in the same *manner* upon the heart of Mr. Smith, as nature had done upon that of Mr. Boylan, who made no religious profession. This latter gentleman used to give my wife, who was a favorite slave, (her mother nursed every one of his own children,) sufficient food and clothing to render her comfortable, so that I had to spend for her but little, except to procure such small articles of extra comfort as I was prompted to from time to time. Indeed Mr. Boylan was regarded as a very kind master to all the slaves about him; that is, to his house servants; nor did he personally inflict much cruelty, if any, upon his field hands. The overseer on his nearest plantation (I know but little about the rest) was a very cruel man; in one instance, as it was said among the slaves, he whipped a man *to death*; but of course denied that the man died in consequence of the whipping. Still it was the choice of my wife to pass into the hands of Mr. Smith, as she had become attached to him in consequence of belonging to the same church, and receiving his religious instruction and counsel as her class-leader, and in consequence of the peculiar devotedness to the cause of religion for which he was noted, and which he always seemed to manifest. — But when she became his slave, he withheld both from her and her children, the needful food and clothing, while he exacted from them to the uttermost all the labor they were able to perform. Almost every article of clothing worn either by my wife or children, especially every article of much value, I had to purchase; while the food he furnished the family amounted to less than a meal a day, and that of the coarser kind. I have no remembrance that he ever gave us a blanket or any other article of bedding, although it is considered a rule at the South that the master shall furnish each of his slaves with one blanket a year. So that, both as to food and clothing, I had in fact to support both my wife and the children, while he claimed them as his property, and received all their labor. She was a house servant to Mr. Smith, sometimes cooked the food for his family, and usually took it from the table, but her mistress was so particular in giving it out to be cooked, or so watched it, that she always knew whether it was all returned; and when the table was cleared away, the stern old lady would sit by and see that every dish (except the very little she would send into the kitchen) was put away, and then she would turn the key upon it, so as to be sure her slaves should not die of gluttony. This practice is common with some families in that region; but with others it is not. It was not so in that of her less pious master, Mr. Boylan, nor was it precisely so at my master's. We used to have corn bread enough, and some meat. When I was a boy, the pot-liquor,[12] in which the meat was boiled for the "great house," together with some little corn-meal balls that had been thrown in just before the meat was done, was poured into a tray and set in the middle of the yard, and a clam shell or pewter spoon given to each of us children, who would fall upon the delicious fare as greedily as pigs. It was not generally so much as we wanted, consequently it was customary for some of the white persons who saw us from the piazza[13] of the house where they were sitting, to order the more stout and greedy ones to eat slower, that those more young and feeble might have a chance. But it was not so with Mr. Smith: such luxuries were more than he could afford, kind and Christian man as he was considered to be. So that by the expense of providing for my wife and children, all the money I had earned and could earn by my night labor was consumed, till I found myself reduced to five dollars, and this I lost one day in going to the plantation. My light of hope now went out. My prop seemed to have given way from under me. Sunk in the very night or despair respecting my freedom, I discovered myself, as though I had never known it before, a husband, the father of two children, a family looking up to me for bread, and I a slave, penniless, and well watched by my master, his wife and his children, lest I should, perchance, catch the friendly light of the stars to make something in order to supply the cravings of nature in those with whom my soul was bound up; or lest some plan of freedom might lead me to trim the light of diligence after the day's labor was over, while the rest of the world were enjoying the hours in pleasure or sleep.

At this time an event occurred, which, while it cast a cloud over the prospects of some of my fellow slaves, was a rainbow over mine. My master died; and his widow,[14] by the will, became sole executrix of his property. To the surprise of all, the bank of which he had been cashier presented a claim against the estate for forty thousand dollars. By a compromise, this sum was reduced to twenty thousand dollars; and my mistress, to meet the amount, sold some of her slaves, and hired out others. I hired my time of her,[I] for which I paid her a price varying from one hundred dollars to one hundred and twenty dollars per year. This was a privilege which comparatively few slaves at the South enjoy; and in this I felt truly blessed.

I commenced the manufacture of pipes and tobacco on an enlarged scale. I opened a regular place of business, labeled my tobacco in a conspicuous manner with the names of *"Edward and Lunsford Lane,"* and of some of the persons who sold it for me,—established agencies for the sale in various parts of the State, one at Fayetteville, one at Salisbury,[15] one at Chapel Hill,[16] and so on,—sold my articles from my place of business, and about town, also deposited them in stores on commission, and thus, after paying my mistress for my time, and rendering such support as necessary to my family, I found in the space of some six or eight years, that I had collected the sum of one thousand dollars. During this time I had found it politic to go shabbily dressed, and to appear to be very poor, but to pay my mistress for my services promptly. I kept my money hid, never venturing to put out a penny, nor to let any body but my wife know that I was making any. The thousand dollars was what I supposed my mistress would ask for me, and so I determined now what I would do.

I went to my mistress and inquired what was her price for me. She said a thousand dollars. I then told her that I wanted to be free, and asked her if she would sell me to be made free. She said she would; and accordingly I arranged with her, and with the master of my wife, Mr. Smith, already spoken of, for the latter to take my money[II] and buy of her my freedom, as I could not legally purchase it, and as the laws forbid emancipation except, for "meritorious services."[17] This done, Mr. Smith endeavored to emancipate me formally, and to get my manumission recorded; I tried also; but the court judged that I had done nothing "meritorious," and so I remained, nominally only, the slave of Mr. Smith for a year; when, feeling unsafe in that

[I] It is contrary to the laws of the State, for a slave to have command of his own time in this way, but in Raleigh it is sometimes winked at. I knew one slave-man who was *doing well for himself,* taken up by the public authorities and hired out for the public good, three times in succession for this offence. The time of hiring in such a case is one year. The master is subject to a fine. But generally as I have said, if the slave is *orderly* and appears to be *making nothing,* neither he nor the master is interfered with.

[II] *Legally,* my money belonged to my mistress; and she could have taken it and refused to grant me my freedom. But she was a very kind woman for a slave owner; and she would under the circumstances, scorn to do such a thing. I have known of slaves, however, served in this way.

relation, I accompanied him to New York whither he was going to purchase goods, and was there regularly and formally made a freeman, and there my manumission was recorded. I returned to my family in Raleigh, and endeavored to do by them as a freeman should. I had known what it was to be a slave, and I knew what it was to be free.

But I am going too rapidly over my story. When the money was paid to my mistress and the conveyance fairly made to Mr. Smith, I felt that I was free. And a queer and a joyous feeling it is to one who has been a slave. I cannot describe it, only it seemed as though I was in heaven. I used to lie awake whole nights thinking of it. And oh, the strange thoughts that passed through my soul, like so many rivers of light; deep and rich were their waves as they rolled; — these were more to me than sleep, more than soft slumber after long months of watching over the decaying, fading frame of a friend, and the loved one laid to rest in the dust. But I cannot describe my feelings to those who have never been slaves; then why should I attempt it? He who has passed from spiritual death to life, and received the witness within his soul that his sins are forgiven, may possibly form some distant idea, like the ray of the setting sun from the far off mountain top, of the emotions of an emancipated slave. That opens heaven. To break the bonds of slavery, opens up at once both earth and heaven. Neither can be truly seen by us while we are slaves.

And now will the reader take with me a brief review of the road I had trodden. I cannot here dwell upon its dark shades, though some of these were black as the pencillings of midnight, but upon the light that had followed my path from my infancy up, and had at length conducted me quite out of the deep abyss of bondage. There is a hymn opening with the following stanza, which very much expresses my feelings:

> "When all thy mercies, Oh my God,
>   My rising soul surveys,
>   Transported with the view, I'm lost
>   In wonder, love, and praise."

I had endured what a freeman would indeed call hard fare; but my lot, on the whole, had been a favored one for a slave. It is known that there is a wide difference in the situations of what are termed house servants, and plantation hands. I, though sometimes employed upon the plantation, belonged to the former, which is the favored class. My master, too, was esteemed a kind and humane man; and altogether I fared quite differently from many poor fellows whom it makes my blood run chill to think of, confined to the plantation, with not enough of food and that little of the coarsest kind, to satisfy the gnawings of hunger, — compelled oftentimes, to hie away[18] in the night-time, when worn down with work, and *steal*, (if it be stealing,) and privately devour such things as they can lay their hands upon, — made to feel the rigors of bondage with no cessation, — torn away sometimes from the few friends they love, friends doubly dear because they are few, and transported to a climate where in a few hard years they die, — or at best conducted heavily and sadly to their resting place under the sod, upon their old master's plantation, — sometimes, perhaps, enlivening the air with merriment, but a forced merriment, that comes from a stagnant or a stupified heart. Such as this is the fate of the plantation slaves generally, but such was not my lot. My way was comparatively light, and what is better, it conducted to freedom. And my wife and children were with me. After my master died, my mistress sold a number of her slaves from their families and friends — but not me. She sold several children from their parents — but my children were with me still. She sold two husbands from their wives — but I was still with mine. She sold one wife from her husband — but mine had not been sold from me. The master of my wife, Mr. Smith, had separated members of families by sale — but not of mine. With me and my house, the tenderer tendrils of the heart still clung to where the vine had entwined; pleasant was its shade and delicious our fruits to our taste, though we knew, and what is more, we *felt* that we were slaves. But all around I could see where the vine had been torn down, and its bleeding branches told of vanished joys, and of new wrought sorrows, such as, slave though I was, had never entered into my practical experience.

I had never been permitted to learn to read; but I used to attend church, and there I received instruction which I trust was of some benefit to me. I trusted, too, that I had experienced the renewing influences of the gospel; and after obtaining from my mistress a written *permit* (a thing *always* required in such a case,) I had been baptised and received into fellowship with the Baptist denomination. So that in religious matters, I had been indulged in the exercise of my own conscience — a favor not always granted to slaves. Indeed I, with others, was often told by the minister how good God was in bringing us over to this country from dark and benighted Africa, and permitting us to listen to the sound of the gospel. To me, God also granted temporal freedom, which man without God's consent, had stolen away.

I often heard select portions of the scriptures read. And on the Sabbath there was one sermon preached expressly for the colored people which it was generally my privilege to hear. I became quite familiar with the texts, "Servants be obedient to your masters."—"Not with eye service as men pleasers."[19]—"He that knoweth his master's will and doeth it not, shall be beaten with many stripes,"[20] and others of this class: for they formed the basis of most of these public instructions to us. The first commandment impressed upon our minds was to obey our masters, and the second was like unto it, namely, to do as much work when they or the overseers were not watching us as when they were. But connected with these instructions there was more or less that was truly excellent; though mixed up with much that would sound strangely in the ears of freedom. There was one very kind hearted Episcopal minister whom I often used to hear; he was very popular with the colored people. But after he had preached a sermon to us in which he argued from the Bible that it was the will of heaven from all eternity we should be slaves, and our masters be our owners, most of us left him; for like some of the faint hearted disciples in early times we said,—"This is a hard saying, who can bear it?"[21]

My manumission, as I shall call it; that is, the bill of sale conveying me to Mr. Smith, was dated Sept. 9th, 1835. I continued in the tobacco and pipe business, as already described, to which I added a small trade in a variety of articles; and some two years before I left Raleigh, I entered also into a considerable business in wood, which I used to purchase by the acre standing, cut it, haul it into the city, deposit it in a yard and sell it out as I advantageously could. Also I was employed about the office of the Governor as I shall hereafter relate. I used to keep one or two horses, and various vehicles, by which I did a variety of work at hauling about town. Of course I had to hire more or less help, to carry on my business.

In the manufacture of tobacco I met with considerable competition, but none that materially injured me. The method of preparing it having originated with me and my father, we found it necessary, in order to secure the advantage of the invention, to keep it to ourselves, and decline, though often solicited, going into partnership with others. Those who undertook the manufacture could neither give the article a flavor so pleasant as ours, nor manufacture it so cheaply, so they either failed in it, or succeeded but poorly.

Not long after obtaining my own freedom, I began seriously to think about purchasing the freedom of my family. The first proposition was that I should buy my wife, and that we should jointly labor to obtain the freedom of the children afterwards as we were able. But that idea was abandoned, when her master, Mr. Smith, refused to sell her to me for less than one thousand dollars, a sum which then appeared too much for me to raise.

Afterwards, however, I conceived the idea of purchasing at once the entire family. I went to Mr. Smith to learn his price, which he put at *three thousand dollars* for my wife and six children, the number we then had. This seemed a large sum, both because it was a great deal for me to raise; and also because Mr. Smith, when he bought my wife and *two* children, had actually paid but five hundred and sixty dollars for them, and had received, ever since, their labor, while I had almost entirely supported them, both as to food and clothing. Altogether, therefore, the case seemed a hard one, but as I was entirely in his power I must do the best I could. At length he concluded, perhaps partly of his own motion, and partly through the persuasion of a friend, to sell the family for $2,500, as I wished to free them, though he contended still that they were worth three thousand dollars. Perhaps they would at that time have brought this larger sum, if sold for the Southern market. The arrangement with Mr. Smith was made in December, 1838. I gave him five notes of five hundred dollars each, the first due in January, 1840, and one in January each succeeding year; for which he transferred my family into my own possession, with a *bond* to give me a bill of sale when I should pay the notes. With this arrangement, we found ourselves living in our own house — a house which I had previously purchased — in January, 1839.

After moving my family, my wife was for a short time sick, in consequence of her labor and the excitement in moving, and her excessive joy. I told her that it reminded me of a poor shoemaker in the neighborhood who purchased a ticket in a lottery; but not expecting to draw, the fact of his purchasing it had passed out of his mind. But one day as he was at work on his last, he was informed that his ticket had drawn the liberal prize of ten thousand dollars: and the poor man was so overjoyed, that he fell back on his seat, and immediately expired.

In this new and joyful situation, we found ourselves getting along very well, until September, 1840, when to my surprise, as I was passing the street one day, engaged in my business, the following note was handed me. "Read it," said the officer, "or if you cannot read, get some white man to read it to you." Here it is, *verbatim*:

> *To Lunsford Lane, a free man of Colour*
> Take notice that whereas complaint has been made to us two Justices of the Peace for the county of Wake and state of North Carolina that you

are a free negro from another state who has migrated into this state contrary to the provisions of the act of assembly concerning free negros and mulattoes now notice is given you that unless you leave and remove out of this state within twenty days that you will be proceeded against for the penalty proscribed by said act of assembly and be otherwise dealt with as the law directs given under our hands and seals this the 5th Sept. 1840.

WILLIS SCOTT JP (Seal)

JORDAN WOMBLE JP (Seal)

This was a terrible blow to me; for it prostrated at once all my hopes in my cherished object of obtaining the freedom of my family, and led me to expect nothing but a separation from them forever.

In order that the reader may understand the full force of the foregoing notice, I will copy the Law of the State under which it was issued:

SEC. 65. It shall not be lawful for any free negro or mulatto to migrate into this State: and if he or she shall do so, contrary to the provisions of this act, and being thereof informed, shall not, within twenty days thereafter, remove out of the State, he or she being thereof convicted in the manner hereafter directed, shall be liable to a penalty of five hundred dollars; and upon failure to pay the same, within the time prescribed in the judgment awarded against such person or persons, he or she shall be liable to be held in servitude and at labor a term of time not exceeding ten years, in such manner and upon such terms as may be provided by the court awarding such sentence, and the proceeds arising therefrom shall be paid over to the county trustee for county purposes: Provided, that in case any free negro or mulatto shall pay the penalty of five hundred dollars, according to the provisions of this act, it shall be the duty of such free negro or mulatto to remove him or herself out of this State within twenty days thereafter, and for every such failure, he or she shall be subject to the like penalty, as is prescribed for a failure to remove in the first instance. — *Revised Statutes, North Carolina, chap.* 111.

The next section provides that if the free person of color so notified, does not leave within the twenty days after receiving the notice, he may be arrested on a warrant from any Justice, and be held to bail for his appearance at the next county court, when he will be subject to the penalties specified above; or in case of his failure to give bonds, he may be sent to jail.

I made known my situation to my friends, and after taking legal counsel it was determined to induce, if possible, the complainants to prosecute no farther at present, and then as the Legislature of the State was to sit in about two months, to petition that body for permission to remain in the State until I could complete the purchase of my family; after which I was willing, if necessary, to leave.

From January 1st, 1837, I had been employed as I have mentioned, in the office of the Governor of the State,[22] principally under the direction of his private Secretary, in keeping the office in order, taking the letters to the Post Office, and doing such other duties of the sort as occurred from time to time. This circumstance, with the fact of the high standing in the city of the family of my former master, and of the former masters of my wife, had given me the friendship of the first people in the place generally, who from that time forward acted towards me the friendly part.

Mr. BATTLE, then private Secretary to Governor Dudley, addressed the following letter to the prosecuting attorney in my behalf:

RALEIGH, Nov. 3, 1840.

DEAR SIR:—Lunsford Lane, a free man of Color, has been in the employ of the State under me since my entering on my present situation. I understand that under a law of the State, he has been notified to leave, and that the time is now at hand.

In the discharge of the duties I had from him, I have found him prompt, obedient, and faithful. At this particular time, his absence to me would be much regretted, as I am now just fixing up my books and other papers in the new office, and I shall not have time to learn another what he can already do so well. With me the period of the Legislature is a very busy one, and I am compelled to have a servant who understands the business I want done, and one I can trust. I would not wish to be an obstacle in the execution of any law, but the enforcing of the one against him, will be doing me a serious inconvenience, and the object of this letter is to ascertain whether I could not procure a suspension of the sentence till after the adjournment of the Legislature, say about 1st January, 1841.

I should feel no hesitation in giving my word that he will conduct himself orderly and obediently.

I am most respectfully,

Your obedient servant,

C. C. BATTLE.

G. W. HAYWOOD, ESQ.[23]

Attorney at Law, Raleigh, N.C.

To the above letter, the following reply was made:

RALEIGH, Nov. 3, 1840.

MY DEAR SIR:—I have no objection so far as I am concerned, that all further proceedings against Lunsford should be postponed until after the adjournment of the Legislature.

The process now out against him is one issued by two magistrates, Messrs. Willis Scott and Jordan Womble, over which I have no control. You had better see them to-day, and perhaps, at your request, they will delay further action on the subject. Respectfully yours,

GEO. W. HAYWOOD.

Mr. Battle then enclosed the foregoing correspondence to Messrs. Scott and Womble, requesting their "favorable consideration." They returned the correspondence, but neglected to make any reply.

In consequence, however, of this action on the part of my friends, I was permitted to remain without further interruption, until the day the Legislature commenced its session. On that day a warrant was served upon me, to appear before the county court, to answer for the sin of having remained in the place of my birth for the space of twenty days and more after being warned out. I escaped going to jail through the kindness of Mr. Haywood, a son of my former master, and Mr. Smith, who jointly became security for my appearance at court.

This was on Monday; and on Wednesday I appeared before the court; but as my prosecutors were not ready for the trial, the case was laid over three months, to the next term.

I then proceeded to get up a petition to the Legislature. It required much hard labor and persuasion on my part to start it; but after that, I readily obtained the signatures of the principal men in the place. Then I went round to the members, many of whom were known to me, calling upon them at their rooms, and urging them for my sake, for humanity's sake, for the sake of my wife and little ones, whose hopes had been excited by the idea that they were even now free; I appealed to them as husbands, fathers, brothers, sons, to vote in favor of my petition, and allow me to remain in the State long enough to purchase my family. I was doing well in business, and it would be but a short time before I could accomplish the object. Then, if it was desired, I and my wife and children, redeemed from bondage, would together seek a more friendly home, beyond the dominion of slavery. The following is the petition presented, endorsed as the reader will see:

To the Hon. General Assembly of the State of North Carolina.

GENTLEMEN: — The petition of Lunsford Lane humbly shews[24] — That about five years ago, he purchased his freedom from his mistress, Mrs. Sherwood Haywood and by great economy and industry has paid the purchase money; that he has a wife and seven children whom he has agreed to purchase, and for whom he has paid a part of the purchase money; but not having paid in full, is not yet able to leave the State, without parting with his wife and children.

Your petitioner prays your Honorable Body to pass a law allowing him to remain a limited time within the State, until he can remove his family also. Your petitioner will give bond and good security for his good behaviour while he remains.

Your petitioner will ever pray, &c.

LUNSFORD LANE.

The undersigned are well acquainted with Lunsford Lane, the petitioner, and join in his petition to the Assembly for relief.

- Charles Manly,
- R. W. Haywood,
- Eleanor Haywood,
- Wm. Hill,
- R. Smith,
- Wm. Peace,
- Jos. Peace,
- Wm. M'Pheeters,
- Wm. Boylan,
- Fabius J. Haywood,
- D. W. Stone,[25]
- T. Meredith,[26]
- A. J. Battle,
- Drury Lacy,
- Will. Peck,
- W. A. Stith,
- A. B. Stith,
- J. Brown,
- William White,
- Geo. Simpson,
- Jno. I. Christophers,
- John Primrose,

- Hugh M'Queen,
- Alex. J. Lawrence,
- C. L. Hinton.

Lunsford Lane, the petitioner herein, has been servant to the Executive Office since the 1st of January, 1837, and it gives me pleasure to state that, during the whole time, without exception, I have found him faithful and obedient, in keeping every thing committed to his care in good condition. From what I have seen of his conduct and demeanor, I cheerfully join in the petition for his relief.

C. C. BATTLE,
P. Secretary to Gov. Dudley.
Raleigh, Nov. 20, 1840.

The foregoing petition was presented to the Senate. It was there referred to a committee. I knew when the committee was to report, and watched about the State House that I might receive the earliest news of the fate of my petition. I should have gone within the senate chamber, but no colored man has that permission. I do not know why, unless for fear he may hear the name of *Liberty*. By and by a member came out, and as he passed me, said "*Well Lunsford, they have laid you out; the nigger Bill is killed.*" I need not tell the reader that my feelings did not enter into the merriment of this honorable senator. To me, the fate of my petition was the last blow to my hopes. I had done all I could do, had said all I could say, laboring night and day, to obtain a favorable reception to my petition; but all in vain. Nothing appeared before me but I must leave the State, and leave my wife and my children never to see them more. My friends had also done all they could for me.

And why must I be banished? Ever after I entertained the first idea of being free, I had endeavored so to conduct myself as not to become obnoxious to the white inhabitants, knowing as I did their power, and their hostility to the colored people. The two points necessary in such a case I had kept constantly in mind. First, I had made no display of the little property or money I possessed, but in every way I wore as much as possible the aspect of poverty. Second, I had never appeared to be even so intelligent as I really was. This all colored people at the south, free and slaves, find it peculiarly necessary to their own comfort and safety to observe.

I should, perhaps, have mentioned that on the same day I received the notice to leave Raleigh, similar notices were presented to two other free

colored people, who had been slaves; were trying to purchase their families; and were otherwise in a like situation to myself. And they took the same
course I did to endeavor to remain a limited time. ISAAC HUNTER, who had
a family with five children, was one; and WALLER FREEMAN, who had six
children, was the other. Mr. Hunter's petition went before mine; and a bill
of some sort passed the Senate, which was so cut down in the Commons, as
to allow him only *twenty days* to remain in the State. He has since, however,
obtained the freedom of his family, who are living with him in Philadelphia.

Mr. Freeman's petition received no better fate than mine. His family were
the property of Judge BADGER, who was afterwards made a member of Mr.
Harrison's cabinet. When Mr. Badger removed to Washington, he took with
him among other slaves this family; and Freeman removed also to that city.
After this, when Mr. B. resigned his office, with the other members of the
cabinet, under President Tyler, he entered into some sort of contract with
Freeman, to sell him this family, which he left at Washington, while he took
the rest of his slaves back to Raleigh. Freeman is now endeavoring to raise
money to make the purchase.

It was now between two and three months to the next session of the court;
and I knew that before or at that time I must leave the State. I was bound
to appear before the court; but it had been arranged between my lawyer
and the prosecuting attorney, that if I would leave the State, and pay the
costs of court, the case should be dropped, so that my bondsman should
not be involved. I therefore concluded to stay as long as I possibly could,
and then leave. I also determined to appeal to the kindness of the friends of
the colored man in the North, for assistance, though I had but little hope of
succeeding in this way. Yet it was the only course I could think of, by which
I could see any possible hope of accomplishing the object.

I had paid Mr. Smith six hundred and twenty dollars; and had a house
and lot worth five hundred dollars, which he had promised to take when I
should raise the balance. He gave me also a bill of sale of one of my children, Laura, in consideration of two hundred and fifty dollars of the money
already paid; and her I determined to take with me to the North. The costs
of court which I had to meet, amounted to between thirty and forty dollars,
besides the fee of my lawyer.

On the 18th of May, 1841, three days after the court commenced its ses-
sion, I bid adieu to my friends in Raleigh, and set out for the city of New
York. I took with me a letter of introduction and recommendation from
Mr. John Primrose, a very estimable man, a recommendatory certificate from

Mr. Battle, and a letter from the church of which I was a member, together with such papers relating to the affair as I had in my possession. Also I received the following:

RALEIGH, N.C. May, 1841.

The bearer, Lunsford Lane, a free man of color, for some time a resident in this place, being about to leave North Carolina in search of a more favorable location to pursue his trade, has desired us to give him a certificate of his good conduct heretofore.

We take pleasure in saying that his habits are temperate and industrious, that his conduct has been orderly and proper, and that he has for these qualities been distinguished among his caste.

> Wm. Hill,
> Weston R. Gales,
> C. L. Hinton,
> R. Smith,
> C. Dewey.

The above was certified to officially in the usual form by the clerk of the Court of Common Pleas and Quarter Sessions.

My success in New York was at first small; but at length I fell in with two friends who engaged to raise for me three hundred dollars, provided I should first obtain from other sources the balance of the sum required, which balance would be one thousand and eighty dollars. Thus encouraged, I proceeded to Boston; and in the city and vicinity the needful sum was contributed by about the 1st of April, 1842. My thanks I have endeavored to express in my poor way to the many friends who so kindly and liberally assisted me. I cannot reward them; I hope they will receive their reward in another world. If the limits of this publication would permit, I should like to record the names of many to whom I am very especially indebted for their kindness and aid, not only in contributing, but in introducing me, and opening various ways of access to others.

On the 5th of February, 1842, finding that I should soon have in my possession the sum necessary to procure my family, and fearing that there might be danger in visiting Raleigh for that purpose, in consequence of the strong opposition of many of the citizens against colored people, their opposition to me, and their previously persecuting me from the city, I wrote to Mr. Smith, requesting him to see the Governor,[27] and obtain under his hand a permit to visit the State for a sufficient time to accomplish this business. I requested

Mr. Smith to publish the permit in one or two of the city papers, and then to enclose the original to me. This letter he answered, under date of Raleigh, 19th Feb. 1841, as follows:

> LUNSFORD:—Your letter of the 5th inst. came duly to hand, and in reply I have to inform you, that owing to the absence of Gov. Morehead, I cannot send you the permit you requested, but this will make no difference, for you can come home, and after your arrival you may obtain one to remain long enough to settle up your affairs. You ought of course to apply to the Governor immediately on your arrival, before any malicious person would have time to inform against you; I don't think by pursuing this course you need apprehend any danger.
>
> We are all alive at present in Raleigh on the subjects of temperance and religion. We have taken into the temperance societies, about five hundred members, and about fifty persons have been happily converted. The work seems still to be spreading, and such a time I have never seen before in my life. Glorious times truly.
>
> Do try and get all the religion in your heart you possibly can, for it is the only thing worth having after all.
> Your, &c.
>
> B. B. SMITH.

The way now appeared to be in a measure open; also I thought that the religious and temperance interest mentioned in the latter portion of Mr. Smith's letter, augured a state of feeling which would be a protection to me. But fearing still that there might be danger in visiting Raleigh without the permit from the Governor, or at least wishing to take every possible precaution, I addressed another letter to Mr. Smith, and received under date of March 12th, a reply, from which I copy as follows:

> "The Governor has just returned, and I called upon him to get the permit as you requested, but he said he had no authority by law to grant one; and *he told me to say to you, that you might in perfect safety come home* in a quiet manner, and remain twenty days without being interrupted. I also consulted Mr. Manly [a lawyer] and he *told me the same thing. Surely you need not fear any thing under these circumstances. You had therefore better come on just as soon as possible.*"

I need not say, what the reader has already seen, that my life so far had been one of joy succeeding sorrow, and sorrow following joy; of hope, of despair, of bright prospects, of gloom; and of as many hues as ever appear on the varied sky, from the black of midnight, or the deep brown of a tempest, to the bright warm glow of a clear noon day. On the 11th of April, it was noon with me; I left Boston on my way for Raleigh with high hopes, intending to pay over the money for my family and return with them to Boston, which I designed should be my future home; for there I had found friends, and there I would find a grave. The visit I was making to the South was to be a farewell one; and I did not dream that my old cradle, hard as it once had jostled me, would refuse to rock me a pleasant, or even an affectionate good bye. I thought, too, that the assurances I had received from the Governor, through Mr. Smith, and the assurances of other friends, were a sufficient guaranty that I might visit the home of my boyhood, of my youth, of my manhood, in peace, especially as I was to stay but for a few days and then to return. With these thoughts, and with the thoughts of my family and freedom, I pursued my way to Raleigh, and arrived there on the 23d of the month. It was Saturday about four o'clock, P.M. when I found myself once more in the midst of my family. With them I remained over the Sabbath, as it was sweet to spend a little time with them after so long an absence, an absence filled with so much of interest to us, and as I could not do any business until the beginning of the week. On Monday morning between eight and nine o'clock, while I was making ready to leave the house for the first time after my arrival, to go to the store of Mr. Smith, where I was to transact my business with him, two constables, Messrs. Murray and Scott, entered, accompanied by two other men, and summoned me to appear immediately before the police. I accordingly accompanied them to the City Hall, but as it was locked and the officers could not at once find the key, we were told that the court would be held in Mr. Smith's store, a large and commodious room. This was what is termed in common phrase, in Raleigh, a "call court." The Mayor, Mr. Loring,[28] presided, assisted by William Boylan and Jonathan Busbye, Esqs. Justices of the Peace. There were a large number of people together—more than could obtain admission to the room, and a large company of mobocratic spirits crowded around the door. Mr. Loring read the writ, setting forth that I had been guilty of *delivering abolition lectures in the State of Massachusetts*. He asked me whether I was guilty or not guilty. I told him I did not know whether I had given abolition lectures or not, but if it pleased the court, I would relate the course I had pursued during my absence from Raleigh. He then said that I was at liberty to speak.

The circumstances under which I left Raleigh, said I, are perfectly familiar to you. It is known that I had no disposition to remove from this city, but resorted to every lawful means to remain. After I found that I could not be permitted to stay, I went away leaving behind everything I held dear, with the exception of one child, whom I took with me, after paying two hundred and fifty dollars for her. It is also known to you and to many other persons here present, that I had engaged to purchase my wife and children of their master, Mr. Smith, for the sum of twenty-five hundred dollars, and that I had paid of this sum (including my house and lot) eleven hundred and twenty dollars, leaving a balance to be made up of thirteen hundred and eighty dollars. I had previously to that lived in Raleigh, a slave, the property of Mr. Sherwood Haywood, and had purchased my freedom by paying the sum of one thousand dollars. But being driven away, no longer permitted to live in this city, to raise the balance of the money due on my family, my last resort was to call upon the friends of humanity in other places, to assist me.

I went to the city of Boston, and there I related the story of my persecutions here, the same as I have now stated to you. The people gave ear to my statements; and one of them, Rev. Mr. Neale, wrote back, unknown to me, to Mr. Smith, inquiring of him whether the statements made by me were correct. After Mr. Neale received the answer, he sent for me, informed me of his having written, and read to me the reply. The letter fully satisfied Mr. Neale and his friends. He placed it in my hands, remarking that it would, in a great measure, do away the necessity of using the other documents in my possession. I then with that letter in my hands went out from house to house, from place of business to place of business, and from church to church, relating, where I could gain an ear, the same heart-rending and soul-trying story which I am now repeating to you. In pursuing that course, the people, first one and then another contributed, until I had succeeded in raising the amount alluded to, namely, thirteen hundred and eighty dollars. I may have had contributions from abolitionists, but I did not stop to ask those who assisted me whether they were anti-slavery or pro-slavery, for I considered that the money coming from either, would accomplish the object I had in view. These are the facts; and now, sir, it remains for you to say, whether I have been giving abolition lectures or not.

In the course of my remarks I presented the letter of Mr. Smith to Mr. Neale, showing that I had acted the open part while in Massachusetts; also I referred to my having written to Mr. Smith requesting him to obtain for me the permit of the Governor; and I showed to the court, Mr. Smith's letters in reply, in order to satisfy them that I had reason to believe I should be unmolested in my return.

Mr. Loring then whispered to some of the leading men; after which he remarked that he saw nothing in what I had done, according to my statements, implicating me in a manner worthy of notice. He called upon any present who might be in possession of information tending to disprove what I had said, or to show any wrong on my part, to produce it, otherwise I should be set at liberty. No person appeared against me; so I was discharged.

I started to leave the house; but just before I got to the door I met Mr. James Litchford, who touched me on the shoulder, and I followed him back. He observed to me that if I went out of that room I should in less than five minutes be a dead man; for there was a mob outside waiting to drink my life. Mr. Loring then spoke to me again, and said that notwithstanding I had been found guilty of nothing, yet public opinion was law; and he advised me to leave the place the next day, otherwise he was convinced I should have to suffer death. I replied, "not to-morrow, but to-day." He answered that I could not go that day, because I had not done my business. I told him that I would leave my business in his hands and in those of other such gentlemen as himself, who might settle it for me and send my family to meet me at Philadelphia. This was concluded upon, and a guard appointed to conduct me to the depot. I took my seat in the cars, when the mob that had followed us surrounded me, and declared that the cars should not go, if I were permitted to go in them. Mr. Loring inquired what they wanted of me; he told them that there had been an examination, and nothing had been found against me; that they were at the examination invited to speak if they knew aught to condemn me, but they had remained silent, and that now it was but right I should be permitted to leave in peace. They replied that they wanted a more thorough investigation, that they wished to search my trunks (I had but one trunk) and see if I was not in possession of abolition papers. It now became evident that I should be unable to get off in the cars; and my friends advised me to go the shortest way possible to jail, for my safety. They said they were persuaded that what the rabble wanted was to get me into their possession, and then to murder me. The mob looked dreadfully enraged, and seemed to lap for blood. The whole city was in an uproar. But the first men and the more wealthy were my friends: and they did everything in their power to protect me. Mr. Boylan, whose name has repeatedly occurred in this publication, was more than a father to me; and Mr. Smith and Mr. Loring, and many other gentlemen, whose names it would give me pleasure to mention, were exceedingly kind.

The guard then conducted me through the mob to the prison; and I felt joyful that even a prison could protect me. Looking out from the prison window, I saw my trunk in the hands of Messrs. Johnson, Scott, and others, who were taking it to the City Hall for examination. I understood afterwards that they opened my trunk; and as the lid flew up, Lo! a paper! a paper!! Those about seized it, three or four at once, as hungry dogs would a piece of meat after forty days famine. But the meat quickly turned to a stone; for the paper it happened, was one *printed in Raleigh*, and edited by Weston R. Gales,[29] a nice man to be sure, but no abolitionist. The only other printed or written things in the trunk were some business cards of a firm in Raleigh — not incendiary.

Afterwards I saw from the window Mr. Scott, accompanied by Mr. Johnson, lugging my carpet-bag in the same direction my trunk had gone. It was opened at the City Hall, and found actually to contain a pair of old shoes, and a pair of old boots! — but they did not conclude that these were incendiary.

Mr. Smith now came to the prison and told me that the examination had been completed, and nothing found against me; but that it would not be safe for me to leave the prison immediately. It was agreed that I should remain in prison until after night-fall, and then steal secretly away, being let out by the keeper, and pass unnoticed to the house of my old and tried friend Mr. Boylan. Accordingly I was discharged between nine and ten o'clock. I went by the back way leading to Mr. Boylan's; but soon and suddenly a large company of men sprang upon me, and instantly I found myself in their possession. They conducted me sometimes high above ground and sometimes dragging me along, but as silently as possible, in the direction of the gallows, which is always kept standing upon the Common, or as it is called "the pines," or "piny old field." I now expected to pass speedily into the world of spirits; I thought of that unseen region to which I seemed to be hastening; and then my mind would return to my wife and children, and the labors I had made to redeem them from bondage. Although I had the money to pay for them according to a bargain already made, it seemed to me some white man would get it, and they would die in slavery, without benefit from my exertions and the contributions of my friends. Then the thought of my own death, to occur in a few brief moments, would rush over me, and I seemed to bid adieu in spirit to all earthly things, and to hold communion already with eternity. But at length I observed those who were carrying me away, changed their course a little from the direct line to the gallows, and hope, a faint beaming, sprung up within me; but then as they were taking me to the woods, I thought they intended to murder me there, in a place where they would be less likely to be interrupted than in so public a spot as where the gallows stood. They conducted me to a rising ground among the trees, and set me down. "Now," said they, "tell us the truth about those abolition lectures you have been giving at the North." I replied that I had related the circumstances before the court in the morning; and could only repeat what I had then said. "But that was not the truth—tell us the truth." I again said that any different story would be false, and as I supposed I was in a few minutes to die, I would not, whatever they might think I would say under other circumstances, pass into the other world with a lie upon my lips. Said one, "you were always, Lunsford, when you were here, a clever fellow, and I did not think you would be engaged in such business as giving abolition lectures." To this and similar remarks, I replied that the people of Raleigh had always said the abolitionists did not believe in buying slaves, but contended that their masters ought to free them without pay. I had been laboring to buy my family; and how then could they suppose me to be in league with the abolitionists?

After other conversation of this kind, and after they seemed to have become tired of questioning me, they held a consultation in a low whisper among themselves. Then a bucket was brought and set down by my side; but what it contained or for what it was intended, I could not divine. But soon, one of the number came forward with a pillow, and then hope sprung up, a flood of light and joy within me. The heavy weight on my heart rolled off; death had passed by and I unharmed. They commenced stripping me till every rag of clothes was removed; and then the bucket was set near, and I discovered it to contain tar. One man, I will do him the honor to record his name, Mr. WILLIAM ANDRES, a journeyman printer, when he is any thing, except a tar-and-featherer, put his hands the first into the bucket, and was about passing them to my face. "Don't put any in his face or eyes," said one.[III] So he desisted; but he, with three other "gentlemen," whose names I should be happy to record if I could recall them, gave me as nice a coat of tar all over, face only excepted, as any one would wish to see. Then they took the pillow and ripped it open at one end, and with the open end commenced the operation at the head and so worked downwards, of putting a coat of its contents over that of the contents of the bucket. A fine escape from the hanging this will be, thought I, provided they do not with a match set fire to the feathers. I had some fear they would. But when the work was completed they gave me my clothes, and one of them handed me my watch which he had carefully kept in his hands; they all expressed great interest in my welfare, advised me how to proceed with my business the next day,

[III] I think this was Mr. Burns, a blacksmith in the place, but I am not certain. At any rate, this man was my *friend* (if so he may be called) on this occasion; and it was fortunate for me that the company generally seemed to look up to him for wisdom.

told me to stay in the place as long as I wished, and with other such words of consolation they bid me good night.

After I had returned to my family, to their inexpressible joy, as they had become greatly alarmed for my safety, some of the persons who had participated in this outrage, came in (probably influenced by a curiosity to see how the tar and feathers would be got off) and expressed great sympathy for me. They said they regretted that the affair had happened—that they had no objections to my living in Raleigh—I might feel perfectly safe to go out and transact my business preparatory to leaving—I should not be molested.

Meanwhile, my friends understanding that I had been discharged from prison, and perceiving I did not come to them, had commenced a regular search for me, on foot and on horseback, every where; and Mr. Smith called upon the Governor to obtain his official interference; and after my return, a guard came to protect me; but I chose not to risk myself at my own house, and so went to Mr. Smith's, where this guard kept me safely until morning. They seemed friendly indeed, and were regaled with a supper during the night by Mr. Smith. My friend, Mr. Battle, (late Private Secretary to the Governor,) was with them; and he made a speech to them setting forth the good qualities I had exhibited in my past life, particularly in my connection with the Governor's office.

In the morning Mr. Boylan, true as ever, and unflinching in his friendship, assisted me in arranging my business,[IV] so that I should start with my family *that day* for the north. He furnished us with provisions more than sufficient to sustain the family to Philadelphia, where we intended to make a halt; and sent his own baggage wagon to convey our baggage to the depot, offering also to send his carriage for my family. But my friend, Mr. Malone, had been before him in this kind offer, which I had agreed to accept.

Brief and sorrowful was the parting from my kind friends; but the worst was the thought of leaving my mother. The cars were to start at ten o'clock in the morning. I called upon my old mistress, Mrs. Haywood, who was affected to weeping by the considerations that naturally came to her mind. She had been kind to me; the day before she and her daughter, Mrs. Hogg, now present, had jointly transmitted a communication to the court repre-

---

[IV] Of course I was obliged to sacrifice much on my property, leaving in this hurried manner. And while I was in the North, a kind *friend* had removed from the wood-lot, wood that I had cut and corded, for which I expected to receive over one hundred dollars; thus saving me the trouble of making sale of it, or of being burdened with the money it would bring. I suppose I have no redress. I might add other things as bad.

senting that in consequence of my good conduct from my youth, I could not be supposed to be guilty of any offence. And now, "with tears that ceased not flowing," they gave me their parting blessing. My mother was still Mrs. Haywood's slave, and I her only child. Our old mistress could not witness the sorrow that would attend the parting with my mother. She told her to go with me; and said that if I ever became able to pay two hundred dollars for her, I might; otherwise it should be her loss. She gave her the following paper, which is in the ordinary form of a *pass*:

RALEIGH, N.C. April 26, 1842.

Know all persons by these presents, that the bearer of this, Clarissa, a slave, belonging to me, hath my permission to visit the city of New York with her relations, who are in company with her; and it is my desire that she may be protected and permitted to pass without molestation or hindrance, on good behavior. Witness my hand this 26th April, 1842.

ELEANOR HAYWOOD.
Witness—J. A. Campbell.

On leaving Mrs. Haywood's, I called upon Mrs. Badger, another daughter, and wife of Judge Badger, previously mentioned. She seemed equally affected; she wept as she gave me her parting counsel. She and Mrs. Hogg and I had been children together, playing in the same yard, while yet none of us had learned that they were of a superior and I of a subject race. And in those infant years there were pencillings made upon the heart, which time and opposite fortunes could not all efface. — May these friends never be slaves as I have been; nor their bosom companions and their little ones be slaves like mine.

When the cars were about to start, the whole city seemed to be gathered at the depot; and among the rest the mobocratic portion, who appeared to be determined still that I should not go peaceably away. Apprehending this, it had been arranged with my friends and the conductor, that my family should be put in the cars and that I should go a distance from the city on foot, and be taken up as they passed. The mob, therefore, supposing that I was left behind, allowed the cars to start.

Mr. Whiting, known as the agent of the railroad company, was going as far as Petersburg, Va.; and he kindly assisted in purchasing our tickets, and enabling us to pass on unmolested. After he left, Capt. Guyan, of Raleigh, performed the same kind office as far as Alexandria, D.C., and then he placed us in the care of a citizen of Philadelphia, whose name I regret to have forgotten, who protected us quite out of the land of slavery. But for this we should have been liable to be detained at several places on our way, much to our embarrassment, at least, if nothing had occurred of a more serious nature.

One accident only had happened: we lost at Washington a trunk containing most of our valuable clothing. This we have not recovered; but our lives have been spared to bless the day that conferred freedom upon us. I felt when my feet struck the pavements in Philadelphia, as though I had passed into another world. I could draw in a full long breath, with no one to say to the ribs, "why do ye so?"

On reaching Philadelphia we found that our money had all been expended, but kind friends furnished us with the means of proceeding as far as New-York; and thence we were with equal kindness aided on to Boston.

In Boston and in the vicinity, are persons almost without number, who have done me favors more than I can express. The thought that I was now in my loved, though recently acquired home — that my family were with me where the stern, cruel, hated hand of slavery could never reach us more — the greetings of friends — the interchange of feeling and sympathy — the kindness bestowed upon us, more grateful than rain to the thirsty earth — the reflections of the past that would rush into my mind, — these and more almost overwhelmed me with emotion, and I had deep and strange communion with my own soul. Next to God from whom every good gift proceeds, I feel under the greatest obligations to my kind friends in Massachusetts. To be rocked in their cradle of Liberty, — oh, how unlike being stretched on the pillory of slavery! May that cradle rock forever; may many a poor care-worn child of sorrow, many a spirit-bruised (worse than lash-mangled) victim of oppression, there sweetly sleep to the lullaby of Freedom, sung by Massachusetts' sons and daughters.

A number of meetings have been held at which friends have contributed to our temporal wants, and individuals have sent us various articles of provision and furniture and apparel, so that our souls have been truly made glad. There are now ten of us in the family, my wife, my mother, and myself, with seven children, and we expect soon to be joined by my father, who several years ago received his freedom by legacy. The wine fresh from the clustering grapes never filled so sweet a cup as mine. May I and my family be permitted to drink it, remembering whence it came!

BILLS OF SALE

I suppose such of my readers as are not accustomed to trade in human beings, may be curious to see the Bills of Sale, by which I have obtained the right to my wife and children. They are both in the handwriting of Mr. Smith. The first—that for Laura is as follows:

State of North Carolina, Wake County.

Know all men by these presents, that for and in consideration of the sum of two hundred and fifty dollars, to me in hand paid, I have this day bargained and sold; and do hereby bargain, sell and deliver unto Lunsford Lane, a free man of color, a certain negro girl by the name of Laura, aged about seven years, and hereby warrant and defend the right and title of the said girl to the said Lunsford and his heirs forever, free from the claims of all persons whatsoever.

In witness whereof, I have hereunto set my hand and seal at Raleigh, this 17th May, 1841.

B. B. SMITH, [seal.]
Witness—ROBT. W. HAYWOOD.

Below is the Bill of Sale for my wife and other six children, to which the papers that follow are attached.

State of North Carolina, Wake County.

Know all men by these presents, that for and in consideration of the sum of eighteen hundred and eighty dollars to me in hand paid, the receipt of which is hereby acknowledged, I have this day bargained, sold and delivered unto Lunsford Lane, a free man of color, one dark mulatto woman named Patsy, one boy named Edward, one boy also named William, one boy also named Lunsford, one girl named Maria, one boy also named Ellick, and one girl named Lucy, to have and to hold the said negroes free from the claims of all persons whatsoever.

In witness whereof, I have hereunto affixed my hand and seal this 25th day of April, 1842.

B. B. SMITH, [seal.]
Witness—TH. L. WEST.

State of North Carolina, Wake County.
Office of Court of Pleas and Quarter Sessions, April 26, 1842.

The execution of the within bill of sale was this day duly acknowledged before me by B. B. Smith, the executor of the same.

In testimony whereof, I have hereunto affixed the seal of said Court, and subscribed my name at office in Raleigh, the date above.
[L. S.][30]

JAS. T. MARRIOTT, Clerk.

State of North Carolina, Wake County.

I, Wm. Boylan, presiding magistrate of the Court of Pleas and Quarter Sessions for the county aforesaid, certify that James T. Marriott, who has written and signed the above certificate, is Clerk of the Court aforesaid, —that the same is in due form, and full faith and credit are due to such his official acts.

Given under my hand and private seal (having no seal of office) this 26th day of April, 1842.

WM. BOYLAN, P. M. [seal.]

The State of North Carolina.

To all to whom these presents shall come, Greeting:

Be it known, that William Boylan, whose signature appears in his own proper hand writing to the annexed certificate, was at the time of signing the same and now is a Justice of the Peace and the Presiding Magistrate for the county of Wake, in the State aforesaid, and as such he is duly qualified and empowered to give said certificate, which is here done in the usual and proper manner; and full faith and credit are due to the same, and ought to be given to all the official acts of the said William Boylan as Presiding Magistrate aforesaid.

In testimony whereof, I, J. M. Morehead, Governor, Captain General and Commander in Chief, have caused the Great Seal of the State to be hereunto affixed, and signed the same at the city of Raleigh, on the 26th day of April, in the year of our Lord one thousand eight hundred and forty-two, and in the sixty-sixth year of the Independence of the United States.

[L. S.]

J. M. MOREHEAD.

By the Governor.

P. REYNOLDS, Private Secretary.

Notes

1. Joshua Pollard Blanchard (1782–1868), a Boston merchant, was an abolitionist, peace advocate, and reformer. Blanchard's poem, as it appeared in Lane's original text, was divided into two sections, half appearing before the title page, the other half appearing at the end of the text.

2. Sherwood Haywood (1762–1829) served as clerk of the North Carolina State Senate from January 4, 1786, to December 24, 1798. He worked as an agent for the Bank of New Bern in Raleigh.

3. Clarissa Haywood (?-1859) was manumitted by Eleanor Hawkins Haywood in 1842. She moved to Boston with her son Lunsford and his family before settling in Wrentham, Massachusetts, with her husband, Edward.

4. Edward Lane (?-1859) belonged to John Haywood, the brother of Sherwood Haywood. Manumitted at the death of John circa 1830, Edward remained with the Haywood family for fourteen years as steward before going north to join his family in Massachusetts, where he died in Wrentham.

5. A measure of length equal to 5 yards or 16 feet or 5.029 meters.

6. Fayetteville is located in Cumberland County, North Carolina.

7. Richard Bennahan (1743-1825), a merchant and planter, built Stagville Plantation in 1800, one of the largest plantations in North Carolina at 4,000 acres. Orange County is located in the central Piedmont area of North Carolina.

8. A North Carolina statute passed in 1788 required that a slave possess written permission from his master for each act of trading. This was due to the concern that trading would encourage slaves to steal from their masters in order to trade. In 1826, the legislature created a specific list of articles that a slave could not sell without written permission. These included cotton, tobacco, corn, pork, farming utensils, meal, and liquor.

9. A dealer in tobacco, especially retail.

10. Thomas Pollock Devereux (1793-1869), owner of several large plantations in North Carolina, served as U.S. attorney for the District of North Carolina as well as a justice of the peace and presiding justice of the Halifax, North Carolina, County Court.

11. William Boylan, editor of the *North Carolina Minerva* and publisher of *Boylan's Almanack*.

12. Vegetable cooking water.

13. The verandah of a house.

14. Eleanor Hawkins Haywood.

15. Salisbury is located in Rowan County in central North Carolina.

16. Chapel Hill is located in Orange County, North Carolina, and is home to the University of North Carolina at Chapel Hill, established in 1793.

17. In 1741, the North Carolina legislature passed a measure allowing a master to emancipate a slave, but requiring proof that the slave had performed "meritorious services." In 1830, the state established a new procedure for freeing slaves, requiring a master to submit a petition including the slave's name, sex, and age to the superior courts of the state. In addition to giving notice to the county courthouse and the *State Gazette* six weeks in advance, a master was also obliged to post a bond of $1,000 that would be forfeited if the slave did not behave "honestly and correctly" while he or she remained in the state.

18. To hasten, speed, go quickly.

19. "Servants be obedient to your masters . . . Not with eye service, as men pleasers" (Ephesians 6:5).

20. Luke 12:47.

21. "This is a hard saying, who can bear it?" (John 6:60).

22. Edward Bishop Dudley (1789–1855), a leader in the formation of the Whig Party in North Carolina and a two-term governor of the state from 1836 to 1840.

23. George Washington Haywood (1802–90), a lawyer in Raleigh.

24. "Shews" is an archaic spelling of "shows."

25. David Williamson Stone, a Raleigh business and political leader and the son of David Stone (1770–1818), who served as governor and U.S. senator from North Carolina.

26. Thomas Meredith (1795–1860), a minister who was one of the fourteen founders of the North Carolina Baptist State Convention in 1830 and the editor of the *Biblical Recorder*. Meredith College in Raleigh is named after him.

27. John Motley Morehead (1796–1866), a two-term governor of the state from 1841 to 1845.

28. Thomas Loring, the mayor of Raleigh, was a native of Massachusetts and former editor of the *North Carolina Standard*.

29. Weston R. Gales (1803–48), the owner and editor of the *Raleigh Register*.

30. L.S. stands for *Locus Sigilii* (Latin: in place of the seal).

Narrative of
the Life of
Moses Grandy

INTRODUCTION

Andreá N. Williams

When he confronted his master Enoch Sawyer in 1827, North Carolina slave Moses Grandy felt justified in demanding his freedom. Already, Grandy had been shuffled from owner to owner and had paid for his freedom twice, only to be sold back into slavery each time before the manumission was made official. Now Sawyer had demoted Grandy from boat captain on the Dismal Swamp—a position that afforded relative independence from his master—to field hand, underfed and overworked. Grandy was blunt: "I could not stand his field work any longer." Denying Grandy's petitions, Sawyer conceded more food for all field hands. "But I was not satisfied," Grandy insisted. "I wanted liberty."

Moses Grandy would not gain his liberty until purchasing himself a third time, three years and $650 later, around 1830. Still, his confrontation with Sawyer constitutes a self-defining point in Grandy's pursuit of freedom. Previously, after settling for meager improvements in his condition, Grandy had "[come] out shouting for joy, and [had gone] to work with delight." However, this time, by refusing to report to duty in the cornfield, Moses Grandy dared suggest a limit as to how much mistreatment he could take. His resistance asserted that he was not a mere physical body whose problems could be solved by an offer of more food. Grandy identified himself as a complete *human*—body, mind, and soul—and expected the corresponding human right of freedom.

The distinction that Grandy evokes in his *Narrative*, by viewing himself as a complete person instead of an instrument of labor, lay at the heart of nineteenth-century debates about the nature and proper status of African Americans. Proslavery proponents reasoned that because of their supposed inferior nature, people of color were suited only to be servants, who actually benefited from the civilizing effects of slavery. Conversely, abolitionists argued that perpetual bondage, not nature, made "rational, accountable, immortal beings, into goods and chattels, and implements of husbandry!"[1] Antislavery supporters argued that African Americans were essentially the same as white Americans, a premise perhaps best illustrated in the popular antislavery emblem of a kneeling, chained black man proclaiming, "Am I not a man and a brother?"

Moses Grandy elicits his readers' reply to this crucial question in the course of offering his own affirmative response in his autobiography. Dictating the narrative to an abolitionist in London in 1842, Grandy presents telling incidents of southern life to enable readers to reach an antislavery conclusion while he maintains apparent impartiality. Yet the *Narrative of the Life of Moses Grandy* goes beyond reiterating the popular antislavery arguments about universal human brotherhood or slavery's inherent evil, as commonly proposed by other slave narratives and abolitionist texts of the 1830s and 1840s.

At the heart of Grandy's narrative, in the silences between his humble self-portrayal and his objective depiction of slavery, he introduces the more daring claim that because of his equality to the white man, he, too, may justly demand the rights and responsibilities of American manhood. Contrary to contemporary racist thought that categorized black males, with white women, as dependent and in need of supervision by white men,[2] Grandy contends that black men are true men, deserving not only emancipation but additional privileges of American citizenship reserved for males. The narrator of Grandy's autobiography portrays himself as a model of black men's worthiness, calling special attention to his own manly character in episodes that reveal him as a family man, earnest Christian, and diligent, upwardly mobile worker. To the extent that his narrative reached beyond the expected antislavery theme to advocate black men's civil rights, it risked offending many white readers — even liberal antislavery whites — who either feared or resented the social equality that Grandy envisioned as true freedom. By positing black manhood rights as the subtext of his otherwise conventional slave account, Grandy took a measured, but genuine, risk, raising the stakes of his narrative's rhetorical agenda well above the more modest sociopolitical claims of predecessors in the genre.

Beyond the details his autobiography provides, we know little about the life of Moses Grandy, especially in the years following the publication of his narrative in 1842. The text seldom dates events to specific years, but the narrator's references to some names and current events make it possible to trace a biographical timeline. Born around 1786 in Camden County, North Carolina, Grandy proved himself "industrious and persevering" through his increasingly skilled labor in various sea-based industries along the Albemarle Sound and the Dismal Swamp of North Carolina. He earned $1,850, an enormous sum at the time, especially for a slave, with which he intended to buy his freedom; yet, one master after another took Grandy's money and resold him into bondage. Having begun his attempts at self-purchase while a young man, probably in his twenties, Grandy did not legally gain his liberty until he was about forty-four years old.

Relocating to the North in 1831 or 1832, Grandy lived in Boston for nearly a decade before sharing his American experiences abroad in his narrative. The Boston City Directory for 1840 and 1841, the two years preceding his trip to the British Isles, lists Grandy as a local laborer,[3] but he also continued to work as a seaman as he had in the South. For African American men in the United States during the eighteenth and early nineteenth centuries, maritime occupations such as Grandy pursued in Boston were a primary means of earning the money that would bolster a masculine ego and affirm a respectable black manhood. Black seamen, who often interacted with white sailors and earned the same wages as they did, experienced more racial tolerance and egalitarianism aboard ship than onshore.[4]

Moses Grandy's arrival in Boston in the early 1830s coincided with the blossoming of New England antislavery activism. In 1831, prominent white Boston reformer William Lloyd Garrison, with the support of many African American readers, began publishing the *Liberator*, a weekly newspaper devoted to the immediate demise of slavery. When the New England Anti-Slavery Society formed the following year in 1832, the all-black Massachusetts General Colored Association, which had been independently promoting abolitionism since 1826, joined as an auxiliary to the new Garrison-led organization. Other antislavery societies sprang up in succession including the Massachusetts Anti-Slavery Society, the first state-level abolitionist movement in the nation, in 1832 and the American Anti-Slavery Society in 1833.[5] Besides agitating for the mass emancipation of southern slaves, both white and black abolitionists in Boston worked to smooth the transition of newly freed slaves in the North and to improve race relations within the city. Most relevant to Grandy's primary aim on his arrival in the North, sympathetic individuals and antislavery societies often provided funds or helped raise them for purchasing the freedom of fugitives or reuniting separated families.

The nature of Grandy's involvement in these domestic antislavery movements remains uncertain. He likely delivered speeches about his slave experience several times in the Boston area between 1832 and 1842 before gaining the endorsements of New England reformers to represent the antislavery cause abroad. After Grandy purchased his wife around 1833, his "many friends in the Northern States" helped to redeem one of his sons whom he had left behind in the South. Still, neither his supporters' resources nor Grandy's own work as a seaman and manual laborer could fund fully his ambition to rescue all of his family. The burden on his American benefactors may have been a primary factor prompting Grandy's British tour, but the antislavery movement also stood to gain from his travels. While offering Grandy financial assistance, British antislavery societies could capitalize on the former slave's experience, using him to propagate abolitionism by authenticating claims about American slavery.

When Moses Grandy began his journey to the British Isles in August 1842, he traveled the path of several antislavery crusaders bridging American and English agendas. Garrison completed his first tour of the British Isles in the spring of 1833; among African American abolitionists, former North Carolina slave Moses Roper preceded Grandy in 1835 for an extended stay overseas.[6] In the 1840s, antislavery traffic increased between America and England after the latter ended slavery in its West Indies colonies in 1833 and could turn its attention toward helping to emancipate slaves in the United States.[7] Bearing letters of introduction from various New England supporters, Grandy made connections with British antislavery leaders on his arrival in late August or September 1842. John Scoble, then secretary of the British and Foreign Anti-Slavery Society, England's preeminent abolitionist agency, functioned as Grandy's liaison to schedule speaking engagements, introduce Grandy to the British public, and collect funds from sales of the narrative. George Thompson, a highly publicized abolitionist and close friend of Garrison, served as the enthusiastic editor for Grandy's autobiographical project. "Just get him to tell you his narrative," one of Grandy's American recommenders suggested to Thompson, "and if you happen to have an Anti-slavery Meeting, let him tell his tale to a British audience."

Transcribing Grandy's narrative fit well with the goals Thompson established for his abolitionist activism. Born in Liverpool in 1804 and raised in London, Thompson began lecturing as an agent for the London Anti-Slavery Society in 1830. After accepting an invitation from Garrison and the New England Anti-slavery Society, Thompson traveled to the United States and conducted a lecture tour from 1834 to 1835. His vitriolic speeches against slaveholding as Christian hypocrisy incited proslavery mobs wherever he spoke, especially because many Americans considered him an intrusive foreigner. Forced to flee for his life in late 1835, Thompson defended his radicalism in a parting letter to Garrison, explaining, "yet shall I, if spared, deem it my duty to publish aloud [America's] wide and fearful departures from rectitude and mercy. I shall unceasingly proclaim the wrongs of her en-

slaved children. . . . Upon these topics I shall write, and speak, and print. . . .
I shall guard against the charge of misrepresentation, by founding all I say
upon abundant and incontrovertible evidence."[8] In Moses Grandy, George
Thompson found his "incontrovertible evidence" as well as the opportunity
to write and print charges against American slavery. What evidence could be
more "incontrovertible" than a former subject of the "peculiar institution,"
bearing witness to enslavement with physical wounds and mental scars?

The partnership between Grandy and Thompson demonstrated how
antislavery propagandizing required cooperation between involved blacks
and whites. African Americans offered an experiential knowledge of slavery
that whites were eager to share, while the latter possessed resources to promote black concerns. However, the exchange was not wholly mutual, as African Americans sometimes relied more heavily on their white counterparts
than vice versa. In order to promote their interests beyond the black community, African American abolitionists needed the influence of white advocates
who had political clout and established relationships with white reform net-
works.[9] For Grandy, the welfare of his still enslaved family depended on
assistance from British sympathizers who likely would have neither wel-
comed him to lecture nor contributed funds without Scoble or Thompson
sanctioning his mission.

Seeing that Thompson had influence over both the composition of the
narrative and the success of his English mission, Moses Grandy, as an un-
lettered former bondman, may have felt constrained when detailing his life
history to an unfamiliar white man on foreign soil.[10] Under such circumstances, the former slave had every reason to represent himself as wholly dignified and reputable, excluding any details that might mar his carefully managed self-portrait. Thompson as editor professes no desire to interfere with
Grandy's autobiographical agenda, assuring his reader, "I leave the touching story of the self-liberated captive to speak for itself." Thus, Thompson
states, he published Grandy's story "as nearly as possible in the language of
Moses himself." With Grandy and Thompson working together, the *Narrative of the Life of Moses Grandy; Late a Slave in the United States of America*
was completed and published hastily. Thompson dated the final touch—
his authenticating introduction to the text—as October 18, 1842; less than
a month later, London newspapers announced the book's release.

Despite Thompson's assertion that he let Grandy speak for himself in
their literary collaboration, the composition history of the *Narrative of the
Life of Moses Grandy* requires that readers treat this text with some care,
minding both what it says and what it does not say, or, perhaps, what it says

only by implication. On first reading, Grandy's autobiography seems, in Thompson's own words, an "artless tale." Composed of episodic vignettes, the narrative betrays little deliberate design. Nevertheless, the narrative's understatements, digressions, and sequencing and juxtapositions of episodes enable us to infer an argument in what appears to be merely "a touching story." More than trying simply to persuade readers of the need to abolish slavery, Grandy's narrative intends to show that African American men, like himself, can be capable contributors to free society, demonstrating the qualities of manhood that were most valued in the nineteenth century.

Notes from the London World's Anti-Slavery Convention in June 1843 reflect the attention Moses Grandy drew as an unusual attraction for whites: "Mr. Scoble presented to the Convention Moses Grandy, a black from North Carolina, who had purchased his freedom, 'three times over,' at 1,800 dollars. [He was a fine, tall, full-grown man, apparently about 45 years of age.] His appearance and narrative excited great interest."[11] As he toured the British Isles from 1842 to 1843 lecturing and fund-raising, audiences sympathized with his noble cause, but they were equally interested in him as a spectacle that perhaps contradicted their previous notions about black manhood. Immediately before Grandy stood before the London convention, delegates had agreed "there was no real distinctive difference in point of talent or ability between the black and white races of the human family."[12] Still, with a mixture of doubt and fascination about Grandy's self-determined accomplishment of buying himself out of slavery, conference attendees needed to evaluate this black man before pronouncing him as an acceptably "fine" man.

Antebellum whites—including antislavery advocates—more willingly accepted black males as human than acknowledged that they could be men, possessing all the self-sufficiency, worth, and power that the title "man" implied. To many in the antislavery movement in the 1830s, blackness and manliness still seemed contradictory terms. The same binary of rationality versus emotion that was usually ascribed to maleness and femaleness extended to racial difference, which allowed even some abolitionists to assume that white Americans possessed greater intellectual capacity and aptitude than people of color, who were granted as compensation a more intense excitability in matters of the emotions and religion. This kind of racialism suggested that black people, both male and female, were, for better and for worse, essentially feminine in character, as epitomized in Harriet Beecher

Stowe's eponymous character Uncle Tom.[13] Although abolitionists indicted slavery for refusing to let black men fulfill their traditional gender roles as husbands and fathers, antislavery advocates treated their African American cohorts on the lecture circuit as requiring the paternalistic guidance of whites. Observers seemed unable to accept self-determined black men without seeing them as exotic primitives or white men at heart unfortunately misplaced "under the slave's garb and this African skin."[14] In the eyes of whites, to be wholly black and wholly man, as Grandy claimed to be, posed a problem.

In his autobiography, as in his oral antislavery presentations, Moses Grandy seemed at pains to prove himself a "fine . . . full-grown man." Grandy's *Narrative* does not explicitly state that the former slave's attempts to gain freedom and equality were designed to assert his manhood. Still, the themes, tone, and emphases of the text suggest that Grandy, like many black leaders of his time, considered freedom and equality as human rights and, more specifically, as "manhood rights," which slavery and racial discrimination hindered.[15] As a slave, Moses Grandy inevitably experienced the frustration and fear of humiliation that, according to literary critic David Leverenz, prompt a marked concern with manhood.[16] He endured multiple calamities at the hands of his masters, including separation from family, physical abuse, and misuse of his hard-earned money. Each injustice reiterated Grandy's degraded status as the legal property of another man. In reaction, to the extent that he could, Grandy aimed to prove himself a man according to the same markers of middle-class manhood by which his masters claimed superiority over him: self-sufficiency, self-control, economic competition, and freedom.[17]

Perhaps anticipating white readers' uneasiness with the issue of black manhood and certainly with black violent resistance, Grandy proclaims his manhood by humbly suggesting his own worthiness compared to that of the characters surrounding him, especially southern slave masters. Evaluating the white male behavior that he does not want to emulate, the narrator describes his masters as a "hard-drinking man," a "severe man," a "great gambler," and a "very wicked young man," the last denoted as such not only because of his slaveholding practices but also because he curses a lady, exhibiting less than gentlemanly courtesy. In contrast, the narrator is too thrifty and pious to spend his money on morally corrupting activities like drinking and gambling. Details throughout the text vouch for the wise accumulation and expenditure of all Grandy's money. With industrialization and the expansion of the capitalist system in the mid-1800s, a man's value was increasingly determined by workplace competition for power and dominance,[18] and in the context of these social and economic changes, Grandy's diligent work ethic served as one of the strongest points for establishing his claim to responsible manhood.

Grandy's narrative challenges claims of superior white manhood by highlighting his masters' failure in the capitalist marketplace, an expected arena of manly achievement. The narrator clarifies how slaveholders' financial mismanagement—not the slaves' misbehavior—usually led to slaves being sold away. Describing the sale of his brother and of his wife, Grandy uses almost identical wording to explain the similar circumstances. Seeing his brother chained and bound for sale, Grandy inquired "what he had been doing, and was told that he had done nothing amiss, but that his master had failed, and he was sold towards paying the debts." Likewise, when Grandy's wife is sold, he asks the master about her offense: "he said she had done nothing, but that her master wanted money." Finally, in describing his own frequent sale despite his loyalty to masters, Grandy emphasizes the financially exploitative nature of slavery. When one of his masters defaults on a loan and Grandy is sold as compensation, Grandy's new owner explains, "[Trewitt] had failed, and was not worth a cent, and he, Mews, must have his money." Without the slaves, whose bodies and labor underwrote their enslavers' fortunes, the slaveholders' idea of their own manhood was severely jeopardized.

Grandy's upstanding character, which weathers all the economic reversals that slavery brings to him, implicitly repudiates the premise of white male superiority that justifies slaveholding. Grandy's economic savvy, perseverance, and honesty gain him the favor of white "gentlemen" of high social standing. Slaveholders on the other hand—whom the narrator mockingly differentiates by labeling them as "men," never "gentlemen"—feel uneasy with Grandy when his reputation exceeds their own. James Grandy, the first owner to cheat Grandy out of his $600 deposit, admits that he sold Grandy to defend his own ego and humble the black entrepreneur. "He said it was because people had jeered him, by saying that I had more sense than he had," Grandy recalls. James Grandy needed to play the role of wise master to ensure his own self-worth. Moses Grandy, by contrast, would rather be a self-man made, relying on his own talent to make a name for himself. Grandy's defenders "would not suffer [the master] to remain in the boarding house, but turned him out, there and then, with all his trunks and boxes." Disgusted by the slaveholder's weakness, the "gentlemen" endorse Grandy's worth, allowing the black man to emerge with a stronger character than his white master. Here, as elsewhere in the text, Grandy relies on understatement so that a potentially self-commending statement instead seems merely to report simple facts. Yet just as the people within the drama of the narrative recognize Grandy's merit, the narrator of the story intends that his readers will as well.

Grandy seems able to ingratiate himself with whites so that, even as they continually deny him freedom, they afford him some compensatory privileges beyond those permitted other blacks. Through his own ingenuity, Grandy finds opportunities to promote himself even when his masters seem intent on holding him back. Grandy recognized that by negotiating slavery's tenuous power dynamics, an African American could gain leverage on the powers and benefits of freedom. His skills in this regard emerged in his boyhood when, as a special playmate for James Grandy, born at almost the same time, young Moses avoided being sold and enjoyed prolonged time in his mother's care. As an adult, he used the coincidence of his birth as a bargaining point against his boyhood friend and "reminded him that we had been playfellows." Though Grandy's narrative repeatedly discredits slavery as a paternalistic institution, he knew how to manipulate the supposed affection between master and slave; twice he voiced his fellow slaves' complaints in order to get more food for himself and his fellow workers. He proves especially adept at carefully negotiating his restricted freedoms, which in turn become gains for him and his community.

Grandy often identifies himself with the concerns of the larger black community, noting many of his experiences as "the usual treatment" or "the usual manner." But throughout the narrative, there remains a tension between the role of Grandy as an average slave and his depiction as an exceptional black man. On the one hand, some of his successes are due in large part to special circumstances.[19] For instance, because he was allowed to hire his time as a slave, Grandy had the unusual opportunity to save for his own manumission profits from his work that exceeded what he owed his master each month. In this regard, Grandy stood apart from the rank and file of the slave community in his region, most of whom worked as field hands, rarely participating in a cash economy. Grandy also established alliances with helpful whites at each stage of his struggle for betterment. Yet it is not the purpose of Grandy's narrative to portray him as fortunate or special, since he is also intent on convincing his audience that he shared slavery's indignities with the majority of African Americans in the South. Grandy also wants to be sure that his audience sees that he is typical, not exemplary, of the potential for productivity and success inherent in his fellow slaves if they had his opportunities. Grandy's difficulty in balancing these two perspectives leads to a concise autobiographical narrative that celebrates an individual slave's remarkable accomplishments, interspersed with broadly based discussions of American slavery, especially in the last quarter of the text, when the narrator signals his intention: "Having thus narrated what has happened to myself, my relatives, and near friends, I will add a few matters about slaves and coloured persons in general."

Both when detailing his own history and when providing overviews of black experience, Grandy articulates his concern with manhood by illustrating that the selfhood and familial relationships of black men are not recognized or respected by slaveholders in the South and prejudiced whites in the North. The narrator regrets not only that slavery reduces rational, humane African Americans to "brutes," but also that the institution denies black males the right to practice their authority as protectors and leaders. More than once Grandy asserts that many enslaved men would rather live on another plantation away from their families than to bear the humiliation of helplessness as their children and wives are sold or misused. "If a man have a wife . . . he will not be in the same field if he can help it," the narrator explains, "for with his hardest labour, he often cannot save her from being flogged, and he is obliged to stand by and see it; he is always liable to see her taken home at night, stripped naked, and whipped before all the men." Hinting at sexual impropriety between masters and their female slaves, Grandy highlights the shame that black men feel in being unable to protect their loved ones.

Similarly, the narrator is sensitive to insults that free men of color incur in the northern states. Massachusetts emancipated its slaves in the 1780s;[20] but when Grandy first relocated there in the early 1830s, segregation laws perpetuated residual racism, which he interprets as an offense to both his human rights and manliness. In the South, where his kin were legal property of another man, the black husband and father could not protect his loved ones from physical injury. In Boston, Grandy could not ensure the dignity and comfort of his relatives. Voicing indignation on behalf of many northern black men, Grandy adds, "we had to be content with the decks of steamboats in all weathers . . . not even our wives or children being allowed to go below, however it might rain, or snow, or freeze; in various other ways, we were treated as though we were of a race of men below the whites." Even as a free man with money, Grandy still could not fully enact the role of family protector, a disappointment that likely motivated his participation in reform efforts in the North.

In Grandy's text, the themes of manhood and family unity correspond, allowing the narrator to argue that black manhood reinforces domesticity and traditional ideas of social order centering on the family. Given white New England's long-standing distrust of free blacks as disorderly and indifferent to white norms regarding the sacredness of the family,[21] Grandy's determination to ensure the stability of his family would have communicated an important message about black men's social priorities in the so-called free states.

Interestingly, in his concern for black men's rights to protect themselves and their families, the narrator of the *Narrative of the Life of Moses Grandy* seems very deliberately to avoid the association between asserting one's manhood and using physical violence. Nowhere in his narrative is Grandy a combative, physical threat to his masters in the South or his economic competitors in the North. The narrator signifies his disavowal of violence by highlighting how his own restrained, nonviolent responses often were more effective than physical resistance. When Grandy witnesses the brutal beating of his sister Tamar, who had previously run away from her master only to be recaptured, he does not portray himself as interceding on behalf of his sister in a headlong, aggressive way. Instead, he attempts to use his economic means and professional connections to try to negotiate with the white man on his own terms. When Grandy secures a benevolent master to purchase Tamar and her children, rescuing them from bodily harm, the narrator explains that the new master, Mr. Johnson, buys the family "out of friendship for me"; though Grandy had to bear the indignity of seeing his sister abused, his respectable reputation among white gentlemen enabled him later to improve his sister's situation.

While other black abolitionists, impatient with the slow effect of moral suasion, began to endorse active resistance by the 1840s, Grandy seems to maintain that nonviolence and character development are the surest way to achieve freedom and progress. As a narrator, Grandy is less forceful than fugitive slave author Frederick Douglass would be in his self-written 1845 *Narrative of the Life of Frederick Douglass, an American Slave*. Douglass describes himself in slavery as "a man transformed into a brute," but he concludes that his physical resistance against a slave-breaker, the pivotal event in his quest for freedom, "revived within [him] a sense of [his] own manhood."[22] Where Douglass is direct, Grandy suggests; where Douglass strikes out physically, Grandy strikes with the force of character. However, both narrators highlight the same conclusion: freedom and manhood necessarily correspond.

The *Narrative of the Life of Moses Grandy* enjoyed a favorable reception from the British public, due to the narrator's insights into American slavery as well as to his personal self-portrait. Though abolitionists generally blended examples with their moral exhortations, as a former bondman, Grandy provided a more urgent and convincing depiction of the southern institution, inviting both curious and sympathetic readers to learn more about the injustices of slavery. Marketed at antislavery meetings with the aid of John Scoble, Grandy's narrative fulfilled a prediction made earlier by one of his American supporters: "[Grandy's] history is not only authentic, but most extraordinary, and full of thrilling interest. Could it be published, it would make a deep sensation in every quarter." Not only did the autobiography sell well throughout the British Isles, but demand for such first-person slave accounts also prompted three American printings of the *Narrative of the Life of Moses Grandy* in 1844 after Grandy's return to Boston.

Antebellum audiences were attracted to Grandy's autobiography by a quality that modern readers may find least engaging about the text: its straightforward, disengaged reportage of slavery. White audiences especially expected this plain, unassuming style from African American lecturers and authors who needed first to prove their character before presenting the content of their experience. In his 1849 review in the *Christian Examiner*, Ephraim Peabody prescribed conventions for the developing genre of slave narratives, suggesting, "When men are profoundly in earnest, they are not apt to be extravagant. The more earnest, the more rigidly true."[23] The *Anti-Slavery Reporter*, in its November 16, 1842, review of Grandy's narrative, commended the autobiography for showing such earnestness and lack of extravagance: "The glimpses which it affords of slavery in the United States are most affecting, as well as instructive. At the same time the entire narrative has been thrown into language of beautiful simplicity and purity, so that it can minister no offence to the nicest taste."[24]

As a novice educated only "in the horrible school of slavery," Grandy dared not take too much liberty in enlightening his readers. Careful not to offend or seem indignant, the narrator subsumes hints of any personal philosophizing or self-interest beneath his persona of trustworthy informant offering unembellished views of slavery.

Yet the tone of Grandy's narrative seems to exceed the measure of objectivity needed to verify his honesty. The narrator seems almost cold as he graphically details injustices toward both enslaved and free people of color, including his own relatives. With simplicity and detachment, he recounts, "One very cold day [Mr. Tyler, a master] sent my brother out, naked and hungry, to find a yoke of steers: the boy returned without finding them, when the master flogged him, and sent him out again . . . but it seems again without success. He piled up a heap of leaves, and laid himself down in them, and died there. He was found through a flock of turkey buzzards hóvering over him; these birds had pulled his eyes out." When recalling a painful incident decades after it occurred, Grandy maintains the emotional numbness that allowed him to cope with cruel circumstances while in slavery. Offering no personal response to the incident, the narrator immediately shifts to the next topic, detailing another snapshot of typical life in slavery.

The *Narrative of the Life of Moses Grandy* presents him in a reserved manner not only to show his reliability as narrator, but also to maintain an appropriate manly disposition. As a seaman used to constant exposure to danger and separation from loved ones, and especially because of his former experiences with the harshness of slavery, the narrator eschews any sorrow or tenderness that might reinforce stereotypes of black people's feminine emotionalism. He occasionally expresses intense emotion, as when climaxing the narrative with memories of his final self-purchase. "[M]y feelings were greatly excited," Grandy recalls. "I felt to myself so light, that I almost thought I could fly, and in my sleep I was always dreaming of flying over woods and rivers." Yet the narrator immediately rationalizes his sentimentality as being a logical, appropriate response to gaining one's manhood rights. "Slavery will teach any man to be glad when he gets freedom," Grandy soberly adds, turning his touching nostalgia into a more objective observation.

The narrator also refrains from showing any signs of anger or bitterness about his former experiences. Taking cues from middle-class ideals of masculine self-restraint, he demonstrates his ability to rise above the pettiness of resentment. When recalling his fellow slaves' response to a white thief's flogging, Grandy admits, "pleased enough were the coloured people to see a white back for the first time subject to the lash." Yet, by not using the first person plural "we," the narrator distinguishes himself from "the coloured people" who demonstrate vindictiveness, a trait unbefitting the role of the dignified Christian man that Grandy consciously maintains. Rather than harboring animosity that might threaten whites, Grandy as bondman and free man is more interested in cooperating with whites as he aspires to self-sufficiency. Preoccupied with his future rather than his past, he portrays himself as a self-controlled man, willing and able to make a peaceful transition into mainstream American society.

Only when looking beyond the narrator's need for propriety and male stoicism can readers get brief glimpses of Moses Grandy as a feeling person—one whose conflicting dignity and pain could overwhelm him if his emotion were not kept in check. Ashamed of his inability, as a male adult, to help defend his sibling, Grandy avoided facing his mother with the news that his brother had been sold. "I feared to tell her what had happened to my brother," he explains. "I got a boy to go and tell her." Sending the boy in his stead, the narrator admits his frustration with slavery's attempt to humble black men to a childlike status. At other points, Grandy records behavior that intimates his fear. He preferred risking self-mutilation than work as an overseer for a certain master. Later, suspecting himself in danger of being reenslaved, he contemplated throwing himself overboard from a ship. Still the restrained tone of the narrative continually overshadows these moments of personal reflection.

As Grandy negotiates the expectations of his readers and his own investments, the *Narrative of the Life of Moses Grandy* becomes as fascinating in its implicit messages as in its overt story line. Occupying a precarious position as narrator, Grandy challenges antebellum stereotypes by presenting African Americans as more logical than emotional, more manly than childlike. At the same time, he must exhibit some emotional responsiveness to show African Americans as feeling human beings instead of mere bodies. After all, the very impetus of his lecturing and publishing endeavors —raising money to redeem his relatives and restore the family—rested on the premise that antebellum African Americans were humans with feelings and needs that could only be fully gratified in liberty. Without romanticizing Grandy's narrative as an "artless tale" as did many of its well-intentioned nineteenth-century readers, contemporary readers can appreciate his autobiography as a straightforward account of Grandy's individual experience and of America's national dilemma. As the *Narrative of the Life of Moses Grandy* suggests, that dilemma was not only whether or not to end slavery, but also how to respond to African American males as brothers in the human family and as equal men.

Note on the Text
During his fund-raising mission to the British Isles, Moses Grandy sought the assistance of British abolitionist George Thompson when composing

his autobiography in the fall of 1842. Grandy, illiterate since slavery, dictated his life history to Thompson; and though Thompson exerted influence over the text as its transcriber and editor, he insisted that Grandy maintained authorial control. Thompson limited his commentary to a single footnote and sparse parenthetical clarifications, claiming in his introduction to the narrative that "I have carefully abstained from casting in a single reflection or animadversion of my own." Comparison of Thompson's own letters and lectures with the style of Grandy's autobiography substantiates the editor's disclaimer.[25] Thus, while Grandy did not manually draft the narrative, its content and structure can be attributed to him.

The text of the *Narrative of the Life of Moses Grandy* reprinted here is that of the first edition, published in London in 1843. The original punctuation and British spellings have been preserved. As Thompson explains in his editorial note, the text includes some nonstandard spellings, especially of proper names, since he aimed to present the narrative exactly as Grandy had spoken it. Dialect variations between Grandy, a former American southerner, and his British amanuensis likely caused some discrepancies, as Thompson relied on phonetic spelling. For example, based on the narrator's pronunciation, Thompson reported that Grandy sailed on a ship called the *James Murray*. Referencing the Boston Ship Register of 1833, historian David Cecelski has verified the vessel's name as the *James Maury*. Likewise, Grandy's former master "Mr. Mews" was most likely William T. Muse, a traceable Pasquotank County, North Carolina, slaveholder.[26] In another case, the amanuensis recorded Grandy's term "mare" and afterward inserted the standard spelling "mayor" in parentheses. Yet, with both its unintentional and deliberate misspellings, Thompson's transcription seems to intend authenticity rather than derision of Grandy's language.

After its initial publication in London, Grandy's narrative appeared in three American reprintings in 1844. These editions, published by Boston abolitionist Oliver Johnson, differ in a few respects from the British precedent. Most notably, the Boston editions target an American audience and, accordingly, exclude the special recognition and forwarding address of John Scoble, Grandy's British liaison. As noted above, Scoble, secretary of the British and Foreign Anti-Slavery Society, served as Grandy's sponsor, arranging speaking engagements and managing financial accounts during the North Carolinian's travels abroad. Meanwhile, proceeds from the American printing of the narrative would most likely have been handled in Grandy's home city, Boston. Thus the American editions omit the instructions directing possible donors to Scoble.

Instead, in concluding the Boston editions of the narrative, Grandy supplies an account ledger of his accumulated spending for buying himself and his relatives out of slavery. Dated January 19, 1844, this receipt legitimizes Grandy's use of solicited revenue and his requests for additional funding to purchase his sibling, Mary. This receipt is reprinted as an appendix to the current edition.

The three American versions of the narrative were all printed consecutively in 1844. The *Liberator*, headquartered in Boston, announced the release of the "First American from the last London" edition on the front page of its February 23, 1844, issue. Shortly afterward, Oliver Johnson released two second editions of the *Narrative of the Life of Moses Grandy* — one subtitled "late a slave in the United States" and the other subtitled "formerly a slave in the United States."

The latter two American versions introduced punctuation changes that affected the style of Grandy's narrative. The second editions often substitute semicolons where colons existed in the British and first American issues. This change may be slight, suggesting only a translation from British syntax to a more American style; after all, the Boston editor also substitutes dollar equivalents for British pounds. The punctuation change, then, may only reflect editor Johnson's attempt to standardize the text or make it more sophisticated.

Nevertheless, the repeated use of colons to conjoin two complete sentences, as in the London and first American editions, more probably replicates the conversational style of oral narration and implies a dialogic collaboration between Grandy and Thompson. As Grandy narrated his story, recounting details that would have been so familiar to him, perhaps Thompson prompted the former slave to provide further specificity. In this case, the colon highlights the dramatic build of details in Grandy's narrative. An excerpt illustrates how narrative development is accentuated by punctuation, leading from cause to effect: "My mother, frantic with grief, resisted their taking her child away: she was beaten and held down: she fainted; and when she came to herself, her boy was gone." Thompson's dependence on colons is noteworthy because he seems to adopt the style especially for drafting Grandy's narrative; neither his introduction to the narrative nor his personal correspondence employs such a deliberate punctuation style.

Because this stylistic feature highlights the orality of Grandy's narrative and because the first edition more closely represents the initial collaboration between Grandy and Thompson, the 1843 London edition has been selected for reprinting here in preference to any of the three similar American editions.

Notes

1. William Lloyd Garrison, ed., "Mr. Thompson in England," in *Lectures of George Thompson* (Boston: I. Knapp, 1836), v.

2. Mia Bay, *The White Image in the Black Mind: African American Ideas about White People, 1830–1925* (New York: Oxford University Press, 2000), 40; George M. Fredrickson, *The Black Image in the White Mind: The Debate on Afro-American Character and Destiny, 1817–1914* (New York: Harper and Row, 1971), 114. Bay and Fredrickson note that antebellum ideas of white men's racial and gender superiority precluded both black men and white women from obtaining American citizenship. Uniting against white males as their common foe, black men and white women often collaborated in abolitionist and feminist movements.

3. James de T. Abajian, comp., *Blacks in Selected Newspapers, Censuses, and Other Sources: An Index to Names and Subjects* (Boston: G. K. Hall, 1977), 2:64.

4. W. Jeffrey Bolster, "'To Feel like a Man': Black Seamen in the Northern States, 1800–1860," in *A Question of Manhood: A Reader in U.S. Black Men's History and Masculinity*, ed. Darlene Clark Hine and Earnestine Jenkins (Bloomington: Indiana University Press, 1999), 361.

5. William Gienapp, "Abolitionism and the Nature of Antebellum Reform," in *Courage and Conscience: Black and White Abolitionists in Boston*, ed. Donald M. Jacobs (Bloomington: Indiana University Press, 1993), 34.

6. See elsewhere in this volume the discussion of Roper and his *Narrative of the Adventures and Escape of Moses Roper from American Slavery*.

7. C. Peter Ripley, ed., *The Black Abolitionist Papers* (Chapel Hill: University of North Carolina Press, 1985–92), 1:6.

8. George Thompson to William Lloyd Garrison, November 27, 1835, in *Letters and Addresses by George Thompson, during his mission in the United States, from Oct. 1st, 1834, to Nov. 27, 1835* (Boston: I. Knapp, 1837), 119–20.

9. Ripley, *The Black Abolitionist Papers*, 3:8.

10. William L. Andrews, *To Tell a Free Story: The First Century of Afro-American Autobiography, 1760–1865* (Urbana: University of Illinois Press, 1988), 21. Andrews makes this assertion specifically about Grandy and Thompson's interaction, although scholars have assumed similar power dynamics existed between other slave narrators, literate or not, and their white sponsors and editors.

11. "Proceedings from General Anti-Slavery Convention," in *The British and Foreign Anti-Slavery Reporter* (London: Kraus Reprint, 1969), 4:108.

12. Ibid.

13. Fredrickson, *The Black Image*, 118.

14. Ephraim Peabody, "Narratives of Fugitive Slaves," in *The Slave's Narrative*, ed. Charles T. Davis and Henry Louis Gates Jr. (New York: Oxford University Press, 1985), 25.

15. James O. Horton and Lois E. Horton, "The Affirmation of Manhood: Black Garrisonians in Antebellum Boston," in *Courage and Conscience*, ed. Jacobs, 134.

16. David Leverenz, *Manhood and the American Renaissance* (Ithaca, N.Y.: Cornell University Press, 1989), 73.

17. Paul Gilmore, *The Genuine Article: Race, Mass Culture, and American Literary Manhood* (Durham, N.C.: Duke University Press, 2001), 42, 59.

18. Leverenz, *Manhood and the American Renaissance*, 72.

19. John W. Blassingame notes that most slave narrators of published autobiographies were "among the most perceptive and gifted of the former slaves" and therefore perhaps not wholly representative of the average slave experience. See Blassingame, "Using the Testimony of Ex-Slaves: Approaches and Problems," in *The Slave's Narrative*, ed. Davis and Gates, 83.

20. Richard S. Newman, *The Transformation of American Abolitionism: Fighting Slavery in the Early Republic* (Chapel Hill: University of North Carolina Press, 2002), 35. While 1783 often is identified as the legal end of Massachusetts slavery, historians now question whether the decision in slave Quok Walker's successful 1783 freedom suit more broadly established the unconstitutionality of slavery in Massachusetts. Newman generalizes that Massachusetts ended slavery "in the early 1780s." For scholarly arguments about this discrepancy, see Arthur Zilversmit, "Quok Walker, Mumbet, and the Abolition of Slavery in Massachusetts," *William and Mary Quarterly* 75, no. 4 (October 1968): 614–24.

21. Joanne Pope Melish, *Disowning Slavery: Gradual Emancipation and "Race" in New England, 1780–1860* (Ithaca, N.Y.: Cornell University Press, 1998), 119–41, discusses how African Americans' behavior—and their very presence as free people among whites—signaled "disorder" or disruption to intolerant white northern communities. By asserting black men's ability to "conduct ourselves with propriety," the narrator of Grandy's *Narrative* attempts to overcome social stigmas associated with black free men.

22. Frederick Douglass, *Narrative of the Life of Frederick Douglass, an American Slave, Written by Himself* (Boston: Published at the Anti-Slavery Office, 1845), 63, 72.

23. Peabody, "Narratives of Fugitive Slaves," 25. Peabody's review of several 1840s slave narratives omits Grandy's autobiography, seemingly in favor of more popular narratives including *The Life of Josiah Henson, Formerly a Slave, Now an Inhabitant of Canada, as Narrated by Himself* (Boston: Phelps, 1849) and Douglass's 1845 *Narrative*.

Still, the qualities Peabody applauds in these texts, such as Henson's humility as narrator, similarly characterize Grandy's autobiography, which chronologically precedes both Henson's and Douglass's.

24. "Literary Notice: Narrative of the Life of Moses Grandy, Late a Slave in the United States of America," in *The British and Foreign Anti-Slavery Reporter*, 3:186.

25. See *Letters and Addresses by George Thompson*.

26. David S. Cecelski, *The Waterman's Song: Slavery and Freedom in Maritime North Carolina* (Chapel Hill: University of North Carolina Press, 2001), 240, 47.

NARRATIVE

OF THE

LIFE OF

MOSES GRANDY;

LATE A SLAVE

IN THE

UNITED STATES OF AMERICA.

" Slavery is a mass, a system of enormities, which incontrovertably bids
defiance to every regulation which ingenuity can devise, or power effect,
but a Total Extinction. Why ought slavery be abolished? Because it is
incurable injustice. Why is injustice to remain for a single hour ?"

William Pitt.

PUBLISHED AND SOLD FOR THE BENEFIT OF HIS RELATIONS
STILL IN SLAVERY.

LONDON:

C. GILPIN, 5, BISHOPSGATE-STREET.

1843.

It is not improbable that some of the proper names in the following pages are incorrectly spelled. M. G., owing to the laws of the slave states, being perfectly illiterate, his pronunciation is the only guide.

DUBLIN:

PRINTED BY WEBB AND CHAPMAN, GREAT BRUNSWICK-ST.

INTRODUCTION.

ABOUT a fortnight ago, the subject of the following brief Memoir came to me, bearing with him a letter from a dear friend and distinguished abolitionist in the United States, from which the following, is an extract: — "I seize my pen in haste to gratify a most worthy coloured friend of mine, by giving him a letter of introduction to you, as he intends sailing this week (August 8th, 1842,) for Liverpool and London, *via* New Orleans. His name is Moses Grandy. He knows what it is to have been a slave, and what are the tender mercies of the southern slave-drivers. His history is not only authentic, but most extraordinary, and full of thrilling interest. Could it be published, it would make a deep sensation in every quarter. He was compelled to buy his freedom *three times over*! He paid for it 1850 dollars (nearly £400 sterling). He has since bought his wife, and one or two of his children; and before going to England will first go to New Orleans, to purchase some of his other children if he can find them, who are still held in captivity. His benevolence, affection, kindness of heart, and elasticity of spirit are truly remarkable. He has a good head, a fine countenance, and a great spirit, notwithstanding his education has been obtained in the horrible school of slavery. Just get him to tell you his narrative, and if you happen to have an Anti-slavery Meeting, let him tell his tale to a British audience." In the letter of another highly esteemed friend, he is spoken of as "unsurpassed for faithfulness and perseverance." In the letter of a third, as "a worthy and respectable man." On examining a book containing a list of the donations made him by American friends, in aid of his noble design to rescue from the miseries of slavery his relations, I found the names and certificates of persons of the highest respectability. It will be amply sufficient with those who are acquainted with the abolitionists of the United States, for me to name General Fessenden,[1] and Nathan Winslow, Esq., of Portland, Maine; the Rev. A. A. Phelps, Ellis Gray Loring,[2] and Samuel E. Sewall, Esqs., of Boston, Massachusetts. Being satisfied, by these indubitable vouchers, of Moses Grandy's title to credit, I listened to his artless tale with entire confidence, and with a feeling of interest which all will participate, who peruse the following pages. Considering his Narrative calculated to promote a more extensive knowledge of the workings of American slavery, and that its sale might contribute to the object which engages so entirely the mind of Moses, namely, the redemption of those who are in bonds, belonging to his family, I resolved to commit it to the press, as nearly as possible in the language of Moses himself. I have carefully abstained from casting in a single reflection or animadversion of my own. I leave the touching story of the self-liberated captive to speak for itself; and the wish of my heart will be gratified, and my humble effort on his behalf be richly rewarded, if this little book be the means of obtaining for my coloured brother the assistance which he seeks, or of increasing the zeal of those who are associated for the purpose of "breaking every yoke, and setting the oppressed free."[3] GEORGE THOMPSON.[4]

9, Blandford-place, Regent's park,
October 18th, 1842.

LIFE OF MOSES GRANDY.

MY name is Moses Grandy: I was born in Camden County, North Carolina.[5] I believe I am fifty-six years old. Slaves seldom know exactly how old they are: neither they nor their masters set down the time of a birth; the slaves, because they are not allowed to write or read; and the masters, because they only care to know what slaves belong to them.

The master, Billy Grandy, whose slave I was born, was a hard-drinking man: he sold away many slaves. I remember four sisters and four brothers; my mother had more children, but they were dead or sold away before I can remember. I was the youngest. I remember well my mother often hid us all in the woods, to prevent master selling us. When we wanted water, she sought for it in any hole or puddle formed by falling trees or otherwise: it was often full of tadpoles and insects: she strained it, and gave it round to each of us in the hollow of her hand. For food, she gathered berries in the woods, got potatoes, raw corn, &c. After a time the master would send word to her to come in, promising he would not sell us. But at length persons came who agreed to give the prices he set on us. His wife, with much to be done, prevailed on him not to sell me; but he sold my brother, who was a little boy. My mother, frantic with grief, resisted their taking her child away: she was beaten and held down: she fainted; and when she came to herself, her boy was gone. She made much outcry, for which the master tied her up to a peach tree in the yard, and flogged her.

Another of my brothers was sold to Mr. Tyler, Dewan's Neck, Pasquotank County:[6] this man very much ill-treated many coloured boys. One very cold day he sent my brother out, naked and hungry, to find a yoke of steers: the boy returned without finding them, when his master flogged him, and sent him out again; a white lady who lived near, gave him food, and advised him to try again: he did so, but it seems again without success. He piled up a heap of leaves, and laid himself down in them, and died there. He was found through a flock of turkey buzzards hóvering over him; these birds had pulled his eyes out.[7]

My young master and I used to play together; there was but two days' difference in our ages. My old master always said he would give me to him. When he died, all the coloured people were divided amongst his children, and I fell to young master; his name was James Grandy. I was then about eight years old. When I became old enough to be taken away from my mother and put to field-work, I was hired out for the year, by auction, at the Court House, every January; this is the common practice with respect to slaves belonging to persons who are under age.[8] This continued till my master and myself were twenty-one years old.

The first who hired me was Mr. Kemp, who used me pretty well; he gave me plenty to eat and sufficient clothing.

The next was old Jemmy Coates, a severe man. Because I could not learn his way of hilling corn,[9] he flogged me naked with a severe whip made of a very tough sapling; this lapped round me at each stroke, the point of it at last entered my belly and broke off, leaving an inch and a-half outside. I was not aware of it until on going to work again it hurt my side very much, when on looking down I saw it sticking out of my body: I pulled it out and the blood spouted after it. The wound festered, and discharged very much at the time, and hurt me for years after.

In being hired out, sometimes the slave gets a good home, and sometimes a bad one: when he gets a good one, he dreads to see January come; when he has a bad one, the year seems five times as long as it is.

I was next with Mr. Enoch Sawyer of Camden County: my business was to keep ferry, and do other odd work. It was cruel living; we had not near enough of either victuals or clothes; I was half-starved for half my time. I have often ground the husks of Indian corn over again in a hand-mill, for the chance of getting something to eat out of it, which the former grinding had left. In severe frosts, I was compelled to go into the fields and woods to work, with my naked feet cracked and bleeding from extreme cold: to warm them, I used to rouse an ox or hog, and stand on the place where it had lain. I was at that place three years, and very long years they seemed to me. The trick by which he kept me so long was this:—the Court House was but a mile off; on hiring day, he prevented me from going till he went himself and bid for me. On the last occasion, he was detained for a little while by other business, so I ran as quickly as I could, and got hired before he came up.

Mr. George Furley was my next master; he employed me as a car-boy in the Dismal Swamp;[10] I had to drive lumber, &c. I had plenty to eat and plenty of clothes. I was so overjoyed at the change, that I then thought I would not have left the place to go to heaven.

Next year I was hired by Mr. John Micheau of the same county, who married my young mistress, one of the daughters of Mr. Grandy, and sister to my present owner. This master gave us very few clothes, and but little to eat; I was almost naked. One day he came into the field, and asked why no more work was done. The older people were afraid of him; so I said that the reason was, we were so hungry, we could not work. He went home and told the mistress to give us plenty to eat, and at dinner time we had plenty. We came out shouting for joy, and went to work with delight. From that time, we had food enough, and he soon found that he had a great deal more work done. The field was quite alive with the people striving who should do most.

He hired me for another year. He was a great gambler; he kept me up five nights together, without sleep night or day, to wait on the gambling table. I was standing in the corner of the room, nodding for want of sleep, when he took up the shovel, and beat me with it: he dislocated my shoulder, and sprained my wrist, and broke the shovel over me. I ran away, and got another person to hire me.

This person was Mr. Richard Furley, who after that hired me at the Court House every year, till my master came of age. He gave me a pass to work for myself,[11] so I obtained work by the piece where I could, and paid him out of my earnings what we had agreed on; I maintained myself on the rest, and saved what I could. In this way I was not liable to be flogged and ill-used. He paid seventy, eighty, or ninety dollars a year for me, and I paid him twenty or thirty dollars a year more than that.

When my master came of age, he took all his coloured people to himself. Seeing that I was industrious and persevering, and had obtained plenty of work, he made me pay him almost twice as much as I had paid Mr. Furley. At that time, the English blockaded the Chesapeake,[12] which made it necessary to send merchandize from Norfolk to Elizabeth City[13] by the Grand Canal, so that it might get to sea by Pamlico Sound and Ocracock Inlet. I took some canal boats on shares; Mr. Grice, who married my other young mistress, was the owner of them. I gave him one-half of all I received for freight: out of the other half, I had to victual and man the boats, and all over that expense was my own profit.

Some time before this, my brother Benjamin returned from the West Indies, where he had been two years with his master's vessel. I was very glad to hear of it, and got leave to go see him. While I was sitting with his wife and him, his wife's master came and asked him to fetch a can of water: he did so, and carried it into the store. While I was waiting for him and wondering at his being so long away, I heard the heavy blows of a hammer: after a little while I was alarmed, and went to see what was going on. I looked into the store, and saw my brother lying on his back on the floor, and Mr. Williams, who had bought him, driving staples over his wrists and ankles; an iron bar was afterwards put across his breast, which was also held down by staples.

I asked what he had been doing, and was told that he had done nothing amiss, but that his master had failed, and he was sold towards paying the debts. He lay in that state all that night; next day he was taken to jail, and I never saw him again. This is the usual treatment under such circumstances. I had to go by my mother's next morning, but I feared to tell her what had happened to my brother: I got a boy to go and tell her. She was blind and very old, and was living in a little hut, in the woods, after the usual manner of old worn-out slaves:[14] she was unable to go to my brother before he was taken away, and grieved after him greatly.

It was some time after this, that I married a slave belonging to Mr. Enoch Sawyer, who had been so hard a master to me. I left her at home, (that is, at his house,) one Thursday morning, when we had been married about eight months. She was well, and seemed likely to be so: we were nicely getting together our little necessaries. On the Friday, as I was at work as usual with the boats, I heard a noise behind me, on the road which ran by the side of the canal: I turned to look, and saw a gang of slaves coming. When they came up to me, one of them cried out, "Moses, my dear!" I wondered who among them should know me, and found it was my wife. She cried out to me, "I am gone." I was struck with consternation. Mr. Rogerson was with them, on his horse, armed with pistols. I said to him, "for God's sake, have you bought my wife?" He said he had; when I asked him what she had done; he said she had done nothing, but that her master wanted money. He drew out a pistol, and said that if I went near the waggon on which she was, he would shoot me. I asked for leave to shake hands with her, which he refused, but said I might stand at a distance and talk with her. My heart was so full, that I could say very little. I asked leave to give her a dram:[15] he told Mr. Burgess, the man who was with him, to get down and carry it to her. I gave her the little money I had in my pocket, and bid her farewell. I have never seen or heard of her from that day to this. I loved her as I loved my life.

Mr. Grice found that I served him faithfully. He and my young mistress, his wife, advised me as I was getting money fast, to try to buy myself. By their advice, I asked my master what he would take for me. He wanted 800 dollars, and when I said that was too much, he replied, he could get 1000 for me any minute. Mr. Grice afterwards went with me to him: he said to him, that I had already been more profitable to him than any five others of his negroes, and reminded him that we had been playfellows; in this way he got him to consent to take 600 dollars for me. I then went heartily to work, and whenever I paid him for my time, I paid him something also towards my freedom, for which he gave me receipts. When I made him the last payment of the 600 dollars for my freedom, he tore up all the receipts: I told him he ought not to have done so; he replied it did not signify, for as soon as court-day came, he should give me my free papers.[16] On Monday, in court week, I went to him; he was playing at billiards, and would not go with me, but told me to come again the next day: the next day he did the same, and so on daily. I went to his sister, Mrs. Grice, and told her I feared that he did not mean to give them to me; she said she feared so too, and sent for him. He was a very wicked young man; he came, and cursed her, and went out of the house. Mr. Grice was from home; on his return, he went to my master and told him he ought to give me my free papers; that I had paid for myself, and it was court week, so that there was no excuse. He promised he would, instead of which he rode away, and kept away till court was over. Before the next court came, he sold me to Mr. Trewitt for 600 dollars.

The way in which Mr. Trewitt came to buy me, was this. I had left the boats, and had gone with a schooner collecting lumber in Albemarle Sound for the merchants. Coming to Elizabeth City, I found a new store had been opened by Mr. Grice, which Mr. Sutton was keeping: the latter gentleman was glad to see me, and was desirous that I should return to my old employment with the canal boats, as lumber was in great demand at Norfolk. I did so, and sold some cargoes to Mr. Moses Myers of Norfolk. As I was waiting at the door of his store for settlement, he came up with Mr. Trewitt, whom I did not then know. Mr. Myers said to Mr. Trewitt, "here is a captain doing business for you." Mr. Trewitt then asked me who had chartered the boats, and to whom I belonged. I told him Mr. Sutton had chartered me, and that I had belonged to Mr. James Grandy, but had bought myself. He said he would buy me; on which Mr. Myers told him he could not, as I had already bought myself, and further said, I was one of their old war captains, and had never lost a single thing of the property entrusted to me. Mr. Trewitt said, he would buy me, and would see about it as soon as he got to Elizabeth City. I thought no more about it. On my return voyage, I delivered a cargo at Elizabeth City for Mr. Trewitt. I had been at Mr. Grice's, the owner of the boats, and on my going away from him to meet Mr. Trewitt for settlement, he said he would go with me, as he wanted money. Opposite the Custom House[17] we met Mr. Trewitt, who said, "Well, captain, I have bought you." Mr. Grice said, "Let us have no nonsense; go and settle with him." Angry words passed between them, one saying he had bought me, and the other denying that he had, or could, as I had bought myself already. We all went to Mr. Grice's dwelling house; there Mr. Trewitt settled with me about the freight, and then, jumping up, said, "Now I will show you,

Mr. Grice, whether I am a liar or not." He fetched the bill of sale; on reading it, Mr. Grice's colour changed, and he sent for Mrs. Grice. When she read it, she began to cry; seeing that, I began to cry too. She sent me to her brother, who was at Mr. Wood's boarding house. He was playing at billiards. I said to him, "Master James, have you sold me?" He said "No." I said, he had; when he turned round and went into another room, crying; I followed him. All the gentlemen followed us, saying, "Captain Grandy, what is the matter?" I told them Master James had sold me again. They asked him why he had done it: he said it was because people had jeered him, by saying I had more sense than he had. They would not suffer him to remain in the boarding house, but turned him out, there and then, with all his trunks and boxes. Mrs. Grice, his sister, sued him in my name for my liberty, but he gained the cause: the court maintained that I, and all I could do, belonged to him, and that he had a right to do as he pleased with me and all my earnings, as his own property, until he had taken me to the Court House, and given me my free papers, and until, besides that, I had been a year and a day in the Northern States to gain my residence.

So I was forced to go to Mr. Trewitt. He agreed that, if I would pay him the same wages as I paid my late master, and the 600 dollars he gave for me, he would give me my free papers. He bought two canal boats; and taking me out of Mr. Grice's employment, set me to work them on the same terms as I did for my former master. I was two years and a half in earning the 600 dollars to pay for myself the second time. Just when I had completed the payment, he failed. On Christmas eve he gave me a letter to take to Mr. Mews, at Newbegun Creek. I was rather unwilling to take it, wishing to go to my wife;[18] I told him, too, I was going to his office to settle with him. He offered to give me two dollars to take the letter, and said he would settle when I came back: then Mr. Shaw came from another room, and said his vessel was ready loaded, but he had nobody he could trust with his goods; he offered me five dollars to take the vessel down, and deliver the goods to Mr. Knox, who also was at Newbegun Creek. The wind was fair, and the hands on board, so I agreed: it being Christmas eve, I was glad of something to carry to my wife. I ran the vessel down to the mouth of the Creek, and anchored: when the moon rose, I went up the river. I reached the wharf, and commenced taking out the goods that night, and delivered them all safely to Mr. Knox next morning. I then took the letter to Mr. Mews, who read it, and looking up at me said, "Well, you belong to me." I thought he was joking, and said, "How? What way?" He said, "Don't you recollect when Trewitt chartered Wilson Sawyer's brig[19] to the West Indies?" I said, I did. He told me Trewitt then came to him to borrow 600 dollars, which he would not lend except he had a mortgage on me: Trewitt was to take it up at a certain time, but never did. I asked him, whether he really took the mortgage on me? He replied that "he certainly thought Trewitt would have taken up the mortgage, but he had failed, and was not worth a cent, and he, Mews, must have his money." I asked him whether he had not helped me and my young mistress in the Court House, when Master James fooled me before? He said he did help me all he could, and that he should not have taken a mortgage on me, but that he thought Trewitt would take it up. Trewitt must have received some of the last payments from me, after he had given the mortgage, and knew he should fail; for the mortgage was given two months before this time.

My head seemed to turn round and round; I was quite out of my senses; I went away towards the woods; Mr. Mews sent his waiter after me, to persuade me to go back: at first I refused, but afterwards went. He told me he would give me another chance to buy myself, and I certainly should have my freedom this time. He said Mr. Enoch Sawyer wanted to buy me to be his overseer in the Swamp. I replied, I would never try again to buy myself, and that they had already got 1200 dollars from me. My wife,* (this was my second wife) belonged to Mr. Sawyer: he told me that her master would not allow me to go to see her, if I would not consent to what he now preposed: for any coloured person going on the grounds of a white man after being warned off, is liable to be flogged or even shot. I thus found myself forced to go, although no coloured man wishes to live at the house where his wife lives, for he has to endure the continual misery of seeing her flogged and abused, without daring to say a word in her defence.

In the service of Mr. Sawyer, I got into a fair way of buying myself again; for I undertook the lightering[20] of the shingles or boards out of the Dismal Swamp, and hired hands to assist me. But my master had become security

---

*It will be observed that the narrator married a second wife, without having heard of the decease of the first. To explain this fact, it is necessary to state, that the frequent occurrence of cases where husbands and wives, members of Christian societies, were finally separated by sale, led the ministers, some years ago, to deliberate on the subject: they decided that such a separation might be considered as the death of the parties to each other, and they therefore agreed to consider subsequent marriages not immoral. The practice is general. It is scarcely necessary to remark that a more unequivocal and impressive proof of the heinous nature of the system could hardly exist. It breaks up the fondest connexions, it tears up the holiest attachments, and induces the ministers of religion, as much as in them lies, to garble the divine law to suit its own infernal exigencies.

for his two sons-in-law at Norfolk, who failed; in consequence of which, he sold eighteen coloured people, his share of the Swamp, and two plantations. I was one of the slaves he kept, and after that had to work in the corn-field the same as the rest. The overseer was a bad one, his name was Brooks. The horn was blown at sunrise; the coloured people had then to march before the overseer to the field, he on horseback. We had to work, even in long, summer days, till twelve o'clock, before we tasted a morsel; men, women, and children all being served alike. At noon the cart appeared with our breakfast. It was in large trays, and was set on the ground. There was bread, of which a piece was cut off for each person; then there was small hominy boiled, (that is, Indian corn, ground in the hand-mill,) and besides this, two herrings for each of the men and women, and one for each of the children. Our drink was the water in the ditches, whatever might be its state; if the ditches were dry, water was brought to us by boys. The salt fish made us always thirsty, but no other drink than water was ever allowed. However thirsty a slave may be, he is not allowed to leave his employment for a moment to get water; he can only have it when the hands in working have reached the ditch at the end of the rows. The overseer stood with his watch in his hand, to give us just an hour; when he said "rise," we had to rise and go to work again. The women who had children laid them down by the hedge-row, and gave them straws and other trifles to play with: here they were in danger from snakes. I have seen a large snake found coiled round the neck and face of a child, when its mother went to suckle it at dinner time. The hands work in a line, by the side of each other; the overseer puts the swiftest hands in the fore row, and all must keep up with them. One black man is kept on purpose to whip the others in the field; if he does not flog with sufficient severity, he is flogged himself: he whips severely, to keep the whip from his own back. If a man have a wife in the same field with himself, he chooses a row by the side of hers, that with extreme labour he may, if possible, help her. But he will not be in the same field if he can help it; for with his hardest labour, he often cannot save her from being flogged, and he is obliged to stand by and see it; he is always liable to see her taken home at night, stripped naked, and whipped before all the men. On the estate I am speaking of, those women who had sucking children suffered much from their breasts becoming full of milk, the infants being left at home; they therefore could not keep up with the other hands: I have seen the overseer beat them with raw hide, so that blood and milk flew mingled from their breasts. A woman who gives offence in the field, and is large in the family way, is compelled to lie down over a hole made to receive her, and is then flogged with the whip, or beaten with a paddle, which has holes in it; at every hole comes a blister. One of my sisters was so severely punished in this way, that labour was brought on, and the child was born in the field. This very overseer, Mr. Brooks, killed in this manner a girl named Mary: her father and mother were in the field at the time. He also killed a boy about twelve years old. He had no punishment, or even trial, for either.

There was no dinner till dark, when he gave the order to knock off and go home. The meal then was the same as in the morning, except that we had meat twice a-week.

On very few estates are the coloured people provided with any bedding; the best masters give only a blanket; this master gave none. A board, which the slave might pick up anywhere on the estate, was all he had to lie on. If he wished to procure bedding, he could only do so by working at nights. For warmth, therefore, the negroes generally sleep near a large fire, whether in the kitchen, or in their log huts; their legs are often in this way blistered and greatly swelled, and sometimes badly burnt: they suffer severely from this cause.

When the water-mill did not supply meal enough, we had to grind with the hand-mill. The night was employed in this work, without any thing being taken from the labour of the day. We had to take turn at it, women as well as men; enough was to be ground to serve for the following day.

I was eight months in the field. My master, Mr. Sawyer, agreed to allow me eight dollars a month, while so employed, towards buying myself: it will be seen he did not give me even that. When I first went to work in the corn field, I had paid him 230 dollars towards this third buying of my freedom. I told him one night, I could not stand his field-work any longer; he asked, why; I said I was almost starved to death, and had long been unaccustomed to this severe labour. He wanted to know why I could not stand it as well as the rest. I told him, he knew well I had not been used to it for a long time; that his overseer was the worst that had ever been on the plantation, and that I could not stand it. He said he would direct Mr. Brooks to give each of us a pint of meal or corn every evening, which we might bake, and which would serve us next morning, till our breakfast came at noon. The black people were much rejoiced that I got this additional allowance for them. But I was not satisfied; I wanted liberty.

One Sunday morning, as Master was sitting in his porch, I went to him and offered to give him the 230 dollars I had already paid him, if, beside them, he would take for my freedom the 600 dollars he had given for me. He drove me away, saying, I had no way to get the money. I sat down for a time, and went to him again: I repeated my offer to procure the 600 dollars, and he again said, I could not. He called his wife out of the room to the porch, and said to her, "Don't you think Moses has taken to getting drunk?" She asked me if it was so; I denied it, when she inquired what was the matter. Master replied, "Don't you think he wants me to sell him?" She said, "Moses, we would not take any money for you. Captain Cormack put a thousand dollars for you on the supper table last Friday night, and Mr. Sawyer would not touch it: he wants you to be overseer in the Dismal Swamp." I replied, "Captain Cormack never said anything to me about buying me: I would cut my throat from ear to ear rather than go to him. I know what made him say so; he is courting Miss Patsey, and he did it to make himself look big." Mistress laughed and turned away, and slammed to the door: Master shook himself with laughing, and put the paper he was reading before his face, knowing that I spoke the truth. Captain Cormack was an old man who went on crutches: Miss Patsey was the finest of master's daughters. Master drove me away from him again.

On Monday morning, Mr. Brooks, the overseer, blew the horn as usual for all to go to the field. I refused to go. I went to master and told him that if he would give me a paper,[21] I would go and fetch the 600 dollars; he then gave me a paper, stating that he was willing to take that sum for my freedom; so I hired an old horse and started for Norfolk, fifty miles off.

When I reached Deep Creek, I went to the house of Captain Edward Minner. He was very glad to see me, for in former days I had done much business for him: he said how sorry he had been to hear that I was at field-work. He inquired where I was going. I said to Norfolk, to get some of the merchants to let me have money to buy myself. He replied, "What did I always say to you? Was it not, that I would let you have the money at any time, if you would only tell me when you could be sold?" He called Mrs. Minner into the room, and told her I could be sold for my freedom: she was rejoiced to hear it. He said, "Put up your horse at Mr. Western's Tavern, for you need go no farther; I have plenty of old rusty dollars, and no man shall put his hand on your collar again to say you are a slave. Come and stay with me to-night, and in the morning I will get Mr. Garrett's horse, and go with you."

Next morning we set off, and found master at Major Farrance's, at the cross canal, where I knew he was to be that day, to sell his share of the canal. When I saw him he told me to go forward home, for he would not sell me. I felt sick and sadly disappointed. Captain Minner stepped up to him, and shewed him the paper he had given me, saying, "Mr. Sawyer, is not this your handwriting?" He replied, "Mistress said, the last word when I came away, I was not to sell him, but send him home again." Captain Minner said, "Mind, gentlemen, I do not want him for a slave; I want to buy him for freedom. He will repay me the money, and I shall not charge him a cent of interest for it. I would not have a coloured person to drag me down to hell, for all the money in the world." A gentleman who was by said it was a shame I should be so treated; I had bought myself so often that Mr. Sawyer ought to let me go. The very worst man as an overseer over the persons employed in digging the canal, Mr. Wiley M'Pherson, was there: he was never known to speak in favour of a coloured person; even he said that Mr. Sawyer ought to let me go, as I had been sold so often. At length Mr. Sawyer consented I should go for 650 dollars and would take no less. I wished Captain Minner to give the extra 50 dollars, and not to stand about it. I believe it was what M'Pherson said that induced my master to let me go: for he was well known for his great severity to coloured people, so that after even he had said so, master could not stand out. The Lord must have opened M'Pherson's heart to say it.

I have said this M'Pherson was an overseer where slaves were employed in cutting canals. The labour there is very severe. The ground is often very boggy: the negroes are up to the middle or much deeper in mud and water, cutting away roots and baling out mud: if they can keep their heads above water, they work on. They lodge in huts, or as they are called camps, made of shingles or boards. They lie down in the mud which has adhered to them, making a great fire to dry themselves, and keep off the cold. No bedding whatever is allowed them; it is only by work done over his task, that any of them can get a blanket. They are paid nothing except for this overwork. Their masters come once a month to receive the money for their labour: then perhaps some few very good masters will give them two dollars each, some others one dollar, some a pound of tobacco, and some nothing at all. The food is more abundant than that of field slaves; indeed it is the best allowance in America: it consists of a peck of meal, and six pounds of pork per week; the pork is commonly not good, it is damaged, and is bought as cheap as possible at auctions.

M'Pherson gave the same task to each slave; of course the weak ones often failed to do it. I have often seen him tie up persons and flog them in the morning, only because they were unable to get the previous day's task done: after they were flogged, pork or beef brine was put on their bleeding backs, to increase the pain; he sitting by resting himself, and seeing it done. After being thus flogged and pickled, the sufferers often remained tied up all day, the feet just touching the ground, the legs tied, and pieces of wood put between the legs. All the motion allowed was a slight turn of the neck. Thus exposed and helpless, the yellow flies and musquitoes in great numbers would settle on the bleeding and smarting back, and put the sufferer to extreme torture. This continued all day, for they were not taken down till night. In flogging, he would sometimes tie the slave's shirt over his head, that he might not flinch when the blow was coming: sometimes he would increase his misery, by blustering and calling out that he was coming to flog again, which he did or did not, as happened. I have seen him flog slaves with his own hands, till their entrails were visible; and I have seen the sufferers dead when they were taken down. He never was called to account in any way for it.

It is not uncommon for flies to blow the sores made by flogging.[22] In that case, we get a strong weed growing in those parts, called the Oak of Jerusalem;[23] we boil it at night, and wash the sores with the liquor, which is extremely bitter: on this, the creepers or maggots come out. To relieve them in some degree after severe flogging, their fellow-slaves rub their backs with part of their little allowance of fat meat.

For fear the slaves should run away, while unable to work from flogging, he kept them chained till they could work again. This man had from 500 to 700 men under his control. When out of other employment, I sometimes worked under him, and saw his doings. I believe it was the word of this man which gained my freedom. He is dead, but there are yet others like him on public works.

When the great kindness of Captain Minner had set me clear of Mr. Enoch Sawyer, I went to my old occupation of working the canal boats. These I took on shares as before. After a time, I was disabled for a year from following this employment by a severe attack of rheumatism, caught by frequent exposure to severe weather. I was anxious however to be earning something towards the repayment of Captain Minner, lest any accident unforeseen by him or me, should even yet deprive me of the liberty for which I so longed, and for which I had suffered so much. I therefore had myself carried in a lighter up a cross canal in the Dismal Swamp, and to the other side of Drummond's Lake. I was left on the shore, and there I built myself a little hut, and had provisions brought to me as opportunity served. Here, among snakes, bears, and panthers, whenever my strength was sufficient, I cut down a juniper tree, and converted it into cooper's timber.[24] The camp, like those commonly set up for negroes, was entirely open on one side; on that side a fire is lighted at night, and the person sleeping puts his feet towards it. One night I was awoke by some large animal smelling my face, and snuffing strongly; I felt its cold muzzle. I suddenly thrust out my arms, and shouted with all my might; it was frightened and made off. I do not know whether it was a bear or a panther, but it seemed as tall as a large calf. I slept of course no more that night. I put my trust in the Lord, and continued on the spot; I was never attacked again.

I recovered, and went to the canal boats again. By the end of three years from the time he laid down the money, I entirely repaid my very kind and excellent friend. During this time he made no claim whatever on my services; I was altogether on the footing of a free man, as far as a coloured man can there be free.

When, at length, I had repaid Captain Minner, and had got my free papers, so that my freedom was quite secure, my feelings were greatly excited. I felt to myself so light, that I almost thought I could fly, and in my sleep I was always dreaming of flying over woods and rivers. My gait was so altered by my gladness, that people often stopped me, saying, "Grandy, what is the matter?" I excused myself as well as I could; but many perceived the reason, and said, "Oh! he is so pleased with having got his freedom." Slavery will teach any man to be glad when he gets freedom.

My good master, Captain Minner, sent me to Providence, in Rhode Island, to stay a year and a day in order to gain my residence. But I stayed only two months. Mr. Howard's vessel came there laden with corn. I longed much to see my master and mistress for the kindness they had done me, and so went home in the schooner. On my arrival, I did not stop at my own house, except to ask my wife at the door how she and the children were in health, but went up the town to see Captain and Mrs. Minner. They were very glad to see me, and consulted with me about my way of getting a living. I wished to go on board the New York and Philadelphia Packets,[25] but feared I should be troubled for my freedom. Captain Minner thought I might venture, and I therefore engaged myself. I continued in that employment till his death, which happened about a year after my return from Providence. Then I returned to Boston; for, while he lived, I knew I could rely on his protection; but when I lost my friend, I thought it best to go wholly to the Northern States.

At Boston I went to work at sawing wood, sawing with the whip-saw,[26] labouring in the coal yards, loading and unloading vessels, &c. After labouring in this way for a few months, I went a voyage to St. John's in Porto Rico, with Captain Cobb, in the schooner, *New Packet*. On the return voyage, the vessel got ashore on Cape Cod: we left her, after doing in vain what we could to right her; she was afterwards recovered. I went several other voyages, and particularly two to the Mediterranean. The last was to the East Indies, in the ship *James Murray*, Captain Woodbury; owner, Mr. Gray. My entire savings up to the period of my return from this voyage amounted to 300 dollars; I sent it to Virginia, and bought my wife. She came to me at Boston. I dared not go myself to fetch her, lest I should be again deprived of my liberty, as often happens to free coloured people.

At the time called the time of the Insurrection, about eight years ago, when the whites said the coloured people were going to rise, and shot, hanged, and otherwise destroyed many of them,[27] Mrs. Minner thought she saw me in the street, and fainted there. The soldiers were seizing all the blacks they could find, and she knew if I were there, I should be sure to suffer with the rest. She was mistaken; I was not there.

My son's master at Norfolk sent a letter to me at Boston to say, that if I could raise 450 dollars, I might have his freedom; he was then fifteen years old. I had again saved 300 dollars. I knew the master was a drinking man, and I was therefore very anxious to get my son out of his hands. I went to Norfolk, running the risk of my liberty, and took my 300 dollars with me, to make the best bargain I could. Many gentlemen, my friends, in Boston, advised me not to go myself: but I was anxious to get my boy's freedom, and I knew that nobody in Virginia had any cause of complaint against me; so, notwithstanding their advice, I determined to go.

When the vessel arrived there, they said it was against the law for me to go ashore. The mayor of the city said, I had been among the cursed Yankees too long. He asked me whether I did not know, that it was unlawful for me to land;[28] to which I replied, that I did not know it, for I could neither read nor write. The merchants for whom I had formerly done business came on board, and said they cared for neither the mare (mayor) nor the horse, and insisted that I should go ashore. I told the mayor the business on which I came, and he gave me leave to stay nine days, telling me that if I were not gone in that time, he would sell me for the good of the State.

I offered my boy's master the 300 dollars: he counted the money, but put it back to me, refusing to take less than 450 dollars. I went on board, to return to Boston. We met with head winds, and put back three times to Norfolk, anchoring each time just opposite the jail. The nine days had expired, and I feared the mayor would find me on board and sell me. I could see the jail full of coloured people, and even the whipping post, at which they were con-stantly enduring the lash. While we were lying there by the jail, two vessels came from Eastern Shore, Virginia, laden with cattle and coloured people. The cattle were lowing for their calves, and the men and women were crying for their husbands, wives, or children. The cries and groans were terrible, notwithstanding there was a whipper on board each vessel, trying to compel the poor creatures to keep silence. These vessels lay close to ours. I had been a long time away from such scenes; the sight affected me very much, and added greatly to my fears.

One day, I saw a boat coming from the shore with white men in it. I thought they were officers coming to take me; and such was my horror of slavery, that I twice ran to the ship's waist, to jump overboard into the strong ebb-tide then running, to drown myself: but a strong impression on my mind restrained me each time.

Once more we got under way for New York; but meeting again with head winds, we ran into Maurice's River, in Delaware Bay. New Jersey, in which that place lies, is not a slave state. So I said to the captain, "Let me have a boat, and set me on the free land once more; then I will travel home overland; for I will not run the risk of going back to Virginia any more." The captain said there was no danger, but I exclaimed, "No! no! captain, I will not try it; put my feet on free land once again, and I shall be safe." When I once more touched the free land, the burthen of my mind was removed: if two ton weight had been taken off me, the relief would not have seemed so great.

From Maurice's Creek I travelled to Philadelphia, and at that place had a letter written to my wife at Boston, thanking God that I was on free land again. On arriving at Boston, I borrowed 150 dollars of a friend, and going to New York I obtained the help of Mr. John Williams to send the 450 dollars to Norfolk: thus, at length, I bought my son's freedom. I met him at New York, and brought him on to Boston.

Six others of my children, three boys and three girls, were sold to New Orleans. Two of these daughters have bought their own freedom. The eldest of them, Catherine, was sold three times after she was taken away from Virginia: the first time was by auction. Her last master but one was a Frenchman: she worked in his sugar-cane and cotton fields. Another Frenchman inquired for a girl on whom he could depend, to wait on his wife, who was in a consumption.[29] Her master offered him my daughter; they went into the field to see her, and the bargain was struck. Her new master gave her up to his sick wife, on whom she waited till her death. As she had waited exceedingly well on his wife, her master offered her a chance of buying her freedom. She objected to his terms as too high; for he required her to pay him four dollars a week out of her earnings, and 1200 dollars for her freedom. He said he could get more for her, and told her she might get plenty of washing at a dollar a dozen; at last she agreed. She lived near the river side, and obtained plenty of work. So anxious was she to obtain her freedom, that she worked nearly all her time, days and nights, and Sundays. She found, however, she gained nothing by working on Sundays, and therefore left it off. She paid her master punctually her weekly hire, and also something towards her freedom, for which he gave her receipts. A good stewardess was wanted for a steam-boat on the Mississippi; she was hired for the place at thirty dollars a-month, which is the usual salary: she also had liberty to sell apples and oranges on board; and commonly, the passengers give from twenty-five cents to a dollar, to a stewardess who attends them well. Her entire incoming, wages and all, amounted to about sixty dollars a-month. She remained at this employment till she had paid the entire sum of 1200 dollars for her freedom.

As soon as she obtained her free papers, she left the steam-boat, thinking she could find her sister Charlotte. Her two first trials were unsuccessful: but on the third attempt she found her at work in the cane-field. She shewed her sister's master her own free papers, and told him how she had bought herself: he said, that if her sister would pay him as much as she paid her master, she might go too. They agreed, and he gave her a pass. The two sisters went on board a steam-boat, and worked together for the wages of one, till they had saved the entire 1200 dollars for the freedom of the second sister. The husband of Charlotte was dead: her children were left behind in the cotton and cane-fields; their master refuses to take less than 2400 dollars for them: their names and ages are as follows: Zeno, about fifteen; Antoinette, about thirteen; Joseph, about eleven; and Josephine about ten years old.

Of my other children, I only know that one, a girl named Betsy, is a little way from Norfolk in Virginia. Her master, Mr. William Dixon, is willing to sell her for 500 dollars.

I do not know where any of my other four children are,[30] nor whether they be dead or alive. It will be very difficult to find them out; for the names of slaves are commonly changed with every change of master: they usually bear the name of the master to whom they belong at the time. They have no family name of their own by which they can be traced. Owing to this circumstance, and their ignorance of reading and writing, to which they are compelled by law, all trace between parents and their children who are separated from them in childhood, is lost in a few years. When, therefore, a child is sold away from its mother, she feels that she is parting from it for ever: there is little likelihood of her ever knowing what of good or evil befals it. The way of finding out a friend or relative, who has been sold away for any length of time, or to any great distance, is to trace him, if possible, to one master after another; or if that cannot be done, to inquire about the neighbourhood where he is supposed to be, until some one is found who can tell that such a person belonged to such or such a master: and the person supposed to be the one sought for, may perhaps remember the names of the persons to whom his father and mother belonged. There is little to be learnt from his appearance, for so many years may have passed away, that he may have grown out of the memory of his parents, or his nearest relations. There are thus no lasting family ties to bind relations together, not even the nearest, and this aggravates their distress when they are sold from each other. I have little hope of finding my four children again.

I have lived at Boston ever since I bought my freedom, except during the last year, which I have spent at Portland, in the state of Maine.

I have yet said nothing of my father. He was often sold through the failure of his successive owners. When I was a little boy, he was sold away from us to a distance: he was then so far off, that he could not come to see us oftener than once a year. After that, he was sold to go still further away, and then he could not come at all. I do not know what has become of him.

When my mother became old, she was sent to live in a little lonely log-hut in the woods. Aged and worn out slaves, whether men or women, are commonly so treated. No care is taken of them, except, perhaps, that a little ground is cleared about the hut, on which the old slave, if able, may raise a little corn. As far as the owner is concerned, they live or die as it happens; it is just the same thing as turning out an old horse. Their children or other near relations, if living in the neighbourhood, take it by turns to go at night, with a supply saved out of their own scanty allowance of food, as well as to cut wood and fetch water for them: this is done entirely through the good feelings of the slaves, and not through the masters' taking care that it is done. On these night-visits, the aged inmate of the hut is often found crying, on account of sufferings from disease or extreme weakness, or from want of food and water in the course of the day: many a time, when I have drawn near to my mother's hut, I have heard her grieving and crying on these accounts: she was old and blind too, and so unable to help herself. She was not treated worse than others: it is the general practice. Some few good masters do not treat their old slaves so: they employ them in doing light jobs about the house and garden.

My eldest sister is in Elizabeth City. She has five children, who, of course, are slaves. Her master is willing to sell her for 100 dollars: she is growing old. One of her children, a young man, cannot be bought under 900 dollars.

My sister Tamar, who belonged to the same master with myself, had children very fast. Her husband had hard owners, and lived at a distance. When a woman who has many children belongs to an owner who is under age, as ours was, it is customary to put her and the children out yearly to the person who will maintain them for the least money, the person taking them having the benefit of whatever work the woman can do. But my sister was put to herself in the woods. She had a bit of ground cleared, and was left to hire herself out to labour. On the ground she raised corn and flax; and obtained a peck[31] of corn, some herrings, or a piece of meat for a day's work among the neighbouring owners. In this way she brought up her children. Her husband could help her but little. As soon as each of the children became big enough, it was sold away from her.

After parting thus with five, she was sold along with the sixth, (about a year and a half old,) to the speculators; these are persons who buy slaves in Carolina and Virginia, to sell them in Georgia and New Orleans. After travelling with them more than 100 miles, she made her escape, but could not obtain her child to take it with her. On her journey homeward, she travelled by night, and hid herself in thick woods by day. She was in great danger on the road, but in three weeks reached the woods near us. There she had to keep herself concealed; I, my mother, and her husband knew where she was: she lived in a den she made for herself. She sometimes ventured down to my mother's hut, where she was hid in a hollow under the floor. Her husband lived twenty-five miles off: he would sometimes set off after his day's work was done, spend part of the night with her, and get back to work before next sunrise: sometimes he would spend Sunday with her. We all supplied her with such provisions as we could save. It was necessary to be very careful in visiting her; we tied pieces of wood or bundles of rags to our feet that no track might be made.

In the wood she had three children born; one of them died. She had not recovered from the birth of the youngest, when she was discovered and taken to the house of her old master.

She was afterwards sold to Culpepper, who used her very cruelly. He was beating her dreadfully, and the blood was streaming from her head and back, one day when I happened to go to his house. I was greatly grieved, and asked his leave to find a person to buy her: instead of answering me, he struck at me with an axe, and I was obliged to get away as fast as I could. Soon after, he failed, and she was offered for sale in Norfolk; there Mr. Johnson bought her and her two children, out of friendship for me: he treated her exceedingly well, and she served him faithfully: but it was not long before she was claimed by a person, to whom Culpepper had mortgaged her before he sold her to Johnson. This person sold her to Long, of Elizabeth City, where again she was very badly treated. After a time, Long sold her to go to Georgia: she was very ill at the time, and was taken away in a cart. I hear from her sometimes, and am very anxious to purchase her freedom, if ever I should be able. Two of her children are now in North Carolina, and are longing to obtain their freedom. I know nothing of the others, nor am I likely ever to hear of them again.

The treatment of slaves is mildest near the borders, where the free and slave states join: it becomes more severe, the further we go from the free states. It is more severe in the west and south than where I lived. The sale of slaves most frequently takes place from the milder to the severer parts: in that direction, there is great traffic in slaves, which is carried on by the speculators. On the frontier between the slave and free states there is a guard; no coloured person can go over a ferry without a pass. By these regulations, and the great numbers of patrols, escape is made very difficult.

Formerly, slaves were allowed to have religious meetings of their own; but after the insurrection which I spoke of before, they were forbidden to meet even for worship. Often they are flogged, if they are found singing or praying at home. They may go to the places of worship used by the whites; but they like their own meetings better. My wife's brother Isaac was a coloured preacher. A number of slaves went privately into the wood to hold meetings; when they were found out, they were flogged, and each was forced to tell who else was there. Three were shot, two of whom were killed, and the other was badly wounded. For preaching to them, Isaac was flogged, and his back pickled; when he was nearly well, he was flogged and pickled again, and so on for some months; then his back was suffered to get well, and he was sold. A little while before this, his wife was sold away with an infant at her breast; and of his six children, four had been sold away by one at a time. On the way with his buyers he dropped down dead; his heart was broken.

Having thus narrated what has happened to myself, my relatives, and near friends, I will add a few matters about slaves and coloured persons in general.

Slaves are under fear in every word they speak. If in their master's kitchen they let slip an expression of discontent, or a wish for freedom, it is often reported to the master or mistress by the children of the family, who may be playing about: severe flogging is often the consequence.

I have already said that it is forbidden by law to teach coloured persons to read or write. A few well disposed white young persons, of the families to which the slaves belonged, have ventured to teach them, but they dare not let it be known they have done so.

The proprietors get new land cleared in this way. They first "dead" a piece of ground in the woods adjoining the plantation. By "deading" is meant killing the trees, by cutting a nick all round each, quite through the bark. Out of this ground each coloured person has a piece as large as he can tend after his other work is done: the women have pieces in like manner. The slave works at night, cutting down the timber and clearing the ground; after it is cleared, he has it for his own use for two or three years, as may be agreed on. As these new clearings lie between the woods and the old cultivated land, the squirrels and racoons first come at the crops on them, and thus those on the planters' land are saved from much waste. When the negro has had the land for the specified time, and it has become fit for the plough, the master takes it, and he is removed to another new piece. It is no uncommon thing for the land to be taken from him before the time is out, if it has sooner become fit for the plough. When the crop is gathered, the master comes to see how much there is of it; he then gives the negro an order to sell that quantity; without that order, no storekeeper dare buy it. The slave lays out the money in something tidy, to go to meeting in, and something to take to his wife.

The evidence of a black man, or of ever so many black men, stands for nothing against that of one white; in consequence of this, the free negroes are liable to great cruelties. They have had their dwellings entered, their bedding and furniture destroyed, themselves, their wives, and children beaten; some have even been taken, with their wives, into the woods, and tied up, flogged, and left there. There is nothing which a white man may not do against a black one, if he only takes care that no other white man can give evidence against him.

A law has lately been passed in New Orleans, prohibiting any free coloured person from going there.[32]

The coasting packets of the ports on the Atlantic, commonly have coloured cooks. When a vessel goes from New York or Boston to a port in the slave-holding estates, the black cook is usually put in jail till the vessel sails again.

No coloured person can travel without a pass. If he cannot show it, he may be flogged by any body; in such a case, he often is seized and flogged by the patrols. All through the slave states there are patrols; they are so numerous that they cannot easily be escaped.

The only time when a man can visit his wife, when they are on different estates, is Saturday evening and Sunday. If they be very near to each other, he may sometimes see her on Wednesday evening. He must always return to his work by sunrise; if he fail to do so, he is flogged. When he has got together all the little things he can for his wife and children, and has walked many miles to see them, he may find that they have all been sold away, some in one direction, and some in another. He gives up all hope of seeing them again, but he dare not utter a word of complaint.

It often happens that when a slave wishes to visit his wife on another plantation, his own master is busy or from home, and therefore he cannot get a pass. He ventures without it. If there be any little spite against his wife, or himself, he may be asked for it when he arrives; and not having it, he may be beaten with thirty-nine stripes, and sent away. On his return he may be seized by the patrol, and flogged again for the same reason, and he will not wonder if he is again seized and beaten for the third time.

If a negro has given offence to the patrol, even by so innocent a matter as dressing tidily to go to a place of worship, he will be seized by one of them, and another will tear up his pass: while one is flogging him, the others will look another way; so when he or his master make complaint of his having been beaten without cause, and he points out the person who did it, the others will swear they saw no one beat him. His oath, being that of a black man, would stand for nothing, but he may not even be sworn; and in such a case his tormentors are safe, for they were the only whites present.

In all the slave states there are men who make a trade of whipping negroes: they ride about inquiring for jobs of persons who keep no overseer; if there is a negro to be whipped, whether man or woman, this man is employed when he calls, and does it immediately; his fee is half a dollar. Widows and other females having negroes, get them whipped in this way. Many mistresses will insist on the slave who has been flogged, begging pardon for her fault on her knees, and thanking her for the correction.

A white man who lived near me in Camden County, Thomas Evidge, followed this business. He was also sworn-whipper at the Court House. A law was passed that any white man detected in stealing should be whipped. Mr. Dozier frequently missed hogs, and flogged many of his negroes on suspicion of stealing them: when he could not in his suspicions fix on any one in particular, he flogged them all round, saying that he was sure of having punished the right one. Being one day shooting in his woods, he heard the report of another gun, and shortly after met David Evidge, the nephew of the whipper, with one of his hogs on his back which had just been shot: David was sent to prison, convicted of the theft, and sentenced to be flogged. His uncle, who vapoured about greatly in flogging slaves, and taunted them with unfeeling speeches while he did it, could not bear the thought of flogging his nephew, and hired a man to do it. The person pitched on, chanced to be a sailor; he laid it well on the thief: pleased enough were the coloured people to see a white back for the first time subjected to the lash.

Another man of the same business, George Wilkins, did no greater credit to the trade. Mr. Carnie, on Western Branch, Virginia, often missed corn from his barn. Wilkins, the whipper, was very officious in pointing out this slave and that, as very likely to be the thief: with nothing against them but his insinuations, some were severely punished, being flogged by this very Wilkins; and others, at his instigation, were sold away. One night Mr. Carnie, unknown to his coloured people, set a steel trap in the barn. Some of the negroes, passing the barn before morning, saw Wilkins standing there, but were not aware he was caught. They called the master, that he might seize the thief before he could escape: he came and teased Wilkins during the night; in the morning he exposed him to the view of the neighbours, and then set him at liberty without further punishment.

The very severe punishments to which slaves are subjected for trifling offences or none at all, their continued liability to all kinds of ill usage without a chance of redress, and the agonizing feelings they endure at being separated from the dearest connexions, drive many of them to desperation, and they abscond. They hide themselves in the woods, where they remain for months, and in some cases for years. When caught, they are flogged with extreme severity, their backs are pickled and the flogging repeated as before described. After months of this torture the back is allowed to heal, and the slave is sold away. Especially is this done when the slave has attempted to reach a free state.

In violent thunder-storms, when the whites have got between feather beds to be safe from the lightning, I have often seen negroes, the aged as well as others, go out, and lifting up their hands, thank God that judgment was coming at last. So cruelly are many of them used, that judgment, they think, would be a happy release from their horrible slavery.

The proprietors, though they live in luxury, generally die in debt: their negroes are so hardly treated, that no profit is made by their labour. Many of them are great gamblers. At the death of a proprietor, it commonly happens that his coloured people are sold towards paying his debts. So it must and will be with the masters, while slavery continues: when freedom is established, I believe they will begin to prosper greatly.

Before I close this Narrative, I ought to express my grateful thanks to the many friends in the Northern States, who have encouraged and assisted me: I shall never forget to speak of their kindness, and to pray for their prosperity. I am delighted to say, that not only to myself, but to very many other coloured persons, they have lent a benevolent helping hand. Last year, gentlemen whom I know bought no less than ten families from slavery, and this year they are pursuing the same good work. But for these numerous and heavy claims on their means and their kindness, I should have had no need to appeal to the generosity of the British public; they would gladly have helped me to redeem all my children and relations.

When I first went to the Northern States, which is about ten years ago, although I was free as to the law, I was made to feel severely the difference between persons of different colours. No black man was admitted to the same seats in churches with the whites, nor to the inside of public convey-ances, nor into street coaches or cabs: we had to be content with the decks of steam-boats in all weathers, night and day, — not even our wives or chil-dren being allowed to go below, however it might rain, or snow, or freeze; in various other ways, we were treated as though we were of a race of men below the whites. But the abolitionists boldly stood up for us, and through them things are much changed for the better. Now, we may sit in any part of many places of worship, and are even asked into the pews of respectable white families; many public conveyances now make no distinction between white and black. We begin to feel that we are really on the same footing as our fellow citizens. They see we can and do conduct ourselves with propri-ety, and they are now admitting us in many cases to the same standing with themselves.

During the struggles which have procured for us this justice from our fellow-citizens, we have been in the habit of looking in public places for some well-known abolitionists, and if none that we knew were there, we ad-dressed any person dressed as a Quaker;[33] these classes always took our part against ill usage, and we have to thank them for many a contest in our behalf.

We were greatly delighted by the zealous efforts and powerful eloquence in our cause of Mr. George Thompson, who came from our English friends to aid our suffering brethren. He was hated and mobbed by bad men amongst the whites; they put his life in great danger, and threatened destruc-tion to all who sheltered him.[34] We prayed for him, and did all we could to defend him. The Lord preserved him, and thankful were we when he es-caped from our country with his life. At that time, and ever since, we have had a host of American friends, who have laboured for the cause night and day; they have nobly stood up for the rights and honour of the coloured man;

but they did so at first in the midst of scorn and danger. Now, thank God, the case is very different. Mr. William Lloyd Garrison,[35] who was hunted for his life by a mob in the streets of Boston has lately been chairman of a large meeting in favour of abolition, held in Fanueil Hall,[36] the celebrated public hall of Boston, called "the Cradle of Liberty."

I am glad to say also, that numbers of my coloured brethren now escape from slavery; some by purchasing their freedom, others by quitting, through many dangers and hardships, the land of bondage. The latter suffer many privations in their attempts to reach the free states. They hide themselves during the day in the woods and swamps; at night they travel, crossing rivers by swimming, or by boats they may chance to meet with, and passing over hills and meadows which they do not know; in these dangerous journeys they are guided by the north-star, for they only know that the land of freedom is in the north. They subsist on such wild fruit as they can gather, and as they are often very long on their way, they reach the free states almost like skeletons. On their arrival, they have no friends but such as pity those who have been in bondage, the number of which, I am happy to say, is increasing; but if they can meet with a man in a broad-brimmed hat and Quaker coat, they speak to him without fear—relying on him as a friend. At each place the escaped slave inquires for an abolitionist or a Quaker, and these friends of the coloured man help them on their journey northwards, until they are out of the reach of danger.

Our untiring friends, the abolitionists, once obtained a law that no coloured person should be seized as a slave within the free states; this law would have been of great service to us, by ridding us of all anxiety about our freedom while we remained there; but I am sorry to say, that it has lately been repealed, and that now, as before, any coloured person who is said to be a slave, may be seized in the free states and carried away, no matter how long he may have resided there, as also may his children and their children, although they all may have been born there. I hope this law will soon be altered again.[37] At present, many escaped slaves are forwarded by their friends to Canada, where, under British rule, they are quite safe. There is a body of ten thousand of them in Upper Canada; they are known for their good order, and loyalty to the British government; during the late troubles, they could always be relied on for the defence of the British possessions, against the lawless Americans who attempted to invade them.

As to the settlement of Liberia on the coast of Africa,[38] the free coloured people of America do not willingly go to it. America is their home: if their forefathers lived in Africa, they themselves know nothing of that country.

None but free coloured people are taken there: if they would take slaves, they might have plenty of colonists. Slaves will go any where for freedom.

We look very much to Great Britain and Ireland for help. Whenever we hear of the British or Irish people doing good to black men, we are delighted, and run to tell each other the news. Our kind friends, the abolitionists, are very much encouraged when they hear of meetings and speeches in England in our cause. The first of August, the day when the slaves in the West Indies were made free,[39] is always kept as a day of rejoicing by the American coloured free people.

I do hope and believe that the cause of freedom to the blacks is becoming stronger and stronger every day. I pray for the time to come when freedom shall be established all over the world. Then will men love as brethren; they will delight to do good to one another; and they will thankfully worship the Father of All.

And now I have only to repeat my hearty thanks to all who have done any thing towards obtaining liberty for my coloured brethren, and especially to express my gratitude to those who have helped me to procure for myself, my wife, and some of my children, the blessing of freedom,—a blessing of which none can know the value but he who has been a slave. Whatever profit may be obtained by the sale of this book, and all donations with which I may be favoured, will be faithfully employed in redeeming my remaining children and relatives from the dreadful condition of slavery. Mr. Scoble,[40] the Secretary of the British and Foreign Anti-slavery Society, has kindly agreed to take charge of whatever money I may be able to raise; and any reference may be made to Mr. Rouse at the office of the above Society, 27, New Broad Street, London; or to Mr. R. D. Webb, 160, Great Brunswick Street, Dublin.

DUBLIN:

PRINTED BY WEBB AND CHAPMAN, GREAT BRUNSWICK-ST.

NOTE.[41]

I have paid the following sums to redeem myself and relatives from slavery, viz:

For my own freedom, ...	$1,850
For my wife's "	300
For my son's "	450
Grandchild's "	400
To redeem my kidnapped son, . . .	60
	——$3,060

I now wish to raise $100 to buy the freedom of my sister Mary, who is a slave at Elizabeth City, N.C. Her master says he will take that sum for her.

M. G.

Boston, Jan. 19, 1844.

Notes

The epigraph on the title page combines and slightly rephrases two excerpts from *The Speech of the Right Honourable William Pitt, on a Motion for the Abolition of the Slave Trade, in the House of Commons, on Monday the Second of April, 1792* (London: James Phillips, 1792), 17, 19. William Pitt the Younger (1759–1806), was a British prime minister (1783–1801, 1804–06) and an antislavery advocate.

1. William Pitt Fessenden (1806–69), an antislavery politician who served as a senator from Maine between 1855 and 1868. Grandy likely met Fessenden during 1841 or 1842 when Grandy lived in Portland.

2. Ellis Gray Loring (1803–1858), an abolitionist lawyer and financial supporter of the abolitionist periodical the *Liberator*.

3. Isaiah 58:5–7.

4. George Thompson (1804–78), an antislavery orator, activist, and ally to black abolitionists touring the British Isles.

5. A county in northeastern North Carolina bounded by the North River, Albemarle Sound, and Pasquotank River.

6. A county in northeastern North Carolina along the coast.

7. Antislavery sympathizer Elizabeth Poole based her poem "The Slave-Boy's Death" on this episode from Grandy's narrative. The poem is featured in the 1844 edition of the *Liberty Bell*, an annual published for the Massachusetts Anti-Slavery Fair.

8. Because Grandy's juvenile master could not manage the plantation, his slaves were leased to neighboring planters. January 1 was the annual auction day on which new one-year contracts were established for leasing slaves.

9. An agricultural technique that heaps earth around the base of the plant to stabilize the roots and eliminate weeds.

10. A swamp region, extending from southeastern Virginia to northeastern North Carolina, used for shipping.

11. By the written permission of an owner, skilled laborers sometimes solicited independent work, though the master gained most of the worker's profit.

12. As a diversionary tactic during the War of 1812 (1812–15), the British navy blockaded the Chesapeake Bay, impeding commercial trade and in effect weakening the American economy.

13. A shipping port in northeastern North Carolina near the Pasquotank River.

14. When disabled, mentally ill, or aged slaves could no longer function on the plan-

tation, masters customarily relocated them to nearby woods. For some slaves, this move, along with a lighter assignment of work, was considered a privilege; instead, Grandy interprets the practice as a cruelty allowing masters to relinquish economic responsibility for unprofitable slaves.

15. A very small amount of something — in this case, money.

16. Papers attesting to the free status of a person of color in the antebellum United States.

17. A governmental building or office where customs are collected and ships are cleared for entering or leaving the country.

18. See Thompson's explanatory footnote in the text.

19. A two-masted, square-rigged sailing vessel used in sea trade.

20. To move cargo using a flat-bottomed barge called a lighter.

21. Grandy requests a written pass or permission slip to travel; without such, any black person on the road could be harassed by the slave patrol. Likewise, free blacks were admonished to carry their free papers at all times to verify their right to travel.

22. Flies blow sores by laying eggs in open wounds on human and animal flesh.

23. A plant used as an herbal remedy to expel intestinal worms and prevent spasms.

24. Wood for making a barrel or tub for storage.

25. Passenger boats usually carrying cargo for trade. Rhode Island, New York, and Philadelphia were high-traffic ports from which African American seaman most often sailed.

26. A saw for two persons used to divide timber lengthwise.

27. Most likely, Grandy is referring to the 1831 slave rebellion led by Nat Turner. Turner and his cohorts killed fifty-seven whites in Southampton County, Virginia. White terrorist retaliation spread throughout North Carolina and the South after Turner's insurrection.

28. The deportation clause of the 1830 North Carolina slave code stipulated that a slave must leave the state within ninety days after emancipation, never to return; Virginia enacted a similar law.

29. This disease, which would now be termed tuberculosis, was characterized by wasting away of the body.

30. These four missing children, plus Grandy's three named daughters and the son he purchases, add up to eight children. However, the number of Grandy's progeny is unclear because earlier the narrator mentions one son and "six others of my children," making seven offspring in all.

31. A dry measure of eight quarts.

32. In an effort to reduce immigration, New Orleans passed a law in 1804 to prohibit free blacks from entering the city. In 1826, North Carolina instituted a similar act on the state level.

33. A member of the Society of Friends, the first religious denomination in the United States to condemn slavery and the first to require its members to free their slaves.

34. During Thompson's 1834–1835 antislavery tour in the United States, proslavery mobs assembled at his lectures and even threatened to abduct him. Thompson returned to England in December 1835.

35. William Lloyd Garrison (1805–1879), the editor of the antislavery newspaper the *Liberator*, a long-time leader of the American Anti-Slavery Society, and the best-known American abolitionist in the nineteenth century.

36. Opened in 1742 as a market and meeting hall, Faneuil Hall later became a political meeting place.

37. Some northern states attempted to counter the Fugitive Slave Act of 1793 by enacting personal liberty laws to protect runaways. Congress ruled that the constitutional act superseded state-level laws, and in 1850 Congress passed a more stringent fugitive slave act as part of the Compromise of 1850.

38. A republic in West Africa founded by freed American slaves in 1822. Many abolitionists opposed the American Colonization Society (founded 1817) and its attempts to export freed blacks to Liberia and other African colonies.

39. The Emancipation Act of 1833 (August 1, 1833) declared the abolition of slavery in the British West Indian colonies.

40. John Scoble (1799–c. 1867), a Congregational minister and antislavery activist who in 1831 was appointed lecturer of the Agency Committee, an organization founded by the Anti-Slavery Society for purposes of public agitation. Scoble helped found the British and Foreign Anti-Slavery Society in 1839 and was appointed its secretary in 1842.

41. This receipt, which appeared in the later Boston 1844 editions rather than the first London publication, itemizes Grandy's accumulated spending. Dated January 1844, this note is also one of the last records of Grandy's public fund-raising efforts.

The Experience of

Rev. Thomas H. Jones

UNCLE TOM'S

CABIN.

INTRODUCTION.

A suffering brother would affectionately present this simple story of deep personal wrongs to the earnest friends of the slave. He asks you to buy and read it, for in so doing you will help one who needs your sympathy and aid, and will receive, in the perusal of this simple narrative, a more fervent conviction of the necessity and blessedness of toiling for the members of the one great brotherhood, who may suffer and die, ignorant and despairing, in the vast prison-land of the South. "Whatsoever ye would that men should do unto you, do ye also unto them. THE AUTHOR.

Frontispiece of Experience and Personal Narrative of Uncle Tom Jones *(1855)*

INTRODUCTION

David A. Davis

In 1855, Thomas H. Jones, a fugitive slave from North Carolina living in Massachusetts, published a brief sketch of his life in slavery under the title *Experience and Personal Narrative of Uncle Tom Jones, Who Was for Forty Years a Slave*. The frontispiece to the publication depicts a middle-aged black man wearing a stovepipe hat and smoking a pipe. Below this image is a pastoral scene depicting a log cabin framed with the inscription "Uncle Tom's Cabin." By directly associating Jones's narrative with the long-suffering character from Harriet Beecher Stowe's famous 1853 novel, Jones and the abolitionists who sponsored his narrative's publication capitalized on the social and commercial success of *Uncle Tom's Cabin*.[1] Equating Jones with Uncle Tom supplied readers sympathetic to the abolitionist cause with a context for their encounter with Jones, who, like Uncle Tom, endured the cruel injustices of slavery through an unwavering Christian faith. But, beyond these general characteristics, Jones's story diverges markedly from the tale of Uncle Tom as an idealized slave martyr. Jones is instead a complex person who struggles to lift himself above the degrading conditions of slavery by learning to read, becoming a minister, escaping to the North, and agitating for abolition. Jones published several editions of his narrative leading up to the final 1885 edition reprinted here, but the allusion to Uncle Tom does not appear in any subsequent edition. The fictional character is replaced with a real man, Rev. Thomas H. Jones.

Jones was born on John Hawes's plantation near Wilmington, North Carolina, in 1806. Hawes sold Thomas in 1815 to a shopkeeper named Jones, whose surname was attached to Thomas, separating the nine-year-old child from his family. While working in Jones's store, Thomas managed to learn to read and to become a Christian despite his master's disapproval. After Mr. Jones died in 1829, his estate sold Thomas to Owen Holmes, an attorney in Wilmington, who hired Thomas out as a stevedore loading and unloading ships in the city port. At some point between Thomas Jones's purchase in 1829 and his escape in 1849, Holmes allowed his slave to preach to other slaves in the vicinity of Wilmington. By scrupulously saving his earnings during this period, Jones was able to purchase his wife's freedom and send her and their children, except for his son Edward, to New York in 1849. A few months later, Jones escaped from Wilmington and rejoined his family in New York. In the North he became involved in the antislavery movement, but when the Fugitive Slave Act went into effect in 1850 he moved to Canada, where he preached in the Maritime Provinces for four years. Although the date of Jones's death is as yet unknown, he apparently spent the remainder of his life in Boston, publishing the final version of his narrative in 1885.

The antebellum publication of *The Experience of Rev. Thomas H. Jones* had an overt political agenda: to publicize the inhumane treatment of slaves in order to arouse support for the abolitionist movement. Heralded by forceful exposés such as *A Narrative of the Adventures and Escape of Moses Roper, from American Slavery* (1837) and the narratives of celebrated fugitives — among them Frederick Douglass, William Wells Brown, and James W. C. Pennington — made the 1840s a decade of strong interest in slave-generated writing and, consequently, of considerable literary production by former slaves, especially men. Published at a time when the fugitive slave narrative as a genre was at its commercial zenith, *The Experience of Rev. Thomas H. Jones* can be read today as almost a textbook example of nineteenth-century black America's most lasting contribution to literature.

In a survey of the characteristics that many of the most famous antebellum slave narratives hold in common, the critic James Olney reports that more than a dozen narratives, including classic texts by Douglass and Brown, open with the same phrase that begins Jones's narrative: "I was born a slave."[2] Olney goes on to describe a number of normative elements in fugitive slave narratives, all of which are represented in Jones's narrative. Yet, while it reflects the genre's conventions, when compared to the narratives that have been the subject of literary and historical study since the 1960s — particularly those of Douglass, Brown, Pennington, and Harriet Jacobs — Jones's narrative is both less introspective and inventive as autobiography and less politically militant as a weapon in the war against slavery. This is probably the reason why scholars of African American literature, history, and culture have focused slight attention on antebellum editions of Jones's narrative.

Jones's narrative merits the interest of anyone interested in antebellum African American life, however, because his story, published in numerous editions over thirty years, represents a period of momentous change both in America's history and in one remarkable individual's life. The first editions, published soon after his escape, were published as pamphlets circulated among abolitionist organizations. In a later publication, printed by J. E. Farwell of Boston in 1855, Jones's story, couched in the trappings of *Uncle*

Tom's Cabin, was paired with an excerpt from Richard Hildreth's novel *The Slave; or, Memoirs of Archy Moore*, which tells the tragic story of Wild Tom, a slave from South Carolina who killed an overseer and was lynched.[3] The two stories form a diptych contrasting Jones's subtle self-determination with Wild Tom's futile resistance. In 1857 the printer Henry J. Howland of Worcester published a revised and expanded edition of Jones's narrative. This version includes some scenes not included in the first edition, such as the whipping of Jones's sister Sarah, and testimonials from prominent abolitionists and religious leaders, as well as copies of several letters exchanged between Jones and his wife during the period when she lived in New York before his escape. Jones published additional editions of this version of his narrative in 1858, 1862, 1868, 1871, and 1880, presumably to capitalize on what he and his publishers must have felt was the lingering currency of his story. In 1885, Jones and his printer E. A. Anthony and Sons of New Bedford, Massachusetts, published the final edition of his narrative, the version reprinted here, which includes a second part written late in Jones's life that expands and comments on the content of his original narrative.

When we consider the little-known 1885 version of Jones's narrative, which appears to have escaped the attention of most scholars and critics, we find a remarkable dialogue representing Jones's pre- and post–Civil War perspectives on what was most memorable and important about his experience as a slave. The two parts of his 1885 narrative can be read as discrete documents. The first part, the antebellum version of his life as a slave, demonstrates the conventions of the fugitive slave narrative genre. The second part of the 1885 narrative reexamines the same period of Jones's life but from the perspective of freedom; a cursory look at this part indicates that Jones the freeman was intent on revisiting his ministry among the slave communities of coastal North Carolina. When read in dialogue with each other, the two parts of the 1885 narrative reveal a complex and multifaceted representation of a former slave's life that rewards our attention today for two important reasons. First, by augmenting his original story so as to shed light on his spiritual journey, Jones allowed his 1885 autobiography to expand the form and transcend the conventions of the slave narrative. Second, the two parts of Jones's story create a complementary pre- and post–Civil War description of the experience of slavery from two curiously divergent perspectives, that of the abolitionists, whose agenda dominates first part of the text, and that of Jones's personal experience, which pervades the second part the story. This implicit dialogue within the text is both rare and valuable, giving modern readers an unusually candid, multidimensional glimpse into both the secular and spiritual sides of one enslaved man's life in antebellum North Carolina.

In the first part of his narrative Jones describes his memories of growing up on Hawes's plantation in New Hanover County, where, he says, he was conditioned to feel "inferior and degraded." As a child, he suffered from malnutrition, exposure, and overwork, and he felt vulnerable to the arbitrary violence that masters inflicted on slaves. In one of his earliest memories, he recalls how his sister was stripped naked, lashed to a beam in the smokehouse, and whipped. When he was only nine years old, he was literally snatched from his mother's arms by a slave driver sent to deliver him to a new master. This pattern of violence and separation is a recurring theme in Jones's narrative. He describes several beatings he suffered at the hands of his master, Mr. Jones, including one occasion when his master struck him simply for arguing with a white boy. Jones explains that "it is thought necessary to enforce this habit of obsequious submission on the part of the colored people to the whites, in order to maintain their supremacy over the poor, outraged slaves." A few years later, Jones decided to marry another slave, Lucilla Smith, who belonged to a woman from Wilmington, even though he realized slave marriages were subject to arbitrary dissolution. Together Thomas and Lucilla had three children before the family was separated when Lucilla's owner moved first to New Bern, North Carolina, and then to Alabama. Jones was never reunited with his first family, and he demonstrates his frustration over this loss in the opening of the second part of his narrative. After marrying a second time, he determined to purchase his new wife's freedom and send her north to safety, but ironically his success in this regard left him once again bereft of family. Consistent with the emphasis of many antebellum slave narratives on the blighting effect of slavery on the family, Jones made his repeated separations from his own family central to his protest against human bondage while also rendering these experiences key to the image of himself in his narrative as a dignified and sympathetic family man.

To overcome the sense of degradation his masters tried to impose on him, Jones contrived to learn to read and write. Because slaves were forbidden to learn to read in much of the antebellum South, literate whites were reluctant to offer him any assistance. His master would have likely beaten him if he had caught Jones reading. But, in spite of these circumstances, Jones managed to find learning materials and get lessons from literate whites. His methods resemble those used by Frederick Douglass, who learned to read by bribing white school children with food.[4] Jones paid a white boy six cents a week for illicit instruction until he could read and write competently. He took a great risk by daring to learn to read, and on one occasion he suffered a severe beating rather than allow his master to discover his book. Like Douglass, Jones equated literacy with manhood, explaining that as he learned to read "I felt . . . that I was really beginning to be a *man*, preparing myself for a condition in life better and higher and happier than could belong to the ignorant *slave*." The distinction Jones makes between a literate man and an ignorant slave indicates that learning to read gave Jones a sense of intrinsic value that helped to liberate his self-estimate from the artificial economic value of the master class, who assessed his worth based solely on his laboring ability.

Jones explains that literacy represented to him "the way to freedom, influence, and real, secure happiness." Portraying literacy as the gateway to the goals in life that white American readers held dear was a common theme in antebellum slave narratives, especially the more famous ones, such as Douglass's. The achievement of literacy could demonstrate that slaves, dehumanized in the propaganda of proslavery advocates, had an innate ability to reason and express themselves on a par with whites. A slave who authored his own life story would refute myths of Negro inferiority purveyed by such influential European philosophers as Immanuel Kant in "On the Different Races of Men."[5] By learning to read and relating their experience in their own words, slave narrators like Jones made a strong case for equality with whites and competence in freedom.

To practice his reading, Jones secretly studied a book of essays that included several pieces on religious themes. Reading about God, sin, and forgiveness made him curious about religion, leading him to seek advice from other slaves about becoming a Christian. In his recounting of the experience of his conversion, Jones portrays himself as a person who struggled righteously for his faith.[6] He wrestled with his own soul to find belief, attending several church meetings before he finally felt himself moved by the Holy Spirit. After each service that he attended, he suffered a severe beating from his master, who strongly discouraged him from becoming involved with the church. The cycle of internal and external conflict went on for an extended period before climaxing in a final confrontation between Jones and his master in 1823, when Thomas was seventeen years old. Such a moment of confrontation between an aspiring slave and a repressive master is a common element in the most famous slave narratives and is epitomized in the physical struggle Douglass recounts between himself and Edward Covey, a slave-breaker on Maryland's Eastern Shore. Jones, however, effectively triumphs over his master by penitently accepting his beating, which causes his abusive master to feel ashamed and guilty. He makes a point of noting that this episode marked the last beating he ever received from his master.

Frequently in slave narratives, the story of escape to the North dominates the text, providing a natural plot climax and a transition from descriptions of insufferable bondage to jubilant freedom. Some slave narrators became celebrities because of their ingenious escape plans, enjoying popular success recounting their experiences on the lecture circuit in the North and in Europe. For example, *Narrative of the Life of Henry Box Brown, Written by Himself* (1851), the story of a man who shipped himself from slavery in Richmond to freedom in Philadelphia in a wooden box, and *Running a Thousand Miles for Freedom; or, The Escape of William and Ellen Craft from Slavery* (1860), the story of a married couple who masqueraded as a white man and his servant on their travels from Georgia to Boston, each sold thousands of copies.[7] In the case of Jones's narrative, however, the actual escape is anticlimactic, at least from our perspective today. After working for a few years as a stevedore, he saved enough money to purchase his wife and children, and they lived for a time in the free black section of Wilmington. Fearing that she and their children might be forced back into slavery, Jones sent them to New York in 1849 to await his arrival. A few months later, he stowed away on a ship bound for New York, but the crew discovered him before the ship set anchor. Undeterred, Jones soon escaped from the ship on a makeshift raft. Unlike many slaves escaping to the North with no resources and contacts, Jones went directly to his family. By the end of his first week in New York he had begun speaking on the abolitionist circuit.

Although literate, Jones did not write his narrative himself. Instead, the title page describes the text as "written by a friend, as related to him by Brother Jones." Jones never names his amanuensis, but the amanuensis obviously had connections with the abolitionist movement and knowledge of the fugitive slave narrative genre. Perhaps this amanuensis made decisions about the narrative's form, following the paradigm for slave narratives already established by the popularity of Frederick Douglass's and William Wells Brown's texts.[8] The amanuensis likely encouraged Jones to focus his story on his mistreatment and not to discuss the more humane side of his experience in slavery, which might have undermined the antislavery argument. At one point, to explain stylistic inconsistencies between the text of the narrative and the wording of several personal letters included in the story, the narrator, an amalgam of the amanuensis and Jones, says, "The kind friend who has written this narrative for me, has corrected some mistakes in the construction and spelling of these letters, and some he has left uncorrected."

Considering that Jones's narrative developed over a number of years, more than one person may have collaborated with him on the various editions of his autobiography. Since almost three decades elapsed between the writing of the first part and the writing of the second part, it is plausible that another person assisted Jones with the composition of the second part. Stylistically, the second part shows evidence of rhetorical training, but the structure is much looser than the first part and the frequent use of italics for emphasis disappears, which suggests a lack of authorial continuity. While it is conceivable that Jones wrote the second part alone, the rhetorical style is not consistent with the style of Jones's personal letters, and it seems unlikely that a mature adult's writing style would change dramatically. It is likely, therefore, that Jones composed the second part with the assistance of another amanuensis.

Every edition of Jones's narrative that was published before 1885 was written for the dual purpose of furthering the cause of emancipation and contributing to Jones's family income. The fact that Jones published an extended revision in 1885 with the same printer who published the 1868 and 1871 versions strongly suggests that a mutually beneficial relationship had developed between the two parties. Since the second part of Jones's narrative was written twenty years after emancipation, it no longer had a direct antislavery agenda. Hence, by 1885, Jones probably felt more at ease about divulging details of his experience in slavery that might not have earlier advanced the abolitionist cause. While the first portion of the 1885 narrative exemplifies the slave narrative genre, the second part follows the vein of Reconstruction-era African American autobiography.[9]

Most post-Emancipation African American autobiographies describe the author's struggle to gain acceptance in American society and to find success in freedom. The benchmark for this particular genre is Booker T. Washington's *Up from Slavery* (1901). Jones, however, chooses not to discuss his life in freedom in the final version of his autobiography, leaving the details of his life in the North—including his work with the American Anti-Slavery Society, his family's circumstances, and his occupation—largely a mystery. One could conjecture a number of possible reasons for this decision. Perhaps Jones considered his life in freedom relatively unimportant when compared to his life in slavery and his ministry. Perhaps the amanuensis who assisted him with the composition of the second part discouraged him from carrying the narrative farther. Perhaps Jones intended the second part to complement the first part, placing important aspects of his life in slavery in a fresh light. The emphasis in the second part on Jones's ministry in particular may signal his desire to break away from the antebellum slave narrative's portrayal of the slave as an object of abuse and exploitation in order to depict himself, even in slavery, as a man of purpose and spiritual power, an agent of God's will in the midst of circumstances that sought to deny Jones a will of his own.

Just as there is every reason to believe that Jones had a purpose in composing his earlier autobiographical narrative in accordance with the antebellum slave narrative tradition, there is equally reason to think that Jones meant for a heretofore underdeveloped dimension of his life as a slave to find fuller expression in the second part of his 1885 narrative. The first part of his story brings with it a familiar representation of slavery that accentuates the exploitation and arbitrary violence endemic in the institution: masters are described as cruel, slaves are described as heroic, and white southerners who are actually sympathetic to blacks are rare. But in the second part of his narrative Jones offers his reader another perspective on slavery, allowing a depth of characterization of the slaveholder as well as the slave that in the antebellum era was seldom wanted or expected in antislavery writing by blacks or whites. Jones describes his last master, Owen Holmes, as genuinely kind and, without a trace of irony, calls him an abolitionist. Such a representation in a pre–Civil War slave narrative would have challenged conventional notions about slaveholders and slavery and would have likely undermined the abolitionist agenda behind the story's publication. In a similarly unconventional fashion, the second part of Jones's 1885 narrative portrays a relatively comfortable existence for Jones and his family in Wilmington between the 1830s and their abrupt departure in 1849. Most saliently, Holmes, a devout Christian, encouraged Jones's ministry among the coastal North Carolina slave community, even extricating him from trouble on a few occasions. Since Holmes did not fit the villainous image of slaveholders represented by Simon Legree in *Uncle Tom's Cabin*, a balanced portrayal of him would no doubt have seemed out of place to antebellum abolitionists. But by recasting his relationship to Holmes in slavery after more than three decades in freedom, Jones allows his reader to consider a North Carolina slaveholder with regard to both his guilty complicity in human bondage and his attempts to mitigate the injustice he did to men like Jones through his participation in the institution of slavery. Jones's treatment of Holmes in the second part of the narrative testifies to a spirit of forgiveness that underscores Jones's religious faith and reinforces the redemptive theme that concludes the 1885 edition.

The differing but in some ways complementary perspectives on slave experience represented in the two parts of *The Experience of Rev. Thomas H. Jones* provide a vivid image of life as a slave along the North Carolina coast before 1849. At different times, Jones worked in the three most prominent economic ventures in the area—farming, trading, and shipping. Thus his story represents a broad spectrum of experiences. Based on his recollection, plantation work took the hardest toll on slaves. Under the domination of overseers in the field from dusk to dawn, the slaves were worked to exhaustion and given only the barest necessities to enable them to survive. Slaves working in the home, as Jones did for a while, enjoyed somewhat better conditions, although they were still at the mercy of their masters' impulses. Working in a store, however, allowed Jones a relative degree of freedom. While his master still beat him arbitrarily, he had enough latitude and leisure to learn to read and to attend religious services. As a stevedore loading ships on the dock, Jones worked long hours, but he set his own terms for employment and kept some of his income, which put him on par with free blacks. Based on Jones's experience, one can see that for town slaves the quality of their living conditions often depended on their employment and interchange with the public. Slaves isolated in fields and farmhouses could expect few amenities, while slaves working in cities and in trades fared better, if only because their masters learned that maximizing the profits from skilled slaves usually required giving them a measure of economic autonomy.

The quality of a slave's life also depended on the temperament of his or her master, as Jones makes clear. His first master, John Hawes, owned many slaves on a large plantation and regarded them as barely sentient draft animals. Family bonds were frequently sundered without regard for maternal or filial instincts, and overseers drove slaves in the field to extract maximum labor with minimal investment. In contrast, Mr. Jones, the storekeeper whose last name became Thomas's, kept few slaves and worked in direct proximity to them. Although Mr. Jones beat Thomas on several occasions, he treated his slave most of the time with a modicum of dignity, allowing him to work unsupervised for long periods and to leave the store frequently. Owen Holmes, Thomas Jones's last owner, treated him only nominally as a slave, working with him instead as a virtual business partner. Holmes allowed Jones mostly unrestricted freedom and encouraged him to minister to slave communities in the Wilmington area. Jones describes Holmes in the second part of his 1885 narrative in terms that seem incongruous with the institution of human bondage: "I found in him all that any slave could desire. He did for me more and better than my own father could have done. He protected and provided for me as though I had been one of his own household. The memory of my relations to him and his dear family will ever be a pleasure to me while life shall last." While Jones hardly mentions him in the first part of his narrative, he discusses Holmes at length in the second part, particularly in the context of his ministry among the slave community.

Recognizing Jones's religious convictions, Holmes encouraged him to preach to slave congregations in the vicinity of Wilmington despite the fact that the idea of slaves' attending services without supervision disturbed many slaveholders. After the Southampton insurrection of 1831, incited by the preaching of Nat Turner, many southern state legislatures, including North Carolina's, explicitly outlawed unsupervised slave preaching on the grounds that such meetings could be used for agitation.[10] Consequently, although an underground religious network existed, open meetings were rare. Since Jones had the authorization of his master to visit and preach in the area and since Holmes usually made arrangements with other planta-tion owners to allow slaves to attend, Jones's meetings were an exception. In most cases, his congregations were large and animated. By way of example, he describes one occasion when, as he began to pray, his voice "was soon drowned by the voices of the multitudes who pleaded for mercy on their own behalf." His descriptions of the sequence of events in an African Ameri-can religious service provide insight into a practice officially marginalized by the white church in the South. Jones indicates that many slaveholders who were Christian were pleased to have their slaves gain some exposure to religion.

The local authorities, however, did not officially accept Jones's minis-try. On numerous occasions patrollers searching for slaves away from their masters without permission interrupted his meetings. At least once, Jones used Owen Holmes's name and protection to discourage the patrollers from accosting the members of his congregation, but more often the patrollers disrupted services and checked each slave present for a written pass. Slaves caught without a pass were bound and lashed with a whip on the spot. Jones himself was not immune to such punishment. Once, while on his way to give a funeral sermon at the burial of a deceased slave, he was accosted by patrollers who demanded his pass, which he discovered he had forgotten. Jones's punishment was to be stripped to the waist, tied to a tree, and given fifteen lashes. Regardless, the slave pastor resumed his journey and deliv-ered the funeral sermon. This episode implicitly compares the suffering of Christian slaves with the persecution of early Christians, who also fre-quently met in secrecy and were frequently beaten for practicing their faith.

After his escape from slavery and an evidently brief reunion with his family in New York, Jones went to Canada in 1850 to continue his ministry while evading the Fugitive Slave Act. There he spoke at numerous churches, raising funds and support for the antislavery movement in America. While in Canada Jones experienced the feeling of racial equality for the first — and possibly only — time in his life. He preached to mostly white congregations of several denominations and collected large sums of money as a testament to his ability as a speaker and the righteousness of his cause. Yet he makes clear that he found the fellowship of whites and blacks united under a Christian mantle amazing. He tells of one occasion when, tired from his journey, he visited the home of a French-speaking family who lived along the highway. Although Jones and his host could not communicate, he received all the hospitality the family could offer, including a simple, nourishing meal and a carriage ride to his destination. Jones describes his benefactor as an agent of God sent to care for a poor wanderer, and the anecdote illustrates his unstated position that the bonds of Christian faith transcend the prejudices of race.

After four years in Canada, Jones returned to his family in Boston in 1854. His narrative foreshortens the next eleven years of his life to only a few sentences. Jones says almost nothing about his preaching and antislavery lecturing in the North before and during the Civil War except that "everywhere I went I proclaimed my belief that I should some day witness the downfall of slavery. . . . Praise God that end is now accomplished." Instead of celebrating the war and the fall of slavery, Jones turns in the final pages of his story back to his parents and his resolute determination to be reunited with them in the last years of his enslavement. Structurally, this anecdote places the narrative within a symmetrical framework that begins in the first part with his forced separation from his parents and ends in the second part with their reunion, effected by Jones's purchase and support of them until their deaths. Thus *The Experience of Rev. Thomas H. Jones* concludes with a tribute to a son's devotion to his parents, whom he would not leave in slavery despite his own desire for freedom. It is striking that each of Jones's antebellum narratives ends with his escape from slavery, saying nothing of the fate of his parents or his role in liberating them. The final statement of his postbellum narrative, however, reveals what may have come to represent, for Jones in his old age, the most telling testimonial to his faithfulness and dedication to liberty: "I said when a slave I would never leave my old father and mother to suffer, and I kept my word."

Jones's antebellum narrative reflects the militancy of a fugitive slave campaigning for abolition. He adopts many of the conventions of the slave narrative popularized by Douglass and others to add his voice to a growing chorus of black dissenters working with white northern abolitionists to advance a major change in America's economic and human rights policies. To that end, Jones's antebellum narrative is a political document, crafted in accordance with reformist objectives that superseded a thorough and inclusive rendering of the full record of Jones's personal history in slavery. Consistent with the reformist agenda of the antebellum slave narrative, the early versions of Jones's life omit important events and individuals that might have detracted from the polemical value of his text. Writing more than twenty years after emancipation, however, Jones returned to the experiences of his life in slavery with a new set of objectives, which were more personal than political. The second part of the 1885 narrative, therefore, probably reflects Jones's own values more completely, as he describes the events and individuals that were most important to him, such as his ministry, his relationship to Owen Holmes, and the pride he felt when he purchased his parents' freedom.

Read holistically, *The Experience of Rev. Thomas H. Jones* provides unusually clear and compelling insights into the history of slavery in North Carolina and the life of a remarkable individual. Yet Jones's narrative is perhaps most important as a story of faith and courage. Like readers in Jones's time, we can identify with his struggle to believe in a righteous, redemptive God in the face of mass injustice. Refusing to demonize his masters, Jones finds a way by 1885 to offer them forgiveness and understanding, thereby demonstrating the tenacity of his conviction that he could "see now the hand of God in it all." Unlike Uncle Tom, to whom he was compared in the original version of his narrative, Jones found a way to preserve his religious faith and his human dignity while protecting his family, emancipating his parents, *and* escaping slavery.

Note on the Text

The version of Jones's narrative printed here follows the text of *The Experience of Rev. Thomas H. Jones, Who Was a Slave for Forty-three Years, Written by a Friend, as Given to Him by Brother Jones*, published in 1885 by E. A. Anthony and Sons in New Bedford, Massachusetts. Several versions of Jones's narrative are known, beginning with the original *Experience of Uncle Thomas Jones, Who Was for Forty Years a Slave*, published by Henry Howland of Worcester, Massachusetts, in 1849 and reprinted by D. Laing of Boston in 1850. Jones's narrative reappeared as *The Experience and Personal Narrative of Uncle Tom Jones, Who Was for Forty Years a Slave*, in printings by H. B. Skinner of Boston, H. B. Taylor of Springfield, and Holbrook of

New York in 1854 and in printings by J. E. Farwell of Boston in 1855 and 1858. Most early versions of the narrative include only the first chapter of the first part minus a few scenes, such as the whipping of Sarah. Henry J. Howland published *The Experience of Thomas H. Jones, Who Was a Slave for Forty-three Years* in 1857, a version that includes all of chapter 1 and chapter 2 except for the last paragraph about Jones's decision to go to Canada to escape the Fugitive Slave Act. In 1862, the Boston firm of Bazin and Chandler published Jones's narrative under the same title with only the addition of the last paragraph of chapter 2. E. A. Anthony and Sons reprinted this same text under the same title in 1868 and 1871 and then published the expanded 1885 text; A. T. Bliss and Company of Boston reprinted the same edition in 1888. While the final version was printed twenty years after the war, almost all of the material in the expanded text concerns Jones's life in North Carolina before his escape, with the exception of a brief discussion of his ministry in Canada. With each publication, no deletions or significant revisions were made other than the additions previously mentioned. The 1885 version is, therefore, the most complete edition of the text and the most interesting.

Notes

1. Harriet Beecher Stowe, *Uncle Tom's Cabin; or, Life among the Lowly* (1853; reprint, New York: Penguin, 1981).

2. James Olney, "'I Was Born': Slave Narratives, Their Status as Autobiography and as Literature," in *The Slave's Narrative*, ed. Charles T. Davis and Henry Louis Gates Jr. (New York: Oxford University Press, 1985), 148–75.

3. Richard Hildreth, *The Slave; or, Memoirs of Archy Moore* (Boston: John H. Eastburn, 1836).

4. Frederick Douglass, *Narrative of the Life of Frederick Douglass, an American Slave, Written by Himself* (1845; reprint, New York: Norton, 1997), 47–51.

5. Immanuel Kant, "On the Different Races of Men," in *Race and the Enlightenment*, ed. Emmanuel Eze (Cambridge, Mass.: Blackwell, 1997), 38–48.

6. For more on the African American conversion narrative, see Graham Russell Hodges, *Black Itinerants of the Gospel: The Narratives of John Jea and George White* (Madison, Wis.: Madison House, 1993), and William L. Andrews, *Sisters of the Spirit* (Bloomington: Indiana University Press, 1986).

7. Henry Box Brown, *Narrative of Henry Box Brown* (1849; reprint, New York: Oxford University Press, 2002), and William Craft, *Running a Thousand Miles for Freedom* (1860; reprint, Baton Rouge: Louisiana State University Press, 1999).

8. William Wells Brown, *Narrative of William Wells Brown, an American Slave* (London: C. Gilpin, 1849).

9. For more on Reconstruction-era African American autobiography, see William L. Andrews, "The Representation of Slavery and the Rise of Afro-American Literary Realism, 1865–1920," in *Slavery and the Literary Imagination*, ed. Deborah E. McDowell and Arnold Rampersad (Baltimore: Johns Hopkins University Press, 1989), 62–80.

10. For more on the Southampton insurrection, see Henry Irving Tragle, *The Southampton Slave Revolt of 1831* (Amherst: University of Massachusetts Press, 1971).

THE EXPERIENCE

OF

REV. THOMAS H. JONES,

WHO WAS

A SLAVE

FOR FORTY-THREE YEARS.

WRITTEN BY A FRIEND,

AS RELATED TO HIM BY BROTHER JONES.

NEW BEDFORD:

E. ANTHONY & SONS, PRINTERS.

1885.

THE EXPERIENCE OF

REV. THOMAS H. JONES.

Frontispiece of The Experience of Rev. Thomas H. Jones *(1885)*

A suffering brother would affectionately present this simple story of deep personal wrongs to the earnest friends of the Slave. He asks you to buy and read it, for, in so doing, you will help one who needs your sympathy and aid; and you will receive, in the perusal of this simple narrative, a more fervent conviction of the necessity and blessedness of toiling for the desolate members of the one great brotherhood who now suffer and die, ignorant and despairing, in the vast prison land of the South. "Whatsoever ye would that men should do to you, do ye even so to them."

THOMAS H. JONES.

TO THE FRIENDS OF SUFFERING HUMANITY:

The undersigned take pleasure in certifying that they have formed an acquaintance with Brother Thomas H. Jones, since his escape from slavery; having seen and perused his letters and his certificates of church relations, and made all suitable inquiries, most cordially recommend him to the confidence and aid of all who have a heart to sympathize with a down-trodden and outraged portion of the great brotherhood. We would also say that we have heard Brother Jones lecture before our respective churches, and we only speak the unanimous sentiment of our people when we say that his narrative is one of thrilling interest, calculated to secure the attention of any audience, and to benefit the sympathizing hearts of all who will make themselves acquainted with the present condition and past experience of this true-hearted brother.

E. A. STOCKMAN,
Pastor of the Wesleyan church, Boston.

DANIEL FOSTER,
Pastor of the Free Evangelical church,
North Danvers, Mass.

To whom it may concern: This may certify that the bearer, Thomas H. Jones, has lectured to my people with good success, giving a satisfaction uncommon to one deprived, as he has been, of moral or mental cultivation.

I can cheerfully recommend him to all such as may be inclined to give him a hearing or assistance in any way, in confidence, feeling that he is an honest and upright man.

A. B. FLANDERS,
Pastor of the W. M. church, Exeter, N. H.

Nov. 25, 1849.

NARRATIVE OF A REFUGEE SLAVE.

I was born a slave. My recollections of early life are associated with poverty, suffering and shame. I was made to feel, in my boyhood's first experience, that I was inferior and degraded, and that I must pass through life in a dependent and suffering condition. The experience of forty-three years, which were passed by me in slavery, was one of dark fears and darker realities. John Hawes was my first master. He lived in New Hanover county, N.C., between the Black and South rivers, and was the owner of a large plantation called Hawes's Plantation. He had over fifty slaves. I remained with my parents nine years. They were both slaves, owned by John Hawes. They had six children, Richard, Alexander, Charles, Sarah, myself, and John. I remember well that dear old cabin, with its clay floor and mud chimney, in which, for nine years, I enjoyed the presence and love of my wretched parents.

Father and mother tried to make it a happy place for their dear children. *They* worked late into the night many and many a time, to get a little simple furniture for their home and the home of their children; and they spent many hours of willing toil to stop up the chinks between the logs of their poor hut, that they and their children might be protected from the storm and the cold. I can testify, from my own painful experience, to the deep and fond affection which the slave cherishes in his heart for his home and its dear ones. We have no other tie to link us to the human family, but our fervent love for those who are *with* us and of us in relations of sympathy and devotedness, in wrongs and wretchedness. My dear parents were conscious of the desperate and incurable woe of their position and destiny; and of the lot of inevitable suffering in store for their beloved children. They talked about our coming misery, and they lifted up their voices and wept aloud, as they spoke of our being torn from them and sold off to the dreaded slave-trader, perhaps never again to see them or hear from them a word of fond love. I have heard them speak of their willingness to bear their own sorrows without complaint, if only we, their dear children, could be safe from the wretchedness before us. And I remember, and *now* fully understand, as I did not *then*, the sad and tearful look they would fix upon us when we were gathered round them and running on with our foolish prattle. I am a father, and I have had the same feelings of unspeakable anguish, as I have looked upon my precious babes, and have thought of the ignorance, degradation and woe which they must endure as slaves. The great God, who knoweth all the secrets of the heart, and He only, knows the bitter sorrow I now feel when I think of my four dear children who are slaves, torn from me and consigned to hopeless servitude by the iron hand of ruthless wrong. I love those children with all a father's fondness. God gave them to me; but my brother took them from me, in utter scorn of a father's earnest pleadings; and I never shall look upon them again, till I meet them and my oppressors at the final gathering. Will not the great Father and God make them and me reparation in the final award of mercy to the victim, and of justice to the cruel desolator?

Mr. Hawes was a very severe and cruel master. He kept no overseer, but managed his own slaves, with the help of Enoch, his oldest son. Once a year he distributed clothing to his slaves. To the men he gave one pair of shoes, one blanket, one hat, and five yards of coarse, homespun cotton; to the women a corresponding outfit, and enough to make one frock for each of the children. The slaves were obliged to make up their own clothes, after the severe labor of the plantation had been performed. And other clothing, beyond this yearly supply, which they might need, the slaves were compelled to get by extra work, or do without.

The supply of food given out to the slaves was one peck of corn a week, or some equivalent, and nothing besides. They must grind their own corn, after the work of the day was performed, at a mill which stood on the plantation. We had to eat our coarse bread without meat, or butter, or milk. Severe labor alone gave us an appetite for our scanty and unpalatable fare. Many of the slaves were so hungry after their excessive toil, that they were compelled to steal food in addition to this allowance.

During the planting and harvest season, we had to work early and late. The men and women were called at three o'clock in the morning, and were worked on the plantation till it was dark at night. After that they must prepare their food for supper and for the breakfast of the next day, and attend to other duties of their own dear homes. Parents would often have to work for their children at home, after each day's protracted toil, till the middle of the night, and then snatch a few hours' sleep, to get strength for the heavy burdens of the next day.

In the month of November, and through the Winter season, the men and women worked in the fields, clearing up new land, chopping and burning bushes, burning tar kilns, and digging ditches. They worked together, poorly clad, and suffering from the bitter cold and wet of those Winter months. Women, wives and mothers, daughters and sisters, on that plantation, were compelled to toil on cold, stormy days in the open field, while the piercing wind and driving storm benumbed their limbs, and almost froze the tears that came forth out of their cold and desolate hearts. Little boys, and girls, too, worked and cried, toting brush to the fires, husking the corn, watching the stock, and running on errands for master and mistress, and their three sons, Enoch, Edward, and John, and constantly receiving from them scoldings and beatings as their reward.

Thus passed nine years of my life; years of suffering, the shuddering memory of which is deeply fixed in my heart. Oh, that these happy, merry boys and girls, whom I have seen in Massachusetts since my escape from slavery, whom I have so often met rejoicing in their mercies since I came here, only knew the deep wretchedness of the poor slave child! For then, I am sure, their tender hearts would feel to love and pray for these unhappy ones, on whose early life hopeless sufferings bear down a crushing, killing burden! These nine years of wretchedness passed, and a change came for me. My master sold me to Mr. Jones, of Wilmington, N.C., distant forty-five miles from Hawes's plantation. Mr. Jones sent his slave-driver, a colored man named Abraham, to conduct me to my new home in Wilmington. I was at home with my mother when he came. He looked in at the door and called to me:

"Tom, you must go with me." His looks were ugly, and his voice was savage. I was very much afraid, and began to cry, holding on to my mother's clothes, and begging her to protect me, and not let the man take me away. Mother wept bitterly, and in the midst of her loud sobbings, cried out in broken words, "I can't save you, Tommy; master has sold you, you must go." She threw her arms around me, and while the hot tears fell on my face, she strained me to her heart. There she held me, sobbing and mourning, till the brutal Abraham came in, snatched me away, hurried me out of the house where I was born, my only home, and tore me away from the dear mother who loved me as no other friend could do. She followed him, imploring a moment's delay, and weeping aloud, to the road, where he turned around, and striking at her with his heavy cowhide, fiercely ordered her to stop bawling and go back into the house.

Thus was I snatched from the presence of my loving parents, and from the true affection of the dear ones of home. For thirteen weary years did my heart turn in its yearning for that precious home. And then, at the age of twenty-two, was I permitted to revisit my early home. I found it all desolate; the family all broken up; father was sold and gone; Richard, Alexander, Charles, Sarah and John, were sold and gone. Mother, prematurely old, heart-broken, utterly desolate, weak and dying, alone remained. I saw her, and wept once more on her bosom. I went back to my chains with a deeper woe in my heart than I had ever felt before. There was but one thought of joy in my wretched consciousness, and that was, that my kind and precious mother would soon be at rest in the grave. And then, too, I remember, I mused with deep earnestness on death, as the only friend the poor slave had. And I wished that I, too, might lie down by my mother's side, and die with her in her loving embrace.

I should have related, that one of the earliest scenes of painful memory associated with my opening years of suffering, is connected with a severe whipping which my master inflicted on my sister Sarah. He tied her up, having compelled her to strip herself entirely naked, in the smoke house, and gave her a terrible whipping,—at least, so it seemed to my young heart, as I heard her scream, and stood by my mother, who was wringing her hands in an agony of grief, at the cruelties which her tender child was enduring. I do not know what my sister had done for which she was then whipped; but I remember that her body was marked and scarred for weeks after that terrible scourging, and that our parents always after *seemed* to hold their breath when they spoke of it. Sarah was the last of the family who was sold, and my poor mother never looked up after this final act of cruelty was accomplished. I think of my only sister now, and often try to imagine *where* she is, and *how* she fares in this cruel land of slavery. And oh, my God, how dark and wretched are these pictures! Can I think of that poor sister without a sorrow too great for utterance? Ah, me! how can the generous, loving brother or sister, blessed with freedom, forget the cruel sorrows and wrongs of the slave brother and sister? how fellowship, even in the least act of comity, the atrocious slaveholder? There may be some who do this from ignorance of such cruel wrongs. God grant this simple story may enlighten some who only need to *know* our deep necessities, to give us their willing sympathy and aid and love.

My journey to Wilmington with the heartless Abraham was a very sad one. We walked all the way. I was afraid of my savage companion; and yet my heart felt so desolate, and my longings for sympathy so intense, that I was impelled to turn to my cruel guide for relief. He was striding along in stern gloom and silence, too fast for my young feet to keep pace, and I began to feel that I *must* stop and rest. It was bitter cold, too, and I was poorly clad to bear the keen air of a January day. My limbs were weary with travel, and stiff with cold. I could not go on at the rate I had done, and so I turned to my guide and begged him to take me into some hut and let me rest and get warm. He cursed me, and told me to keep silence and come along, or he would warm me with a cowhide. Oh, I thought, how cruel and hopeless my lot! Would that I could fall down here and die! And I did fall down. We had just passed through a soft, wet place, and it seemed to me that I was frozen. And I fell down on my dark, cold way, unable to proceed. I was then carried into a slave's cabin, and allowed to warm and rest. It was nearly midnight when I arrived, with my conductor, at my place of exile and suffering. And certainly no heart could be more entirely wretched than I was when I threw my weary, aching body, on my cold, hard bed.

The next morning I was called into the presence of Mr. Jones, my new master, and my work was assigned to me. I was to take care of the old gray horse, kept for the use of the family when they wished to ride out, to fetch water from the spring to the house, to go on errands to my master's store, to clean the boots and shoes belonging to the white members of the family and to the white visitors, to sweep the rooms, and to bring wood from the wharf on my head for the fires at the house and store. From the first dawn of day till ten and eleven, and sometimes twelve at night, I could hardly find one moment's time for rest. And oh, how the memory of that year of constant toil and weariness is imprinted on my heart, an impression of appalling sorrow! My dreams are still haunted with the agony of that year. I had just been torn from my home; my yearning heart was deprived of the sweet sympathy of those to whose memory I then clung, and to whom my heart still turns with irrepressible and unutterable longings. I was torn from them and put into a circle of cold, selfish and cruel hearts, and put then to perform labors too great for my young strength. And yet I lived through that year, just as the slave lives on through weary years of suffering, on which no ray of light shines, save that which hope of a better, happier future gives even to the desolate bondman. I lived through it, with all its darkness and sorrow. That year I received my first whipping. I had failed one day to finish my allotted task. It seemed to me that I had done my best; but somehow, that day, thoughts of home came so fresh and tender into my mind, and, along with these thoughts, a sense of my utter hopeless desolation came in and took such a strong hold of my heart, that I sank down, a helpless, heartbroken child. My tasks for that day were neglected. The next morning my master made me strip off my shirt, and then whipped me with a cowhide till the blood ran trickling down upon the floor. My master was very profane, and with dreadful oaths he assured me that there was only one way for me to avoid a repetition of this terrible discipline, and that was to do my tasks every day, sick or well.

And so this year went by, and my duties were changed, and my lot was made a little easier. The cook, Fanny, died, and I was put into her place. I still had to get wood, and keep the fires in the house, and, after the work of cooking, setting the table, clearing away and washing the dishes, there was always something to be done for my mistress. I got but little time to rest; but I got enough to eat, which I had not done the year before. I was by the comfortable fire a good part of the cold Winter weather, instead of being exposed to the cold and wet, without warm clothing, as I had been the year before, and my labor was not so hard the second year as it had been the first.

My mistress complained of me at length, that I was not so obedient as I ought to be, and so I was taken from the house into the store. My business there was to open and sweep out the store in the morning, and get all the things ready for the accommodation of customers who might come in during the day. Then I had to bring out and deliver all heavy articles that might be called for during the day, such as salt, large quantities of which were sold in the store, ship stores, grain, etc. I had also to hold myself ready to run on any errand my master or clerk, David Cogdell, might wish to send me on. While Cogdell remained in the store, I enjoyed a *gleam* of happiness. He was very kind to me, never giving me a cross word or sour look; always ready to show me how to do anything which I did not understand, and to perform little acts of kindness to me. His condescension to me, a poor, despised, homeless and friendless slave, and his tenderness to me, while all others were severe and scornful, sank down a precious bond of grateful emotion into my desolate heart. I seemed to be lifted up by this noble friend at times, from the dark despair which had settled down upon my life, and to be joined once more to a living hope of future improvement in my sad lot. Should these simple words ever meet the eye of David Cogdell, let them assure him of my fervent gratitude and affection for his goodness to me. Let them tell him how infinitely precious to my mourning heart, then and now, his generous treatment and noble kindness to a despised and unhappy boy. And let them say to him, "My early and true friend, Tommy, the poor slave boy, whom you blessed with unfailing kindness, has now grown to be a man, and has run away from the dark misery of bondage. And now, when he calls upon his Father in heaven to pour out rich blessings on the few friends who have aided him, then David Cogdell is remembered with fond and fervent affection." David was one of the few who always regarded the feelings and happiness of others as earnestly as his own; who find their own happiness in making the unfortunate happy by sympathy and kindness, and who would suffer any loss rather than do injustice to the poor and defenseless. I often wondered how there could be such a difference in the character of two men.

as there was between that of my master and my friend and benefactor, David Cogdell. And I often wished that I might pass into the hands of such a man as he was. But his kindness and generosity to the poor slaves was very offensive to my master, and to other slaveholders; and so, at length, Mr. Jones turned him off, though he was compelled to acknowledge, at the same time, that he was the most trustworthy and valuable assistant he ever had in his store.

After my master dismissed Mr. C., he tried to get along with me alone in the store. He kept the books and waited upon the most genteel of his customers, leaving me to do the rest of the work. This went on six months, when he declared that he could not bear this confinement any longer; and so he got a white boy to come and enter as clerk, to stay till he was of age. James Dixon was a poor boy about my own age, and when he came into the store could hardly read or write. He was accordingly engaged a part of each day with his books and writing. I saw him studying, and asked him to let me see his book. When he felt in a good humor, James was very kind and obliging. The great trouble with him was, that his fits of ill-humor were much more frequent than his times of good feeling. It happened, however, that he was on good terms with himself when I asked him to show me his book, and so he let me take it and look at it, and he answered very kindly many questions which I asked him about books and schools and learning. He told me that he was trying to get learning enough to fit him to do a good business for himself after he should get through with Mr. Jones. He told me that a man who had learning would always find friends, and get along very well in the world without having to work hard, while those who had no learning would have no friends and be compelled to work very hard for a poor living all their days. This was all new to me, and furnished me topics for wondering thought for days afterwards. The result of my meditations was, that an intense burning desire to learn to read and write took possession of my mind, occupying me wholly in waking hours, and stirring up earnest thoughts in my soul even when I slept. The question which then took hold of my whole consciousness was, How can I get a book to begin? James told me that a spelling-book was the first one necessary in getting learning. So I contrived how I might obtain a spelling-book. At length, after much study, I hit upon this plan: I cleaned the boots of a Mr. David Smith, Jr.,[1] who carried on the printer's business in Wilmington, and edited the Cape Fear Recorder. He had always appeared to me a very kind man. I thought I would get him to aid me in procuring a spelling-book. He looked at me in silence and with close attention for some time, and asked me what I wanted. I told him I wanted to learn to read. He shook his head, and replied, "No, Thomas, it would not answer for me to sell you a book to learn out of; you will only get yourself into trouble if you attempt it; and I advise you to get that foolish notion out of your head as quickly as you can."

David's brother, Peter Smith, kept a book and stationery store under the printing office, and I next applied to him for a book, determined to persevere till I obtained this coveted treasure. He asked me the same question that his brother David had done, and with the same searching, suspicious look. By my previous repulse I had discovered that I could not get a spelling-book if I told what I wanted to do with it, and so I told a lie in order to get it. I answered that I wanted it for a white boy, naming one that lived at my master's, and that he had given me the money to get it with, and had asked me to call at the store and buy it. The book was then handed out to me, the money taken in return, and I left, feeling very rich with my long-desired treasure. I got out of the store, and looking around to see that no one observed me, I hid my book in my bosom, and hurried on to my work, conscious that a new era in my life was opening upon me through the possession of this book. That consciousness at once awakened new thoughts, purposes, and new hopes—a new life, in fact—in my experience. My mind was excited. The words spoken by James Dixon of the great advantages of learning, made me intensely anxious to learn. I was a slave; and I knew that the whole community was in league to keep the poor slave in ignorance and chains. Yet I longed to be free, and to be able to move the minds of other men by my thoughts. It seemed to me now, that if I could learn to read and write, this learning might—nay, I really thought it would—point out to me the way to freedom, influence, and real, secure happiness. So I hurried on to my master's store, and watching my opportunity to do it safe from curious eyes, I hid my book with the utmost care, under some liquor barrels in the smoke house. The first opportunity I improved to examine my book. I looked it over with the most intent eagerness, turned over its leaves, and tried to discover what the new and strange characters which I saw in its pages might mean. But I found it a vain endeavor. I could understand a picture, and from it make out a story of immediate interest to my mind. But I could not associate any thought or fact with these crooked letters with which my primer was filled. So the next day I sought a favorable moment, and asked James to tell me where a scholar must begin in order to learn to read, and how. He laughed at my ignorance, and, taking his spelling-book, showed me the alphabet in large and small letters on the same page. I asked him the name of the first letter, pointing it out; he told me A; so of the next, and so on through the alphabet. I managed to remember A and B, and I studied and looked out the same letters in many other parts of the book. And so I fixed in a tenacious memory the names of the first two letters of the alphabet. But I found that I could not get on without help, and so I applied to James again to show me the letters and tell me their names. This time he suspected me of trying to learn to read myself, and he plied me with questions till he ascertained that I was, in good earnest, entering upon an effort to get knowledge. At this discovery he manifested a good deal of indignation. He told me, in scorn, that it was not for such as *me* to try to improve, that I was a *slave*, and that it was not proper for *me* to learn to read. He threatened to tell my master, and at length, by his hard language, my anger was fully aroused, and I answered taunt with taunt. He called me a poor, miserable nigger; and I called him a poor, ignorant white servant boy. While we were engaged in loud and angry words of mutual defiance and scorn, my master came into the store. Mr. Jones had never given me a whipping since the time I have already described, during my first year of toil, want and suffering in his service. But he now caught me in the unpardonable offence of giving saucy language to a white boy, and one, too, who was in his employ. Without stopping to make any inquiries, he took down the cowhide and gave me a severe whipping. He told me never to talk back to a white man, on pain of flogging. I suppose this law or custom is universal at the South. And I suppose it is thought necessary to enforce this habit of obsequious submission on the part of the colored people to the whites, in order to maintain their supremacy over the poor, outraged slaves.

I will mention, in this connection, as illustrative of this cruel custom, an incident which I saw just before I ran away from my chains. A little colored boy was carrying along through Wilmington a basket of food. His name was Ben, and he belonged to Mrs. Runkin, a widow lady. A little mischievous white boy, just about Ben's age and size, met him, and purposely overturned the little fellow's basket and scattered his load in the mud. Ben, in return for this wanton act, called him some hard name, when the white boy clinched him to throw him down with the scattered fragments upon his basket in the mud. Ben resisted, and threw down the white boy, proving to be the stronger of the two. Tom Myers, a young lawyer of Wilmington, saw the contest, and immediately rushing out, seized little Ben and dragged him into the store opposite the place of battle. He sent out to a saddler's shop, procured a cowhide, and gave the little fellow a tremendous flogging for the daring crime of resisting a white boy who had wantonly invaded his rights. Is it any wonder that the spirit of self-respect of the poor, ignorant slave, is broken down by such treatment of unsparing and persevering cruelty?

I was now repulsed by James, so that I could hope for no assistance from him in learning to read. But I could not go on alone. I must get some one to aid me in starting, or give up the effort to learn. This I could not bear to do. I longed to be able to read, and so I cast about me to see what I could do next. I thought of a kind boy at the bake-house, near my own age. I thought he would help me, and so I went to him, showed my book, and asked him to teach me the letters. He told their names, and went over the whole alphabet with me three times. By this assistance I learned a few more of the letters, so that I could remember them afterwards when I sat down alone and tried to call them over. I could now pick out and name five or six of the letters in any part of the book. I felt then that I was getting along, and the consciousness that I was making progress, though slow and painful, was joy and hope to my sorrowing heart, such as I never felt before. I could not with safety go to the bake-house, as there I was exposed to detection by the sudden entrance of customers or idlers. I wanted to get a teacher who would give me a little aid each day, and now I set about securing this object. As kind Providence would have it, I easily succeeded, and on this wise: A little boy, Hiram Bricket, ten years old, or about that age, came along by the store one day, on his way home from school, while my master was gone home to dinner, and James was in the front part of the store. I beckoned to Hiram to come round to the back door; and with him I made a bargain to meet me each day at noon, when I was allowed a little while to get my dinner, and to give me instruction in reading. I was to give him six cents a week. I met him the next day at his father's stable, the place agreed upon for our daily meeting; and, going into one of the stalls, the noble little Hiram gave me a thorough lesson in the alphabet. I learned it nearly all at that time, with what study I could give it by stealth during the day and night. And then again I felt lifted up and happy.

I was permitted to enjoy these advantages, however, but a short time. A black boy, belonging to Hiram's father, one day discovered our meeting and what we were doing. He told his master of it, and Hiram was at once forbidden this employment. I had then got along so that I was reading and spelling in words of two syllables. My noble little teacher was very patient and faithful with me, and my days were passing away in very great happiness under the consciousness that I was learning to read. I felt at night, as I went to my rest, that I was really beginning to be a *man*, preparing myself for a condition in life better and higher and happier than could belong to the ignorant *slave*. And in this blessed feeling I found, waking and sleeping, a most precious happiness.

After I was deprived of my kind little teacher, I plodded on the best way I could myself, and in this way I got into words of five syllables. I got some little time to study by daylight in the morning, before any of my master's family had risen. I got a moment's opportunity at noon, and sometimes at night. During the day I was in the back store a good deal, and whenever I thought I could have five minutes to myself, I would take my book and try to learn a little in reading and spelling. If I heard James, or master Jones, or any customer coming in, I would drop my book among the barrels, and pretend to be very busy shovelling the salt or doing some other work. Several times I came very near being detected. My master suspected something, because I was so still in the back room, and a number of times he came very slyly to see what I was about. But at such times I was always so fortunate as to hear his tread or see his shadow on the wall in time to hide away my book.

When I had got along to words of five syllables, I went to see a colored friend, Ned Cowan, whom I knew I could trust. I told him I was trying to learn to read, and asked him to help me a little. He said he did not dare to give me any instruction, but he heard me read a few words, and then told me I should learn if I would only persevere as nobly as I had done thus far. I told him *how* I had got along, and what difficulties I had met with. He encouraged me, and spoke very kindly of my efforts to improve my condition by getting learning. He told me I had got along far enough to get another book, in which I could learn to write the letters, as well as to read. He told me where and how to procure this book. I followed his directions, and obtained another spelling-book at Worcester's store, in Wilmington. Jacob showed me a little about writing. He set me a copy, first of straight marks. I now got me a box which I could hide under my bed, some ink, pens, and a bit of candle. So, when I went to bed, I pulled my box out from under my cot, turned it up on end, and began my first attempt at writing. I worked away till my candle was burned out, and then lay down to sleep. Jacob next set me a copy which he called pot-hooks; then, the letters of the alphabet. These letters were also in my new spelling-book, and, according to Jacob's directions, I set them before me for a copy, and wrote on these exercises till I could form all the letters and call them by name. One evening I wrote out my name in large letters — THOMAS JONES. This I carried to Jacob, in a great excitement of happiness, and he warmly commended me for my perseverance and diligence.

About this time I was at the store early one morning, and, thinking I was safe from all danger for a few minutes, had seated myself in the back store on one of the barrels, to study in my precious spelling-book. While I was absorbed in this happy enterprise, my master came in, much earlier than usual, and I did not hear him. He came directly into the back store. I saw his shadow on the wall just in time to throw my book over in among the barrels before he could see what it was, although he saw that I had thrown something quickly away. His suspicion was aroused. He said that I had been stealing something out of the store, and fiercely ordered me to get what I had thrown away just as he was coming in at the door. Without a moment's hesitation, I determined to save my precious book and my future opportunities to learn out of it. I knew if my book was discovered that all was lost, and I felt prepared for any hazard or suffering rather than give up my book and my hopes of improvement. So I replied at once to his questions, that I had not thrown anything away; that I had not stolen anything from the store; that I did not have anything in my hands which I could throw away when he came in. My master declared in a high passion that I was lying, and ordered me to begin and roll away the barrels. This I did; but managed to keep the book slipping along so that he could not see it, as he stood in the doorway. He charged me again with stealing and throwing something away, and I again denied the charge. In a great rage, he got down his long, heavy cowhide, and ordered me to strip off my jacket and shirt, saying, with an oath, "I will make you tell me what it was you had when I came." I stripped myself and came forward, according to his directions, at the same time denying his charge with great earnestness of tone, and look, and manner. He cut me on my naked back, perhaps thirty times, with great severity, making the blood flow freely. He then stopped, and asked me what I had thrown away as he came in. I answered again that I had thrown nothing away. He swore terribly; said he was certain I was lying, and declared he would kill me if I did not tell him the truth. He whipped me the second time with greater severity, and at greater length than before. He then repeated his question, and I answered again as before. I was determined to die, if I could possibly bear the pain, rather than give up my dear book. He whipped me the third time, with the same result as before, and then seizing hold of my shoulders, turned me round as though he would inflict on my quivering flesh still another scourging, but he saw the deep gashes he had already made, and the blood already flowing under his cruel infliction, and his stern purpose failed him. He said, "Why, Tom, I didn't think I had cut you so bad;" and saying that, he stopped, and told me to put on my shirt again. I did as he bade me, although my coarse shirt touching my raw back put me to a cruel pain. He then went out, and I got my book and hid it safely away before he came in again. When I went to the house my wounds had dried, and I was in an agony of pain. My mistress told the servant girl, Rachel, to help me off with my shirt, and to wash my wounds for me, and put on to them some sweet oil. The shirt was dried to my back so that it could not be got off without tearing off some of the skin with it. The pain, upon doing this, was greater even than I had endured from my cruel whipping. After Rachel had got my shirt off, my mistress asked me what I had done for which my master had whipped me so severely. I told her he had accused me of stealing when I had not, and then had whipped me to make me own it.

While Rachel was putting on the sweet oil my master came in, and I could hear mistress scolding him for giving me such an inhuman beating, when I had done nothing. He said in reply that Tom was an obstinate liar, and that was the reason why he had whipped me.

But I got well of my mangled back, and my book was still left. This was my best, my constant friend. With great earnestness, I snatched every moment I could get, morning, noon, and night, for study. I had begun to read; and, oh! how I loved to study, and to dwell on the thoughts which I gained from reading! About this time I read a piece in my book about God. It said that "God, who sees and knows all our thoughts, loves the good and makes them happy; while he is angry with the bad, and will punish them for all their sins." This made me feel very unhappy, because I was sure I was not good in the sight of God. I thought about this, and couldn't get it out of my mind a single hour. So I went to James Galley, a colored man, who exhorted the slaves sometimes on Sunday, and told him my trouble, asking, "What shall I do?" He told me about Jesus, and told me I must pray the Lord to forgive me and help me to be good and happy. So I went home, and went down cellar and prayed, but I found no relief, no comfort for my unhappy mind. I felt so bad that I could not study my book. My master saw that I looked very unhappy, and he asked me what ailed me. I did not dare *now* to tell a lie, for I wanted to be good, that I might be happy. So I told my master just how it was with me; and then he swore terribly at me, and said he would whip me if I did not give over praying. He said there was no heaven and no hell, and that Christians were all hypocrites, and that there was nothing after this life, and that he would not permit me to go moping round, praying and going to the meetings. I told him I could not help praying, and then he cursed me in a great passion, and declared he would whip me if he knew of my going on any more in that foolish way. The next night I was to a meeting, which was led by Jack Cammon, a free colored man, and a class-leader in the Methodist church. I was so much overcome by my feelings that I stayed very late. They prayed for me, but I did not yet find any relief; I was still very unhappy. The next morning my master came in and asked me if I went the night before to the meeting. I told him the truth. He said, "Didn't I tell you I would whip you if you went nigh these meetings, and didn't I tell you to stop this foolish praying?" I told him he did, and if he would, why, he might whip me, but still I could not stop praying, because I wanted to be good, that I might be happy and go to heaven. This reply made my master very angry. With many bitter oaths, he said he had promised me a whipping, and now he should be as good as his word. And so he was. He whipped me, and then forbade, with bitter threatenings, my praying any more, and especially my going again to meeting. This was Friday morning. I continued to pray for comfort and peace. The next Sunday I went to meeting. The minister preached a sermon on being born again, from the words of Jesus to Nicodemus.[2] All this only deepened my trouble of mind. I returned home very unhappy. Collins, a free man of color, was at the meeting, and told my master that I was there. So on Monday morning my master whipped me again, and once more forbade my going to meeting and praying. The next Sunday there was a class meeting, led by Binney Pennison, a colored free man. I asked my master, towards night, if I might go out. I told him I did not feel well. I wanted to go to the class-meeting. Without asking me *where* I was going, he said I might go. I went to the class. I stayed very late, and I was so overcome by my feelings that I could not go home that night. So they carried me to Joseph Jones's cabin, a slave of Mr. Jones. Joseph talked and prayed with me nearly all night. In the morning I went home as soon as it was light, and, for fear of master, I asked Nancy, one of the slaves, to go up into mistress' room and get the store key for me, that I might go and open the store. My master told her to go back and tell me to come up. I obeyed with many fears. My master asked me where I had been the night before. I told him the whole truth. He cursed me again, and said he should whip me for my obstinate disobedience; and he declared he would kill me if I did not promise to obey him. He refused to listen to my mistress, who was a professor, and who tried to intercede for me. And, just as soon as he had finished threatening me with what he would do, he ordered me to take the key and go and open the store. When he came into the store that morning, two of his neighbors, Julius Dumbiven, and McCauslin, came in too. He called me up and asked me again where I stayed last night. I told him with his boy, Joseph. He said he knew that was a lie; and he immediately sent off for Joseph to confirm his suspicions. He ordered me to strip off my clothes, and, as I did so, he took down the cowhide, heavy and stiff with blood which he had before drawn from my body with that cruel weapon, and which was congealed upon it. Dumbiven professed to be a Christian, and he now came forward, and earnestly interceded for me, but to no purpose, and then he left. McCauslin asked my master if he did not know that a slave was worth more money after he became pious than he was before. And why, then, he said, should you forbid Tom going to meeting and praying? He replied that religion was all a damned mockery, and he was not going to have any of his slaves praying and whining round about their souls. McCauslin then left. Joseph came and told the same story about the night before that I had done; and then he began to beg master not to whip me. He cursed him and drove him off. He then whipped me with great severity, inflicting terrible pain at every blow upon my quivering body, which was still very tender from recent lacerations. My suffering was so great that it seemed to me I should die. He paused at length, and asked me would I mind him and stop praying. I told him I could not promise him not to pray any more, for I felt that I must and should pray as long as I lived. "Well, then, Tom," he said, "I swear that I will whip you to death." I told him I could not help myself, if he was determined to kill me, but that *I must pray while I lived.* He then began to whip me the second time, but soon stopped, threw down the bloody cowhide, and told me to go wash myself in the river, just back of the store, and then dress myself, and if I was determined to be a fool, why, I must be one. My mistress now interceded earnestly for me with my cruel master. The next sabbath was love-feast,[3] and I felt very anxious to join in that feast. This I could not do without a paper from my master, and so I asked mistress to help me. She advised me to be patient, and said she would help me all she could. Master refused to give any paper, and so I could not join in the love-feast the next day.

On the next Friday evening I went to the prayer meeting. Jack Cammon was there, and opened the meeting with prayer. Then Binney Pennison gave out the sweet hymn, which begins in these words:

"Come, ye sinners, poor and needy,
   Weak and wounded, sick and sore."[4]

I felt that it all applied most sweetly to my condition, and I said in my heart, *I* will come *now* to Jesus, and *trust* in him. So when those who felt anxious were requested to come forward and kneel within the altar for prayer, I came and knelt down. While Jack Cammon was praying for me, and for those who knelt by my side, my burden of sorrow, which had so long weighed me down, was removed. I felt the glory of God's love warming my heart, and making me very happy. I shouted aloud for joy, and tried to tell all my poor slave brothers and sisters, who were in the house, what a dear Saviour I had found, and how happy I felt in his precious love. Binney Pennison asked me if I could forgive my master. I told him I could, and did, and that I could pray God to forgive him, too, and make him a good man. He asked me if I could tell my master of the change in my feelings. I told him I should tell him in the morning. "And what," he said, "will you do if he whips you still for praying and going to meeting?" I said, "I will ask Jesus to help me to bear the pain, and to forgive my master for being so wicked." He then said, "Well, then, Brother Jones, I believe that you are a Christian."

A good many of us went from the meeting to a brother's cabin, where we began to express our joy in happy songs. The palace of General Dudley was only a little way off, and he soon sent over a slave with orders to stop our noise, or he would send the patrollers upon us. We then stopped our singing, and spent the remainder of the night in talking, rejoicing and praying. It was a night of very great happiness to me. The contrast between my feelings then, and for many weeks previous, was very great. Now, all was bright and joyous in my relations towards my precious Saviour. I felt certain that Jesus was my Saviour, and in this blessed assurance a flood of glory and joy filled my happy soul. But this sweet night passed away, and, as the morning came, I felt that I must go home, and bear the *slave's heavy cross*. I went, and told my mistress the blessed change in my feelings. She promised me what aid she could give me with my master, and enjoined upon me to be patient and very faithful to his interest, and, in this way, I should at length wear out his opposition to my praying and going to meeting.

I went down to the store in a very happy state of mind. I told James my feelings. He called me a fool, and said master would be sure to whip me. I told him I hoped I should be able to bear it, and to forgive master for his cruelty to me. Master came down, talked with me a while, and told me he should whip me because I had disobeyed him in staying out all night. He had told me he should whip me if ever I did so, and he should make every promise good. So I began to take off my clothes. He called me a crazy fool, and told me to keep my clothes on till he told me to take them off. He whipped me over my jacket; but I enjoyed so much peace of mind that I scarcely felt the cowhide. This was the last whipping that Mr. Jones inflicted upon me.

I was then nearly eighteen years old. I waited and begged for a paper to join the church six months before I could get it. But all this time I was cheerful, as far as a slave can be, and very earnest to do all I could for my master and mistress. I was resolved to convince them that I was happier and better for being a Christian; and my master at last acknowledged that he could not find any fault with my conduct, and that it was impossible to find a more faithful slave than I was to him. And so, at last, he gave me a paper to Ben English, the leader of the colored members, and I joined the love feast, and was taken into the church on trial for six months. I was put into Billy Cochrane's class. At the expiration of six months, I was received into the church in full fellowship, Quaker Davis's class. I remained there three years. My master was much kinder after this time than he had ever been before; and I was allowed some more time to myself than I had been before. I pursued my studies as far as I could, but I soon found the utter impossibility of carrying on my studies as I wished to do. I was a slave, and all avenues to real improvement I found guarded with jealous care and cruel tenacity against the despised and desolated bondman.

I still felt a longing desire to improve, to be free, but the conviction was getting hold of my soul that I was only struggling in vain when seeking to elevate myself into a manly and happy position. And now my mind was fast sinking into despair. I could read and write, and often enjoyed much happiness in poring over the very few books I could obtain; and especially, at times, I found great peace in reading my old worn Testament. But I wanted now that hope which had filled my mind with such joy when I first began to learn to read. I found much happiness in prayer. But here, also, my mind labored in sadness and darkness much of the time. I read in my Testament that Jesus came from the bright heaven of his glory into this selfish and cruel world, to seek and to save the lost. I read and pondered with deep earnestness on the blessed rule of heavenly love which Jesus declared to be the whole of man's duty to his fellow: each to treat his brother as he would be treated. I thought of the command given to the followers of the loving Saviour, to teach all nations to obey the blessed precepts of the gospel. I considered that eighteen hundred years had gone by since Jesus plead for man's redemption and salvation, and, going up to heaven, has left His work of mercy to be finished by His children, and then I thought that I and thousands of my brothers and sisters, loving the Lord and pressing on to a blessed and endless home in His presence, were slaves — branded, whipped, chained; deeply, hopelessly degraded — thus degraded and outraged, too, in a land of bibles and sabbaths and churches, and by professed followers of the Lord of Love. And often, such thoughts were too much for me. In an agony of despair, I have at times given up prayer and hope together, believing that my master's words were true, that "religion is a cursed mockery, and the Bible a lie." May God forgive me for doubting, at such times, his justice and love. There was but one thing that saved me from going at once and fully into dark infidelity, when such agony assailed my bleeding heart—the memory of seasons of unspeakable joy in prayer, when love and faith were strong in my heart. The sweet remembrance of these dear hours would draw me back to Jesus and to peace in his mercy. Oh, that all true Christians knew just how the slave feels in view of the religion of this country, by whose sanction men and women are bound, branded, bought and sold!

About this time my master was taken sick. On Sunday he was prostrated by mortal pains; and on Friday the same week he died. He left fifteen slaves; I was purchased by Owen Holmes [5] for $435. I was then in my twenty-third year. I had just passed through the darkest season of despairing agony that I had yet known. This came upon me in consequence of the visit, which I have already described, to my dear old desolate home. About this time, too, I entered on a new and distinct period of life, which I will unfold in another chapter. I will close this period of sorrow and shame with a few lines of touching interest to my mind:

> Who shall avenge the slave? I stood and cried;
> The earth, the earth, the echoing sea replied.
> I turned me to the ocean, but each wave
> Declined to be the avenger of the slave.
> Who shall avenge the slave? my species cried;
> The wind, the flood, the lightnings of the sky.
> I turned to these, from them one echo ran,
> The right avenger of the slave is man.
> Man was my fellow; in his sight I stood,
> Wept and besought him by the voice of blood.
> Sternly he looked as proud on earth he trod,
> Then said, the avenger of the slave is GOD.
> I looked in prayer towards Heaven, a while 't was still,
> And then methought, God's voice replied, I WILL.[6]

CHAPTER SECOND.

I enter now upon a new development of wrongs and woes which I as a slave was called to undergo. I must go back some two or three years from the time when my master died, and I was sold to Owen Holmes. The bitterness of persecution which Master Jones had kept up against me so long, because I would try to serve the Lord, had passed away. I was permitted to pray and go to our meetings without molestation. My master laid aside his terrible severity toward me. By his treatment to me afterwards, he *seemed* to feel that he had done wrong in scourging me as he had done, because I could not obey his wicked command to stop praying, and keep away from the meetings. For, after the time of my joining the church, he allowed me to go to all the meetings, and granted me many other little favors, which I had never before received from him. About this time I began to feel very lonely. I wanted a friend to whom I could tell my story of sorrows, of unsatisfied longing, of new and fondly cherished plans. I wanted a companion whom I could love with all my warm affections, who should love me in return with a true and fervent heart, of whom I might think when toiling for a selfish, unfeeling master, who shall dwell fondly on my memory when we were separated during the severe labors of the day, and with whom I might enjoy the blessed happiness of social endearments after the work of each day was over. My heart yearned to have a home, if it was only the wretched home of the unprotected slave, to have a wife to love me and to love. It seems to me that no one can have such fondness of love and such intensity of desire for *home* and home affections, as the poor slave. Despised and trampled upon by a cruel race of unfeeling men, the bondman must die in the prime of his wretched life, if he finds no refuge in a dear home, where love and sympathy shall meet him from hearts made sacred to him by his own irrepressible affection and tenderness for them. And so I sought to love and win a true heart in return. I did this, too, with the full knowledge of the desperate agony that the slave husband and father is exposed to. Had I not seen this in the anguish of my own parents? Yea, I saw it in every public auction, where men and women and children were brought upon the block, examined, and bought. I saw it on such occasions, in the hopeless agony depicted on the countenance of husband and wife there separated to meet no more in this cruel world; and in the screams of wild despair and useless entreaty which the mother, then deprived of her darling child, sent forth. I heard the doom which stares every slave parent in the face each waking and sleeping hour of an unhappy life. And yet I sought to become a husband and a father, because I felt that I could live no longer unloved and unloving. I was married to Lucilla Smith, the slave to Mrs. Moore. We *called* it and *we considered* it a *true marriage*, although we knew well that marriage was not permitted to the slaves as a sacred right of the loving heart. Lucilla was seventeen years old when we were married. I loved her with all my heart, and she gave me a return for my affection with which I was contented. Oh, God of love thou knowest what happy hours we have passed in each other's society in our poor cabin! When we knelt in prayer, we never forgot to ask God to save us from the misery of cruel separation, while life and love were our portion. Oh, how we have talked of this dreadful fate, and wept in mingling sorrow, as we thought of our desolation, if we should be parted and doomed to live on weary years, away from each other's dear presence! We had three dear little babes. Our fondness for our precious children increased the current feeling of love for each other, which filled our hearts. They were bright, precious things, those little babes; at least so they seemed to us. Lucilla and I were never tired of planning to improve their condition, as far as might be done for slaves. We prayed with new fervency to our Father in Heaven to protect our precious babes. Lucilla was very proud of me, because I could read and write, and she often spoke of my teaching our dear little ones, and then she would say, with tears, "Who knows, Thomas, but that *they* may yet be *free and happy?*" Lucilla was a valuable slave to her mistress. She was a seamstress, and very expert at her needle; I had a constant dread that Mrs. Moore, her mistress, would be in want of money, and sell my dear wife. We constantly dreaded a final separation. Our affection for each other was very strong, and this made us always apprehensive of a cruel parting. These fears were well founded as our sorrowing hearts too soon learned. A few years of very pure and constant happiness for slaves, passed away, and we were parted to meet but once again till we meet in eternity. Mrs. Moore left Wilmington, and moved to Newbern.[7] She carried with her my beloved Lucilla and my three children, Annie, four years old; Lizzie, two and a half years; and our sweet little babe, Charlie. She remained there eighteen months, and oh, how lonely and dreary and desponding were those months of lonely life to my crushed heart! My dear wife and my precious children were seventy-four miles distant from me, carried away from me in utter scorn of my beseeching words. I was tempted to put an end to my wretched life. I thought of my dear family by day and by night. A deep despair was in my heart, such as no one is called to bear in such cruel, crushing power as the poor slave, severed forever from the objects of his love by the cupidity of his brother. But that dark time of despair passed away, and I saw once more my wife and children. Mrs. Moore left Newbern for Tuscaloosa, Ala., and passing through Wilmington on her journey, she spent one night in her old home. That night I passed with my wife and children. Lucilla had pined away under the agony of our separation, even more than I had done. That night she wept on my bosom, and we mingled bitter tears together. Our dear children were baptised in the tears of agony that were wrung from our breaking hearts. The just God will remember that night in the last award that we and our oppressors are to receive.

The next morning Mrs. Moore embarked on board the packet. I followed my wife and children to the boat, and parted from them without a word of farewell. Our sobs and tears were our only adieu. Our hearts were too full of anguish for any other expression of our hopeless woe. I have never seen that dear family since, nor have I heard from them since I parted from them there. God only knows the bitterness of my agony, experienced in the separation of my wife and children from me. The memory of that great woe will find a fresh impress on my heart while that heart shall beat. How will the gifted and the great meet the charge against them at the great day, as the judge shall say to them, in stern displeasure, "I was sick, destitute, imprisoned, helpless, and ye ministered not unto me; for when ye slighted and despised these wretched, pleading slaves, ye did these acts of scorn against me. Depart, ye workers of iniquity?"

After my purchase by Owen Holmes, I hired my time at $150 per year, paid monthly. I rented a house of Dr. E. J. Desert. I worked, loading and unloading vessels that came into Wilmington, and could earn from one dollar to a dollar and a quarter a day. While my wife and family were spared to bless my home by their presence and love, I was comparatively happy. But I found then that the agony of that terrible thought, "I am a slave, my wife is a slave, my precious children are slaves," grew bitter and insupportable, just as the happiness in the society of my beloved home became more distinct and abounding. And this one cup of bitterness was ever at my lips. Hearts of kind sympathy and tender pity, did I not drain that cup of bitter woe to its very dregs, when my family were carried off into returnless exile, and I was left a heart-broken, lonely man? Can you be still inactive while thousands are drinking that potion of despair every year in this land of schools and bibles? After I parted from my family, I continued to toil on, but not as I had done before. My home was darker than the holds of the ships in which I worked. Its light, the bright, joyous light of love and sympathy and mutual endearments, was quenched. Ah, me, how dark it left my poor heart! It was colder than the winter wind and frost; the warm sunshine was snatched away and my poor heart froze in its bitter cold. Its gloom was deeper than the prison or cave could make it. Were not there the *deserted* chairs and beds, once occupied by the objects of a husband's and a father's love? Deserted! How, and why? Is not the answer the unqualified condemnation of the government and religion of this land? I could not go into my cold, dark, cheerless house; the sight of its deserted room was despair to my soul. So I worked on, taking jobs whenever I could get them, and working often till nearly morning, and never going to my home for rest till I could toil no more. And so I passed four years, and I began to feel that I could not live in utter loneliness any longer. My heart was still and always yearning for affection and sympathy and loving communion. My wife was torn from me. I had ceased to hope for another meeting with her in this world of oppression and suffering; so I sat down and wrote to Lucilla, that I could live alone no longer, and saying to her the sad farewell, which we could not say when we were sundered. I asked Mary R. Moore to come and cheer me in my desolate home. She became my wife, and, thank God, *she* has been rescued from slavery by the blessing of God and my efforts to save her. She is now my wife, and she is with me to-day, and till death parts us, secure from the iron hand of slavery. Three of our dear children are with us, too, in the old Commonwealth. I cannot say they are in a *free* land, for, even here, in the city of Boston, where I am told is kept the old cradle of liberty, *my* precious children are excluded from the public schools, because their skin is black. Still, Boston is better than Wilmington, inasmuch as the rulers of this place permit me to send my children to any school at all. After my second marriage, I hired my wife of her master, and paid for her time $48 a year, for three years. We had one child while Mary was a slave. That child is still in chains. The fourth year, by the aid of a white friend, I purchased my wife for $350. We had before determined to try to accomplish this enterprise in order that our dear babes might be free. Besides I felt that I could not bear another cruel separation from my wife and children. Yet the dread of it was strong and unceasing upon my mind. So we made a box, and through a hole in the top, we put in every piece of money, from five cents up to a dollar, that we could save from our hard earnings. This object nerved us for unceasing toil, for twenty months or about that time. What hopes and fears beset us as those months wore away! I have been compelled to hide that box in a hole dug for it, when I knew the patrollers were coming to search my cabin. For well did I know, if they found my box, I should be penniless again. How often have I started and turned, in sudden and terrible alarm, as I have dropped a piece of money into my box, and heard its loud ring upon the coin below, lest some prowling enemy should hear it, and steal from me my hoarded treasure! And how often have I started up in my sleep as the storm has beat aloud upon my humble home, with the cry of unspeakable agony in my heart, "Then, O God they have taken my box, and my wife and babes are still slaves!" When my box was broken open, I still lacked a little of the $350 necessary to buy my wife. The kind friend who had promised to aid me in the contemplated purchase, made up the deficiency, and I became the owner of my wife. We had three children at this time, and oh, how my crushed heart was uplifted in its pride and joy, as I took them in my arms and thought that they were not slaves! These three children are with me and with their mother now, where the slave's chains and whips are heard no more. Oh, how sweet is freedom to man! But doubly dear is the consciousness to the father's heart, made bitter in its incurable woe by the degradation of slavery, that his dear child is never to be a slave! Would to God the fathers of this nation were all possessed of a true consciousness of these things; for then surely, they would will and secure the immediate ending of human bondage.

After I had purchased my wife, we still worked hard and saved our earnings with great care, in order to get some property in hand for future use. As I saved my earnings, I got a white man whom I thought my friend, (his name I choose to keep back for the present), to lay it out for me. In this way I became the owner of the cabin in which I lived, and two other small houses, all of which were held in the name of this supposed friend. He held them in his own name for me. A slave cannot hold property. I will here remark that I was deceived by this man; and when I ran away from my chains, after sending on my family, I was compelled to sacrifice the whole of this property. I left it, because I could not get my own from his hands, and came off entirely destitute. Thank God, I got away, and now I have no tears to shed over the loss of my houses.

During the winter of 1848-9, a kind lady came and told me that some white men were plotting to enslave my wife and children again. She advised me to get them off to the free States as quickly and secretly as possible. A lawyer of Wilmington told me they were not safe, unless emancipated by a special act of the Legislature. He was a member of the House, and tried to get through the House a bill for their emancipation. But there was so much ill feeling upon this question that he could not do it. The Legislature threw it aside at once. He then advised me to get them off to the free States as my only course to save them. This I determined to do if possible. I kept a good lookout for a vessel. I found one and made a bargain with the captain to take on board for New York a free colored woman and her three children. A kind friend gave me a certificate of their freedom to the captain, and I brought my wife and children on board at night, paid the captain $25 for their fare, and staid on the wharf in torturing fear till about sunrise, when I saw the vessel under way. It was soon out of sight. When I went home, I threw myself on my knees, and poured out my soul to God, to carry that ship and its precious cargo safely and swiftly on to a free haven and to guard and guide me soon to a free home with my beloved family. And so I kept on, praying, working, hoping, pining, for nearly three weeks, when I received the happy news that my dear ones were safe with a true-hearted friend in Brooklyn. I had notified him beforehand that they were coming; and now the good and glorious news came that they were safe with Robert H. Cousins, where the slave-holders could trouble them no more. I had arranged with Mary when she left, to come on myself as soon as I could get the money for my houses and land. She was to write to me as though she had gone to New York on a visit, intending to come back, and she was to speak of New York as if she did not like it at all. I knew my master would be very angry when he heard she had gone unbeknown to him, and I thought he would demand to see the letters my wife should get friends in New York to write to me for her; and so I made ready to meet and quiet his suspicions, while I was plotting my own escape. For more than three months I tried to get the money, or part of it, for my houses; but was put off and deceived, till I found I must come off without a cent of the property I had tried so hard to accumulate. I was required to call and see my master every day, because he suspected me of design to run away. He was taken suddenly sick, and then I started for my wife and children. Before I give a narrative of my escape, I will give copies of the letters which passed between me and my wife, while I remained in the land of bondage after her escape. These letters, with their post marks, are all in my possession, and can be examined by any one who may doubt their authenticity, or the fidelity with which they are here given. The kind friend who has written this narrative for me, has corrected some mistakes in the construction and spelling of these letters, and *some* he has left *uncorrected*. He has also omitted some repititions; otherwise they are given as exact copies. I wrote my own letters; my wife wrote by the help of a friend. I give all my letters, and the two from my wife which I was able to keep. The following was written soon after my wife started for New York:

WILMINGTON, N.C., July 11, 1849.

MY DEAR WIFE. — I write these few lines to inform you that I am well, and hope they may find you and the children well, and all the friends. My dear wife, I long to see you and the children one time more in this world. I hope to see you all soon. Don't get out of heart, for I will come as soon as I can. I hope it will not be long, for God will be my helper, and I feel he will help me. My dear wife, you must pray for me that God may help me. Tell John he must be a good boy till I see him. I must not forget sister Chavis. She must pray for me, that God may help me come out. Tell her I say that she must be faithful to God; and I hope, dear wife, that you will be faithful to God. Tell sister Chavis that Henry will be out soon, and he wants her to keep a good heart and he will send money out to her. Tell her he says she must write to him as soon as she can, for he will not stay long behind her. As soon as he gets his money he will come. I hope to see you all very soon. Tell my Brethering to pray for me, that God may help me get there safe, and make my way clear before me. Help me by your prayers, that God may be with me. Tell brother Robert H. Cousins that he must pray for me; for I long to meet him one time more in this world. Sister Tucker and husband give their love to you and sister Chavis, and say that you must pray for them. Dear wife, you may look for me soon. But what way I will come, I can't tell you now. You may look for me in three weeks from now. You must try and do the best you can till I come. You know how it is with me, and how I have to come. Tell the Church to pray for me, for I hope to reach that land if I live, and I want the prayers of all God's children. I can't say any more at this time; but I remain, your dear husband, till death,

THOMAS JONES.

P.S. — Dear wife, I want you to make out that you don't like New York. When you write to me you must say so. Do mind how you write.

The next letter was written before I had received any certain intelligence of my wife's arrival at New York.

WILMINGTON, N.C., July 17, 1849.

MY DEAR WIFE. — I write to tell you I am well, and I hope these few lines will find you and the children well. I long to see you all one time more. Do pray for me, that God may help me to get to you all. Do ask sister to pray the Lord to help me. I will trust in God, for I know that He is my friend, and He will help me. My dear wife, tell my children I say they must be good till I see them once more. Do give my love to brother R. H. Cousins, and tell him I hope to meet him in two or three weeks from now. Then I can tell him all I want to say to him. Tell sister Chavis I say, do not come back to this place till I come. Her husband says he wants her to stay, and he will come on soon. My dear wife I want you to do the best you can till I come. I will come as soon as I can. You and sister Chavis must live together, for you went together, and you must try to stay together. Do give my love to sister Johnson and husband, and all of my friends. Ask them all to pray for me, that God may be with me in all that I do to meet you all one time more. My dear wife, you know how I told you, you must mind how you write your letters. You must not forget to write as if you did not like New York, and that you would come home soon. You know what I told you to do, and now you must not forget it when you write. I will send you some money in my next letter. I have not sold my houses yet, and if I can't sell, I will leave them all, and come to you and the children. I will trust in that God who can help the poor. My dear, don't forget what I told you to do when you write. You know how I have to do. Be careful how you write. I hope to be with you soon, by the help of God. But, above all things, ask all to pray for me, that God may open the way for me to come safe. I hope to be with you soon, by the help of the Lord. Tell them if I never come, to go on, and may God help them to go forth to glorious war. Tell them to see on the mountain top the standard of God. Tell them to follow their Captain, and be led to certain victory. Tell them I can but sing with my latest breath, happy if I may to the last speak His name, preach Him to all, and cry, in death, "Behold the Lamb." Go on, my dear wife, and trust in God for all things.

I remain your husband,

THOMAS JONES.

Before I wrote the next, I received the happy news that my wife was safe with brother Cousins.

WILMINGTON, N.C., July 25, 1849.

MY DEAR WIFE. — Do tell my children they must be good children till I come to them; and you, my dear wife, must do the best you can; for I don't know how I will come, but I will do the best I can for you. I hope God will help me, for if He don't, I don't know what I will do. My dear wife, I have not sold my houses yet, but I will do the best I can. If I had money I would leave all I have and come, for I know the Lord will help me. It is for want of money that I can't come. But I hope, my dear wife, the Lord will help me out. Tell brother Cousins I hope he and all the people of God will pray for me; and you, my dear wife, must not forget to pray for me. Ask brother Cousins, if he pleases, to put my children to some school. Dear wife, you know the white people will read your letters to me; do mind how you write. No one but God knows my heart. Do pray for me.

I remain your husband till death,

THOMAS JONES.

P.S. — My dear wife, I received your letter the 24th of July, and was truly glad to hear you arrived safe in New York. Please tell brother Cousins I will write to him in a few days, and I will send you some money. My dear wife, do mind how you write. You must not forget I am in a slave place, and I can't buy myself for the money. You know how it is, and you must tell brother Cousins. I have not sold yet, but if I can't sell, I will come somehow, by the help of the Lord. John Holmes is still in my way. I want you to write a letter, and say in it, that you will be home in two months, so I can let them read it, for they think I will run away and come to you. So do mind how you write, for the Lord's sake.

THOMAS JONES.

The next letter was written to sister Chavis, who went on to New York, but got disheartened and came back to Wilmington.

WILMINGTON, N.C., Aug. 4, 1849.

MY DEAR SISTER. — I hope to see you in a few days, and all my friends. I hope, dear sister, you will not forget to pray for me, for by the help of God, I will see you in a few days. Your husband is coming on soon, but I will be on before him. I would have been on before now, but I could not get my money. I have had a hard time to get money to leave with. I am sorry to hear that you think we can't get a living where you are. My dear sister, a smart man can get a living anywhere in the world, if he try. Don't think we can't live out there, for I know God will help us. You know God has promised a living to all his children. Don't forget that God is ever present, for we must trust him till death. Don't get out of heart, for I know we can live out there, if any one can. You may look for me before your husband. Don't leave New York before I come, for you know what I told you before you left Wilmington. If you come back to this place before I get off, it will make it bad for me. You know what the white people here are. Please don't come yet.

I am, your brother in the Lord, till death,

THOMAS JONES.

P.S. — I sent the letter you wrote to Mr. John Ranks. I thought you will wait for a letter from your husband, and I hope you will be better satisfied in your mind that we can get a living out there. Your husband has wrote to you last week; I hope you have got the letter. Oh, that you may trust in God every day, for I know God is your friend, and you must pray night and day that He may help you. I long to see you one time more in this world. We went into the new Church on the 9th day of this month. God was with us on that day, and we had a good time. Though my time with them is short, I hope God will be with them, and may we all meet in the kingdom at last. So pray for me, my dear sister. Aunt Narvey has been dead nearly four weeks. She died happy in the Lord, and is gone home to rest. I hope we may meet in the kingdom at last. Good night, my dear sister.

THOMAS JONES.

The next letter is to my wife and brother Cousins, and explains itself.

WILMINGTON, August 7, 1849.

MY DEAR WIFE, — I long to see you once more in this world, and hope it will not be very long before I am with you. I am trying, my dear wife, to do all I can to get to you. But I hope you will not forget to mind how you write to me. If you should not mind how you write, you will do me great harm. You know I told you to write that you would be home in two months, or three months at the longest. But in two months I told them you would be home. Now, my dear, you must mind, and don't forget, for you know how it is here; a man can't say that his soul is his own; that is, a colored man. So do mind how you write to me. Tell sister Chavis I say she must write to me; and I hope soon I will write my last letter. I will let you know in my next letter how all things are with me. Dear wife, don't get out of heart, for God is my friend. The will of God is my sure defence, nor earth nor hell can pluck me thence, for God hath spoken the word. My dear wife, in reply to your kind letter, received the second day of this month, I have wrote these few lines. I hope you will pray for me. Your dear husband,

THOMAS JONES.

P.S. — To brother Cousins. — My dear brother, I hope you will not think hard of me for not writing to you, for you know how it is with me out here. God knows that I would write to you at any time, if it was not for some things. You know the white people don't like for us to write to New York. Now let me ask your prayers, and the prayers of the Church, and God's children, that I may see you all soon. I know that God is my friend, for He doth my burden bear. Though I am but dust and ashes, I bless God, and often feel the power of God. Oh, my brother, pray for me, who loves you all, for I have found of late much comfort in the word of God's love. When I come where you are, in the work of the Lord, and I hope the time will soon come when the gospel will be preached to the whole of mankind. Then go on, dear brother, and do all you can for the Lord. I hope the Lord will help me to get where you are at work soon. Nothing more, but I remain, your brother in the Lord,

THOMAS JONES.

The next is from my wife.

BROOKLYN, Aug. 10, 1849.

MY DEAR HUSBAND. — I got your kind letter of the 23d July, and rejoiced to hear that you was well. I have been very sick myself, and so has Alexander; but, thanks to the Lord, these lines leave me and the children right well. I hope in God they will find you and my son and my mother, and all enquiring friends, enjoying the same blessings. My dear, you requested me and Mrs. Chavis to stay together, but she has taken other people's advice beside mine and Mr. Cousins', and has gone away. She started for home before we knew a word of it. She left me on the eighth of this month. Do give my love to Betsey Webb and to her husband. Tell her I am sorry she has not come on before now. I am waiting to see her before I start for home. My dear husband, you know you ought to send me some money to pay my board. You know I don't love to live in this way with my children. It is true that brother Cousins has not said anything to me about it. You keep writing that you are going to send it in your next letter; you know I like to act independent, and I wish you to help me do so now, if you please. Do give my compliments to Aunt Moore, and tell her the children all send their love to her. They send their love to you, and say they want to kiss you mighty bad. The children send their love to brother Edward. I long to see you, husband. No more at present, but remain your loving wife till death,

RYNAR JONES.

The next letter is in answer to the letter from my wife given above.

WILMINGTON, N.C., Aug 12, 1849.

MY DEAR WIFE. — I received your paper of the 10th to-day. I am glad to hear that you are well, and the children and friends. I have written to brother Cousins, and told him to tell you that I had not sold out yet. But I hope to sell in a few days, and then I will send you some money. My dear wife, you know that I will do all I can for you and for my children, and that with all my heart. Do try and wait on me a few days, and I hope you will see me and the money too. I am trying to do all I can to sell out, but you know how it is here, and so does brother Cousins. I will do all I know, for I think of you, my dear wife and the children, day and night. If I can get my money, I will see you soon, by the help of God and my good friend, and that is a woman; she is waiting for me to come every day. My dear wife, all I want is money and your prayers, and the prayers of my friends. I know that God will help me out of my trouble; I know that God is my friend, and I will trust to Him. You wrote to me that Mrs. Chavis left New York. She has not got home yet. I hope, dear wife, that you have done all your part for her. Do give my love to brother Cousins; ask him to pray for me, and all God's people to pray for me, a poor slave at this time. My dear wife, since I wrote last I have seen much of the goodness of the Lord. Pray for me, that I may see more, and that I may trust in Him. My dear wife, I want you should pray for me night and day, till you see me. For, by the help of God, I will see you all soon. I think now it will be but a few days. Do give my love to my children, and tell them that I want to kiss them all. Good night, my dear, I must go to bed. It is one o'clock at night, and I have a pain in my head at this time. Do tell brother Cousins that I say he must look out for me on John street, in a few days. Nothing more, but I remain your husband till death,

THOMAS JONES.

Letter from my wife.

BROOKLYN, August 23, 1849.

MY DEAR HUSBAND. — It is with the affectionate feeling of a wife I received your letter of the 19th inst. It found me and the children well, and we were glad to hear that you was well. But we feel very sorry that you have not sold out yet; I was in hopes you would have sold by the time you promised, before I got home. Your letter found Mr. Cousins and his wife very sick. Mr. C. has not been out of the house going on two weeks. He was taken by this sickness, so common, which carries so many people off, but, by the help of God and good attendance, he is much on the mend, and his wife also. You ask how much I pay for board. It is three dollars a week for myself and children. In all the letters you have written to me, you don't say a word of mother or Edward. It makes me feel bad not to hear from them. Husband, I have not paid Mr. Cousins any board, and am waiting for you to send me some money. I will pray for you hourly, publicly and privately, and beseech the Almighty God, till I see you again. I shall trust in God; He will do all things for the best.

I am yours till death do us part.

RYNAR JONES.

Last letter to my wife from the land of bondage.

WILMINGTON, N.C., Aug. 30, 1849.

MY DEAR WIFE. — I have been quite sick for three weeks, but, thank God, I am better at this time, and hope these few lines will find you and the children all well. I hope, my dear wife, that you have not got out of heart looking for me; you know how it is here; I did think I would have my money here before this time. But I can't get it, and I will leave it all and come to you as soon as I can. So don't get out of heart, my dear wife; I have a hard trial here; do pray for me, that the Lord may help me to see you all soon. I think of you day and night, and my dear children; kiss them for me; I hope to kiss them soon. Edward is sold to Owen Holmes; but I think Mr. Josh. Wright will get him from H. I have done all I could for Edward. Don't think of coming back here, for I will come to you or die. But I want you should write one more letter to me, and say you will be home in a month. Mr. Dawson will be in New York next week, and you will see him; mind how you talk before him, for you know how it is, though he is a friend to me. Now, you must mind what I tell you my dear wife, for if you don't you will make it hard for me. Now, my dear wife, you must not come back here for your brother and sister; they talk too much; but mind what I say to you, for you know I will do all I can for you; you must not think that you will not get any money, for you shall have it soon. Don't get out of heart, my dear wife; I hope I shall see you soon. Nothing more, but I remain your husband till death.

THOMAS JONES.

Soon after dispatching this letter, I bargained, while my master lay sick, with the steward of the brig Bell, to stow me away in the hold of the ship, and take me on to New York. I paid him eight dollars, which was all the money I then had or could get. I went into the hold, with an allowance of biscuit and water, and the ship started. She was loaded with turpentine, and I found on the second day that I could not live out the passage there. So I told the steward, and he took me out in a state of great weakness, and stowed me away in one of the staterooms. Here I was discovered by the captain. He charged me with being a runaway slave, and said he should send me back by the first opportunity that offered. That day a severe storm came on, and for several days we were driven by the gale. I turned to and cooked for the crew. The storm was followed by a calm of several days; and then the wind sprung up again, and the captain made for port at once. I had reason to suspect, from the manner in which I was guarded, after the ship came to anchor off New York, that the captain was plotting to send me back. I resolved to peril life in a last effort to get on shore. So, while the captain was in the city, and the mate was busy in the cabin mending his clothes, I made a raft of such loose boards as I could get, and hastily bound them together, and committing myself to God, I launched forth upon the waves. The shore was about a mile distant; I had the tide in my favor, and with its help I had paddled one-fourth the distance, when the mate of the Bell discovered my escape, and made after me in the boat. I waved my old hat for help, and a boat, which seemed to be coming round not far from me, came to my rescue. I was taken on board. They asked me if I was a slave, and told me not to fear to tell the truth, for I was with friends, and they would protect me. I told them my circumstances just as they were. They were as good as their word. When the mate came up they ordered him to keep off, and told him they would prosecute him if he touched me. They took me to brother Cousins, and gave me a little money and some clothes in addition to all their other kindness.

The meeting with my wife and children I cannot describe. It was a moment of joy too deep and holy for any attempt to paint it. Husbands who love as I have loved, and fathers with hearts of fond, devoted affection, may *imagine* the scene and my feelings, as my dear wife lay sobbing in her joy in my arms, and my three dear little babes were clinging to my knees, crying "Pa has come; Pa has come." It was the happy hour of my life. I then felt repaid for all my troubles and toils to secure the freedom of my dear family and my own. O God, would that my other dear ones were here, too. God in mercy speed the day when right shall over might prevail, and all the downtrodden sons and daughters of toil and want shall be free, and pious, and happy.

I have but little more now to say. The Sabbath after my arrival in Brooklyn, I preached in the morning in the Bethel: I then came on to Hartford.[8] A gentleman kindly paid my passage to that place, and sent me an introduction to a true-hearted friend. I stayed in Hartford twenty-four hours; but finding I was pursued, and being informed that I should be safer in Massachusetts than in Connecticut, I came on to Springfield, and from thence to Boston, where I arrived, penniless and friendless, the 7th of October. A generous friend took me, though a stranger, in, and fed and cheered me. He loaned me five dollars to get my dear family to Boston. He helped me to get a chance to lecture in May Street Church, where I received a contribution of $2.58; also in Zion Church, where I obtained $2.33: and in the Bethel Church, where they gave me $3.53. And so I was enabled to get my family to Boston. Entirely destitute, without employment, I now met with a kind friend, who took me with him to Danvers. I lectured and preached in the Free Evangelical Church, and received most generous and opportune aid. They gave me ten dollars, and by their kindness they lifted up a sinking brother. The next Sabbath evening I lectured in the Wesleyan Church in Boston, and received a contribution of $3.33. During the week following I was assisted by the pastor of this church, and by several individual members. The next sabbath I spent with brother Flanders of Exeter, N.H. He gave me a brother's warm welcome. I preached for him in the Wesleyan Church, of which he is pastor, in the morning, and lectured in the evening to a full and attentive house. Here I received a generous contribution of nearly ten dollars. To-morrow is Thanksgiving Day. God will know, and He alone can know, the deep and fervent gratitude and joy with which I shall keep it, as I gather my friends, and my dear family, around me to celebrate the unspeakable goodness of God to me, and to speak with swelling hearts of the kindness of the dear friends who have poured upon our sadness and fears the sunlight of sympathy, love, and generous aid. May the blessing of heaven rest down now and forever upon them, is the prayer of their grateful brother, and of his dear family, by their kindness saved from pinching want.

But alas! it was not long before I found that I was not yet free. I had not yet slipped from the chain. The Fugitive Slave Law[9] drove me from my kind friends in New England, and I found that my wanderings were not yet ended. I took refuge in the British Provinces, where God had provided a house of refuge for the houseless, homeless slave. Tribulation and distress, with many kind dealings of Providence, and wonderful deliverances, have since been my lot. I hope to be able to tell, in another narrative, of my adventures after the close of this story of the kindness of friends, and the goodness of God.

PART SECOND.

Part First of my experience ended with my flight to the British provinces, where I remained four years. Of what transpired there and subsequent to my return to the States I shall hereafter speak somewhat in detail, but before doing so I desire to rehearse a few additional experiences of my life while yet a slave. It will be remembered that on page thirty [page 231 of this edition], Part First, reference is made to the selling of my wife and children. I have repeatedly been requested to give a more particular account of that trans- action. I will endeavor to do so, notwithstanding its memory is peculiarly painful even at this late day. I was living in Wilmington, N.C., at the time, engaged in the business of stevedore, having hired my labor of my master, Mr. Owen Holmes, for that purpose. I had several men in my employ, and on the day of the sale we were at work stowing a vessel. We had partly fin- ished the job when one of my neighbors came on board and said I must go home at once, my wife wanted to see me. I inquired what for. "Oh wait till you get there." he replied. I said, "I can't go just now, the work is so press- ing." He then told me that my wife and children had been sold, and I must go home if I wanted to see them again. "Oh, my God," said I, "can it be so?" I then ran to the companion-way and called to the Captain, but he had gone on shore. I told the mate what I wanted, and he gave me permission to go home. Directing my men to keep at their work until I returned, I set out for my humble cabin. (The events just narrated transpired on board the Brig Mentis, from Philadelphia, owned by Mr. James Patent.) On my arrival home I found my wife's master already there to take her and the little ones away. As I entered the cabin he said, "Well, old man, are these your wife and children?" "Yes sir," I replied. "Well, I have bought them." "But won't you sell them to my master," I inquired, "I know he will buy them?" "Oh no," "I have bought your wife for a seamstress and I can't let her go." "But won't you let her go for the sake of the children," I still entreated. He still refused to part with her. Pretty soon he ordered her to get ready to go. She at once arose, her face bathed in tears, with two of the children clinging to her dress, and the third, a babe nine months old, resting on her arm. I gave a hand to each of the two children, Charlie and Sarah. A few colored friends who were present assisted in carrying some bundles, and thus we proceeded to the vessel that was to bear my dear ones from my sight forever. As we walked along, many of my wife's acquaintances came out to bid her good-bye. This seemed greatly to offend her master, and after a time he ordered her not to stop again to speak to any one. At the landing I found my master waiting for me. I told him what had taken place, and pointed out the man who had purchased my wife and children. He immediately went to him and inquired what he would take for them. The man said he would not sell them at any price. "Will you take a thousand dollars for them?" "No sir, I don't want to sell them." "Well," said my master. "If you won't sell them its no use talking any more, but for my own part I never would separate a slave and his family. I am an owner of slaves myself, but I never have gone as far as that." Then turning to me, he continued, "Well, Peter,[10] I have done all I can for you."

After bidding my wife and children good-bye, he returned to his office, directing me to follow when I got through there. And now comes the sorest trial of my whole life. My wife's master ordered her to go on board. We stepped to the vessel's side, and I passed the little girl over to the mate. She clung to me as long as she could crying "Oh, let me go back to my father!" The little boy soon followed, and was placed on deck beside his sister. I then passed over the little babe; there were tears in the mate's eyes as he received it, and an evident sympathy in his heart which he could not conceal. Having thus disposed of the little ones, I took my wife's arm to assist her on board. Just then her master ordered the mate not to let any more "niggers" get on board. I persisted, however, in accompanying her, and, standing there on the vessel's deck we bade each other a last farewell. From that hour to the present I have neither seen nor heard from any one of them. I shall probably never know their fate until the last great day, when both the master and the slave appear before the judgment seat of Christ. I watched the vessel until it disappeared from view, and then turned my steps in the direction of my master's office. As I entered he inquired if my wife and children had gone. I bowed my head in reply, for I was too full for utterance. He turned to his brother Richard, and with a terrible oath said, "Richard, this is too bad." "Well, we can't help it as I see," his brother replied. "Can't help it," said my master. "Can't help it. There will be some way to help it before long. For my own part I would be willing to let all my slaves go free at once. I know they would never leave me to want for anything. And besides, if compelled to, I can live by my profession." (He was a lawyer.) He then told me not to worry about my wife and he would have her back if money would do it. Her master had not yet left the place, and he would see him again, and see what could be done. Thus encouraged I returned to the vessel to look after my men. The Captain met me as I stepped on board and said he had heard of the sale of my

wife and children, and expressed a hearty sympathy for me in my great af-
fliction. He inquired if my wife was a Christian. I replied that she was. "Well,
Stevedore, you must be faithful, and I hope you will one day meet your dear
ones in a world where partings are unknown." He then came up close to my
side, and in a low tone said, "Stevedore, I believe the time is coming when
you and all your oppressed brethren and sisters will be free. Your friends at
the North are earnestly praying and laboring for the accomplishment of that
end." He also spoke of one Mr. Garrison,[11] who was holding conventions
and delivering lectures for the purpose of arousing public sentiment against
the awful sin of human slavery. I thanked him for the encouraging words he
had spoken, and went down in the hold to look after the men. As soon as
they saw me they began to inquire about my wife and children. I told them
they had gone. I could say no more, for my very heart seemed ready to break
with grief. One of the men, seeing how I felt, said to the others, "Let us go
aft and pray for Uncle Peter." He led the way and we all followed. I could
not control my feelings sufficiently to pray audibly, but such as could did.
And they prayed as only those can pray who have experienced a kindred
sorrow,—prayed that God would sustain and comfort me in that hour of
need. Two of the men were not professing Christians, but they knelt down
with their companions and freely wept while prayer was being offered. At
sunset we quit work. Two of the brethren invited me to go to their houses
for the night, but I declined doing so, preferring to return to my own home
where I could be alone with God. No language can portray the feeling of
desolation that came over me as I entered it that evening; and falling on my
knees, poured forth my soul's deep agony. About midnight I went out into
the garden. The moon and stars shone brightly down upon me as I knelt and
prayed again for strength to bear my heavy burden, wondering the while
if I should ever again behold the loved ones so suddenly and so wickedly
torn from my embrace. Anxiously I waited for the dawn of day, hoping that
my master would succeed in his endeavors to buy back my wife and children, yet fearing all the while that their master would still refuse to part with
them. In the afternoon of the next day my master came to the vessel where I
worked, and told me that he had seen Mr. Moore and offered him fourteen
hundred dollars for them, but he would not let them go at any price. I waited
almost a month, and then I got a white man to write a letter to my wife, directing it to Lucy La Moore, Tuscaloosa, Alabama. Three months passed,
but no answer was received. I then got another white man to write, in his
own name, to Mr. Moore, without referring to me at all. The result was the
same. At last I got my master to write to the postmaster at Tuscaloosa, and

inquired if Mr. Moore resided there. The postmaster replied, that so far as he knew no such person had ever been in that vicinity. With this my efforts to ascertain what had become of my family ceased until after the war.

I remained with Mr. Owen Holmes until his death, and it is proper that I should bear testimony to his uniform kindness in dealing with his slaves. He was at heart an Abolitionist, though he never professed as much in public. His slaves were left him by his father, and though still held as such, their bondage was merely nominal. They were, for the most part, employed on a plantation in Sampson county.[12] A few, myself included, were kept at Wilmington with the family. This plantation was generally left in charge of a trusted slave named Daniel, who took the entire management of its affairs, and paid to the master the profits. Every Spring Mr. Holmes was accustomed to take his family out there, to remain during the sickly season. At such times I went with them, and acted as general waiter for the family. Previous to my first Summer at the plantation, no religious service of any kind had ever been held there. On the very day of my arrival, having obtained my master's permission, I began preparations for holding such a service. I went over the plantation and invited all the slaves to come to the meeting, for I had something good to tell them. At the grain mill I met an old man from a neighboring plantation, named Uncle Bob. He wanted to know what kind of a meeting it was to be to which I had invited him. I replied, "A religious meeting." He seemed very much pleased at what I had said. I asked him if he had ever attended any such meetings. "Oh, yes," he replied, "I often go to the Presbyterian meeting, about eighteen miles from here." "Then you enjoy religion, don't you?" "Oh, yes, I was converted many years ago. I belong to the Baptist church at Six Rivers. Mr. Boswell baptized me." I told him I had been a member of the Methodist church ever since I was twelve years of age. He immediately grasped my hand, and the tears fell thick and fast as he exclaimed, "The Lord has sent you here, and I pray that He will bless your labors in the conversion of many of the slaves in this region." On the way back to the house I met the overseer, and inquired of him what he thought of my purpose to hold religious meetings with the slaves. He replied that he thought it would be a good thing, though he was not a Christian himself. I asked him if we might hold the first meetings in his house, as it was larger than any other place we could get. "Oh, yes," he replied, "you are quite welcome to come there." I informed my mistress of what Daniel had said. She expressed her satisfaction with the arrangements, and directed me to go to Celia, the house girl, and get some candles and candle-sticks with which to light the house. At the appointed time I began the service. The room was nearly filled with people, doubtless drawn thither largely by curiosity, and yet in some measure prepared to profit by what they saw and heard. During the opening prayer the house was still as death. The people evidently were much impressed with a sense of the divine presence. After prayer, I requested Celia and Betsey and Mary, three of the house servants, to join with me in singing a hymn, as we used to do at Wilmington. We sang, as best we could, the hymn beginning:

> "God moves in a mysterious way,
>   His wonders to perform." [13]

After which I prayed again, asking all who would to bow down with me. When we arose I observed that many were in tears. I then gave a short talk, in which I spoke of what Christ had done and would do for all who came to him. In the midst of my talk one of the house servants suddenly cried out, as though in great distress of mind, "O God, have mercy on me!" I immediately ceased talking and invited all who wished to be saved to come and kneel down in the centre of the room, and I would pray for them. A general rush followed, and falling on our knees I began to entreat God to come and save the perishing. My voice, however, was soon drowned by the voices of the multitudes who pleaded for mercy on their own behalf. We continued in alternate prayer and exhortation until a late hour, when the meeting closed. One precious soul had been saved, and many others brought under deep conviction. Uncle Bob, to whom reference has already been made, was greatly revived in spirit, and nearly exhausted himself shouting the praises of God. The news of this meeting soon spread throughout all that region; nothing like it had ever been witnessed before. Next morning Mr. Richard Holmes came over to my master's place and inquired what was going on there the previous evening. My mistress said the slaves were holding a religious meeting. "I thought so," he replied; "I could distinctly hear Peter praying from where I live." His house was some two miles distant. I did not know that I prayed so loud, but I think it quite likely that I did. That morning I went around again among the slaves and gave notice that I would hold family prayers every evening at the overseer's house with all who would meet together there. These and similar services were continued on that and neighboring plantations during all that season, until my master returned to Wilmington, and there is good reason to believe that many slaves were converted to God. It may be of interest to some if I revert to one experience that transpired in connection with the meetings held on my master's plantation. One evening, as we were met together for prayer and praise, word was brought me that the patrol were outside. The patrol in the old days of slavery answered somewhat to the police of the present time. Their duties consisted in patrolling a given section of country in search of any slaves who might be absent from their plantations without leave, or engaging in religious meetings without their masters' permission. If any such were found, it was permitted the patrol to tie them up and administer a given number of lashes on their bare backs. Their appearance at any time was always a terror to the poor slave, for, as a rule, they delighted in nothing more than in an opportunity to exercise their authority. In this instance the slaves were very much frightened, and many of them started to run. I called to them to remain where they were, and I would go outside and speak to the patrol. The moment I did so I discovered a man sitting on the fence at a little distance from the house. I hailed him and inquired his name. He replied, "Master Henry, Uncle Peter." "Well," said I, "what do you want here?" Just then Captain Pope, the leader of the band, came forward and asked if I had any strange negroes inside. I replied by telling him that my master allowed me to hold religious meetings, and told me to say to any one who interfered with them that he could look after his plantation himself. I then directed Duncan, the house boy, to go and call Massa Sam as quick as he could. Hearing this, Captain Pope and his men started off, and were soon out of sight. After they had gone I called the house boy back, and we went on with the meeting. Next morning I told my mistress of the previous evening's experience. She said she would tell Master Holmes about it, and he would see that Captain Pope did not trouble me any more. Master Holmes was very angry at the treatment I had received, and said he would fix Pope so he never would come there again. He was as good as his word. A few days afterward I met Master Sam, and he told me his father had seen Pope, and forbidden him ever to come on his plantation again. Thus the Lord fights the battles of His people for them. He has gained many a victory for me, for which I praise His name.

Soon after these experiences I had occasion to go with Master Holmes on a visit to his mother, a distance of about three miles. As we rode along, he inquired very particularly about a funeral service I had recently conducted at Mr. May's, in the town of Clinton. I gave him a full account of the services, and of the conversation I had with some white people who were present. We also discussed some plans I had formed for future meetings. I told him of several invitations I had received to hold meetings on different plantations in that vicinity, and asked if he would be willing I should go. "Oh, yes," he replied, "if the owner will agree to protect you while there." He promised to give me his permission in writing, so that I could always have it with me when traveling. At his mother's I met an old colored woman named Dinah. She was overjoyed to think that "Massa Owen" had come. "But, aunty," I said, "ain't you going in to see Massa Owen?" "Oh, no, honey," she replied, "he'll be out here very soon, and bring me some backey [tobacco]; he always brings me something when he comes." She then went on to ask about the meetings. "Look here, chile, you tell me all about the meetings you've been holding at Massa Owen's." "Well, aunty," I replied, "I can tell you this much about them: my master gave me permission to hold such meetings, and many have been converted to God as the result of them." "God bless Massa Owen!" she exclaimed; "why, I tell you, honey, he's the best chile in the family." After a little further talk with Aunt Dinah, I left the kitchen and went out to see some of the field hands. On the way I met the overseer. We stopped and talked a little about the meetings, and while thus engaged two of the slaves came running out to meet us. The overseer asked them what they wanted. "Oh, we just wanted to speak to Uncle Peter," they replied. They were two young converts. I asked them how they were getting on in the good way. "Oh, thank God, we are very happy." "And what is it that makes you happy?" I inquired. "Oh, Jesus has forgiven our sins." "Then you think Jesus has indeed saved you?" "Oh, yes, he saves us now." I exhorted them to be faithful, and they returned to their work. The overseer then remarked the great change that had taken place in their behavior; he had no trouble with them now, whereas they had formerly occasioned him a great deal of trouble.

I inquired if the overseer was a Christian. He replied that he was not, but that at the last meeting he had resolved to become one. I encouraged him to persevere, assuring him that the Lord would bless and save. After dinner, my master rode on a few miles farther to the Court House, and got his mail, and then we returned home. The reader will bear in mind that these experiences are given entirely from memory, as I knew nothing in those days about keeping a diary.

Soon after the events just recorded, my master went away, to be gone several weeks. Before going, he gave me the written permit of which I have previously spoken, and directed me to take good care of everything during his absence. The week following his departure I had occasion to drive over to Clinton[14] with my mistress. While there I chanced to meet Col. Sellen. He said he had been wanting to see me for several weeks; he wanted to make some arrangement for a meeting at his plantation. I told him I had my master's written permit to go anywhere and hold meetings when I was not needed at home. "That is good," he replied; "I wish your master was a Christian. Have you ever talked with him on the subject?" "Oh, yes, I have talked with him many times, and I am earnestly praying that God will convert his soul." The next Sunday I went over to Col. Sellen's and held a meeting. I found a large company assembled. They had been waiting nearly an hour. As I entered the house, they all arose and exclaimed, "Thank God, the brother has come!" We sang the hymn beginning,

"A charge to keep I have,
  A God to glorify."[15]

After which I requested a young colored brother named Tom McCoy to lead in prayer. And such a prayer I have seldom heard. Almost the entire congregation was moved to tears. After prayer we sang another hymn, and I commenced my discourse. I took my text from Matt. xi, 28.[16] The subject was, "God's exceeding great and precious promises to such as put their trust in him." The people were powerfully moved during the preaching. Col. Sellen and his family, and a few other white persons, sat with the congregation, and paid good attention to all that was said. Near the close of my remarks, I said, "I am now recruiting soldiers for the army of the Lord," and requested all who desired to enlist to raise their hands. Many responded to the invitation. After a short prayer, in which the anxious were remembered at a throne of grace, I closed the meeting. Twenty-six persons professed to have found peace in believing. It may be of interest to some to read the hymn sung at the close of this, and in fact of nearly every meeting we held. It was as follows:

"Until we meet again,
  Until we meet again,
  I'll meet you in the heavens,
  When we'll part no more.
  So fare you well,
  So fare you well:
  God Almighty bless you,
  Until we meet again."[17]

During the singing there was a general hand-shaking, in which Col. Sellen and his family joined. He was deacon of a Baptist church, and a most excellent Christian man.

Following this meeting there were several others held at different times on the various plantations in that vicinity, several of which I will mention. And first, one at a Mr. Joseph Moore's plantation. There were but few persons present at this meeting, except his own slaves. Mr. Moore, his wife and one daughter attended, and seemed much interested in what was said. At the close of the service they expressed a wish that I might come again. There were no cases of conversion at this meeting, but the good seed was sown which, I doubt not, in due time bore its fruit to the glory of God. About three weeks later I held another meeting at a Mr. Blackman Crumpling's. They were Methodist people. My remarks at this meeting were based upon the Scripture, "O Lord, revive thy work." And the Lord did revive it in mighty power. Large numbers of both white and colored persons were stricken down and led to cry for mercy at God's hand. I observed that during the sermon Mr. Crumpling was very much affected. I afterwards learned the cause; he was burdened for a neighbor who was present. When I gave the usual invitations to the anxious to come forward for prayer, this neighbor was one of the first to come. Mr. Crumpling immediately stepped to his side, and putting his arm around his neck, exclaimed, "Thank God, my prayers are answered." We continued the meeting to a very late hour in the evening. Many were converted, and returned to their homes shouting the praises of God. One of Mr. Crumpling's daughters exhorted and shouted praises until her strength gave way, and she fell to the ground in a dead faint. It was one of the best meetings I ever attended. I afterwards became well acquainted with Mr. Crumpling's family, and I ever found them warm-hearted and devoted Christian people.

There is one incident of which I would like to speak just here. One day my master sent me to do an errand at Mr. Crumpling's. When I reached the house I found the family at dinner, and to my great surprise I observed that the slaves were eating at the same table with the white people. I had never beheld the like before, the almost universal custom being for the master and his family to eat by themselves. It was regarded as beneath the dignity of a white person to associate with a slave on anything like terms of equality. What I beheld at Mr. Crumpling's was due to the grace of God; it makes all one, regardless of color or condition. The next meeting of which I will speak was held at Mr. Owen Bennett's. Mr. Bennett was not a Christian himself, but he permitted his slaves to hold religious services whenever they desired to do so. The attendance at his place was not large, neither were the meetings held there especially interesting, and yet there was a measure of good resulting from them.

In this connection I may refer to a meeting held at Squire McCoy's. He had given me a very particular invitation to visit his plantation, promising to have everything in readiness when I arrived. A very good number were present. At the opening of the service we sang one of our plantation songs, after which Bro. Tom McCoy led in prayer. I spoke for about twenty minutes, and then Bro. Tom exhorted for a short time, after which the services closed. Nothing of unusual interest occurred in connection with this meeting. The next one was held at a Mr. May's, in an old barn on his plantation. There were nearly as many whites as blacks present at this meeting. The whites were for the most part from the poorer class. Many of them were not as well or as tidily dressed as were some of the blacks. Mr. May's son, Henry, read a portion of Scripture, and made a few remarks at the opening of the service. He was listened to very closely, and with frequent responses on the part of his hearers. After he had done speaking, I talked for a short time, taking occasion to refer to Uncle Billy, whose funeral I had attended on that plantation a few weeks previous. At the mention of Uncle Billy's name there was a general clapping of hands, and many shouted, "We'll meet him in the better land!" At the conclusion of the preaching service, I invited all who could do so to remain at a class-meeting. I requested Henry May to lead the class, but he declined doing so, because he said Uncle Billy had always done that, and he could not control his feelings sufficiently to stand in his place. He and Uncle Billy were very warm friends. As there was no one else to act as leader, I was forced to take that part myself.

In the course of the meeting, I came upon several young people sitting in a seat together. They were not Christians. I exhorted them to come to Christ at once and be saved. One of the number signified her willingness to do so. Laying my hand very gently on her shoulder, I said, "That is right, my daughter, give your heart to the Saviour now." She immediately fell on her knees, and began to cry to God for mercy. At the close of the meeting I had some further conversation with her. She appeared deeply in earnest. I promised to remember her in my prayers. Since that hour I have never seen her, but I doubt not we shall one day meet with the blood-washed throng in glory. Just now let me add a word respecting Henry May. Though reared amid slave-holding influences, he was as fine a young man as I ever wish to see. He gave promise of a successful and useful life,—a promise which, I doubt not, he fully realized. I expect to meet him in the better land.

The next meeting I will mention was held at Parker's meeting-house, in Cumberland co. I had a regular appointment at that place the fourth Sunday in each month. Christians of all denominations were accustomed to unite in the services. At the meeting of which I am now speaking, the congregation was composed of both whites and blacks, and both classes seemed to have an equal interest in the worship of God's house. All of a sudden, in the midst of the sermon, an old class-leader named Sampson White sprang from his seat, ran up the aisle to the altar, and shouted, "My God, preach the truth, brother, preach the truth!" Soon after he sat down, an old colored sister arose and exclaimed, "Lord Jesus, let it come, let the power come!" Next came a white brother with an occasional "Amen," and they were the longest Amens that I ever heard from human lips. But none of these things moved me, except to push me right along in the good work. I never in all my life have felt more of the power of God upon me than I did that day. At the close of the sermon we held a prayer-meeting. As many as could be accommodated came and knelt at the altar, and the season of prayer that followed was one never to be forgotten. There was a perfect Babel of sound. Everybody was engaged in prayer, either for themselves or some one else. Whites prayed for blacks, and blacks for whites. All distinctions as between the different races seemed to have disappeared altogether, and everybody recognized a common bond of interest and endeavor. I let the meeting continue in this way for a short time, and then I called the brethren and sisters to order. Several persons still remained prostrate on the floor, too much exhausted to rise. I addressed a few words to such as could give me their attention, asking any who felt that they had been blessed that day to bear testimony to the fact. The first one to rise was a young lad about sixteen years of age. He shouted at the top of his voice, "Glory to God, Jesus has blessed my soul!" He then commenced shaking hands with those who stood near him. Thirteen others also testified to having obtained a hope in Christ.

I will mention only one more meeting in this connection. It was held at Col. Sellen's, and was the last of the season. The service lasted all night. Twenty-three professed conversion. In the morning I bade them all farewell, and returned to my home. The results of that Summer's labor I shall never know in this life, but I confidently expect to meet in the life to come many who then found peace in believing in Jesus. The sickly season having now passed, my master and his family soon began preparations for a return to Wilmington. As usual, I accompanied them. It took two days for the journey. The first day we went as far as Little Washington, where we put up for the night. Before retiring, my master told me to have the horses fed and groomed, and ready for an early start the next morning. Accordingly I arose about three o'clock. As I stepped out of doors I discovered that the stars were falling in all directions. I ran to the kitchen and shouted to the cook that the heavens were all on fire. I then ran to the great house and awoke my master. He came out doors, looked at the heavens for a few moments, and then asked me what I thought it was. "I don't know," I replied, "unless it is the day of judgment." He soon returned to his room and awoke the other members of his family. I turned to go back to the kitchen. As I did so I saw the cook standing outside the door, swinging her arms, and shouting at the top of her voice, "Glory to God! glory to God!" supposing that the end of the world had come. By this time the whole plantation was awake, and every-body was out gazing, some in fear and some in joy at the strange appearance of the heavens. The tavern-keeper came out and asked me if I could not stop the cook making so much noise. I got a man to help me, and we carried her into the kitchen. We could not stop her shouting. She begged us to let her go out again; she wanted to see the Saviour when he came. I went back to the tavern-keeper and told him we could do nothing with her. "Well, let her alone, then," he replied. As day began to dawn the fiery red of the heavens began to disappear, and at sunrise it was all gone. I went to my master and told him the horses were ready for a start at any moment. He replied that he did not know how soon we could get anything to eat, the cook was so wild over the falling of the stars. I went to the kitchen and found the tavern-keeper's wife there getting the breakfast ready. While waiting, I conversed with many of the slaves about the strange things we had witnessed. Large numbers of them were under deep conviction, and declared their purpose to seek the Lord without delay. I gave them such counsel as seemed proper, and left them with the hope that their impressions might prove abiding. Soon after eight o'clock we resumed our journey. Master Holmes rode on ahead in his sulky, while I followed on behind in the carriage with the rest of the family. Young Master Sam asked me if I was not frightened when I saw the stars falling. "Oh, no," I replied, "I was not at all frightened." "Well, we were all dreadfully frightened. Almost every person I saw was crying." "Crying, who was crying?" "Oh, mother and sister, and almost everybody." His mother then told him he need not talk any more about that matter. We continued our journey, stopping only for dinner, and reached Wilmington about eight o'clock in the evening. For a few days I was quite busy putting things to rights, after which I arranged with my master to go to work on my own account.

It is proper that I should here state that nearly all the suffering I endured while in slavery occurred previous to my becoming the property of Owen Holmes. I found in him all that any slave could desire. He did for me more and better than my own father could have done. He protected and provided for me as though I had been one of his own household. The memory of my relations to him and his dear family will ever be a pleasure to me while life shall last.

Wilmington afforded many advantages to a slave who could improve them. By hiring my time of my master I was able to lay by quite a sum of money during the years I was there. I have earned as high as three dollars per day, stowing cotton and other commodities. At one time I made fifty dollars in eight days, an average of over six dollars per day, clear of all expenses. The reader will see at a glance how I could lay up money, as I had only one hundred and fifty dollars per year to pay for my time. My master usually made the contracts for me, but during his absence a Mr. John Whittier, nephew of the poet Whittier,[18] acted for him. This was a necessity, because no contract made by a slave was binding unless ratified by a white man. In all cases of dispute either my master or Mr. Whittier would interpose his authority and compel a just settlement. I will present just here a single case by way of illustration.

A captain by the name of Adams refused to settle with me according to agreement, for stowing his vessel. I took the case at once to my master. He inquired if I had charged the captain too much. I gave him the terms of the agreement, — the captain was to pay me one hundred and fifty dollars, and I was to furnish all the help. My master figured up the expenses, and said that if an educated white man had allowed an ignorant slave to impose upon him, he ought to be made to bear it. He then went to his private drawer, and took out a pistol and a long dirk-knife. I remarked that there was no need of those things. "Oh, never you mind," he replied, "I'm going to get your money for you."

We went first to the vessel, but the captain had gone up town, and up town we went in search of him. We soon found him, and I demanded a settlement. He replied that when I was ready to settle his way he would settle with me. I told him I would not settle his way. "Well, then, we cannot settle at all." My master then stepped forward, and I told him what the man had said. He inquired if I had done the work according to agreement. The captain replied that I had. "Well, why don't you pay the boy, then?" "Because he asks too much." "But why did you make such a bargain to begin with?" "Because I thought it would cost that sum." "Well, pay for it, then, as you agreed to do." "I have offered to pay the boy for his work, but he will not take the money." In reply to this statement I remarked that he had offered me only a part of the sum agreed upon. "Well," said my master, "if you will not settle with my boy I shall put an attachment on your vessel, and she shall not leave the wharf until you do." At that instant the captain's partner came out of the office, and told him to pay the bill and have no more talk about it. The captain then took out the money and passed it first to my master, but he refused to take it, and ordered him to hand it to me. He did so; I counted it and found it all right. This little incident will serve as an illustration of my master's manner of treating his slaves. He always looked after their interests as carefully as though they were his own. While he lived I got along very well.

I will now give some account of the religious meetings I was accustomed to hold in the vicinity of Wilmington. I had regular appointments in Hanover county during the Winter, and in Sampson county during the Summer. One of these appointments was at a place called Stump Sound, on John Jones' plantation. The meetings were held in an old barn. Mr. Jones was a good man, and very kind to his slaves. One of his slaves, an old man, and very zealous in the cause of Christ, obtained permission for me to come there. The first meeting was so good that they invited me to come again, and come as often as I could. I told them I would try and come over again watch-night and hold a watch-meeting.[19] In the afternoon of the same day I went to Mr. James Price's plantation and held another service. When I arrived the people had all come together, and were engaged in singing. Uncle Sam, an old class leader, told me that a great many had got tired and gone away, but would be back again in the evening. I had a good time preaching. Only one person professed a desire to be saved. This was on Sunday. Monday evenings we generally held a Union Temperance meeting in Wilmington. A Mr. Northrup and Captain Stowe, northern men, and Mr. Blake, a southerner, together with a colored man named White, and myself, were the founders of this meeting. It was conducted on the old Washingtonian plan.[20] My work in the cause of temperance began here. As the results of our labors, many hundreds of drinking men and women signed the pledge, and ever afterwards led lives of virtue and temperance. Scott Hill was another place where I used to hold meetings. The first time I went there I was invited to do so by a Mr. Stephen Foy. He wrote to my master asking him to let me come and preach a funeral discourse, occasioned by the death of one of his slaves, familiarly known as Uncle John. It was the custom in those days to bury the body at once, and have the funeral service at some future time. In this case, death had occurred several days previous to my going there to preach. On my arrival I found a large company assembled. After the usual opening exercises, I announced my text: "Mark the perfect man and behold the upright, for the end of that man is peace." Uncle John was such a man — perfect and upright — and his end was peace. I talked for about one half hour, after which we held a prayer-meeting. Two persons professed conversion, and many others were brought under deep conviction. At the close of this service I went directly home, to meet an appointment in the meeting-house of the Protestant Methodist church. The meeting was a good one. I used to hold meetings once in a while at Fort Fisher,[21] also at a place called The Forks, in Brunswick county. The meetings at The Forks were held on Mr. Joseph Eagle's plantation. There was a colored Baptist church in that vicinity, of which a colored man named Minger Eagles was pastor. This man also acted as overseer on his master's plantation. One day, when at Wilmington, he proposed to me to come to his place and hold a watch-meeting. I consented to do so. The meeting began at nine o'clock on Saturday evening, and continued all that night and all the next day. An immense congregation was present during the entire service. At midnight I invited the anxious to come forward for prayers, and the number was so large as to fill the entire body part of the church. Many anxious ones were obliged to remain outside, and a portion of the brethren went out there and prayed for them. At one time during the season of prayer that followed, forty-three persons lay on the floor insensible. One after another, they all came out into the light and blessing of the gospel.

Sunday was a regular camp-meeting service. At ten o'clock there was preaching. Bro. Minger Eagles took charge of the meeting. In the midst of the sermon a young girl sprang to her feet and shouted, "I've found Jesus precious to my soul." At once the whole house was in an uproar. Everybody commenced shouting, and those outside commenced crowding in in such numbers that we were compelled to leave the house altogether. At the close of the morning service thirty-nine persons professed conversion. In the afternoon Bro. Sampson preached, and several more persons were converted. During the preaching there was so much noise and confusion that the speaker was forced to pause in his discourse. Bro. Eagles told the people to be as quiet as possible until the preacher got through. One good old colored woman shouted back, "Why, chile, how can we be quiet when the Lord is here?" After a short pause Bro. Sampson began again, and talked for about twenty minutes longer. At the close of the sermon we dismissed the congregation, telling them to go to their homes at once, so that their masters would have no occasion to find fault with them. This was the best meeting, I think, that I ever attended.

The next meeting of which I will speak was held at a place called Smithville, in a Methodist church. Soon after the commencement of the service I observed that many of the audience were in tears. As I did not know the cause, I thought it best to pause and invite all who desired salvation to come forward and be prayed for. A large number came to the altar and knelt down. While we were praying, the patrol suddenly came in upon us, and said we must stop our noise. One of the band stepped up to an old colored man who was engaged in prayer, and struck him a heavy blow on the head. At this a white man came forward and ordered him to leave the house. He did so at once, but instead of going home he went to his store, locked himself in and laid down to sleep. The next morning, when the servants went to look for him, he was found dead. That blow was the last one God ever permitted him to give a poor slave, whose only offence was his love for Christ and his cause. This circumstance produced a marked effect upon both white and colored people. Many of the whites were led to protest against the system of patrols. One of the band of which the deceased had been a member resigned his position, and declared that he would sooner pay his fine than enter the service again. Thus God often makes the wrath of men to praise him, and the remainder of the wrath he restrains. This was the last meeting I ever held in Smithville. Town Creek Bridge was another place where I used sometimes to hold religious meetings. The first time I went there was in connection with the funeral of Father George Baker, a colored preacher. In order to reach the place I had to cross the Cape Fear and Brunswick rivers. A freshet had just carried away the bridge on the latter river, so that I had to take off my clothes and swim across it. The service was held in the open air, as there was no house large enough to accommodate the immense congregation that had assembled. It is not permitted us always to know the why and wherefore of certain things that God permits to be. He had permitted Father Baker to suffer untold agonies on account of his fidelity to Christ. Many times he had been severely whipped because he would continue to preach and pray in the interest of the poor slaves about him. As a last resort, his master cut his heel-cords so that he could not walk. But even this did not prevent him from doing what he felt to be his duty. He once crawled on his hands and knees a distance of five miles, in order to attend a meeting. He died in the triumphs of Christian faith. I was told that a short time before his death he shouted so loud as to be heard at a distance of nearly a mile. There were five preachers in attendance upon the funeral, and as was the custom at such times, they each occupied a few moments. A young son of Father Baker's master was present, and wept like a child. He had known of the treatment the good man had received, and the remembrance of it affected him deeply. At the conclusion of the services we all formed in procession and marched to the grave, singing as we went a funeral hymn:

"And let the body faint,
  And let it faint and die,

My soul shall quit this mournful vale
And soar to worlds on high."[22]

At the grave a few words were spoken, and then the congregation dispersed. I expect to meet Father Baker by-and-by in the kingdom of God. He was a sincere Christian, and I doubt not he has entered into rest.

Another of my appointments was at Mr. Young's plantations. The services were held on Saturday evenings, in an old barn-loft. At one of those meetings we began about dark and held continuous services until noon of the next day, different brethren taking turns in leading them. If some of our northern brethren and sisters had been present they might have thought us crazy, and it is possible we were a little beside ourselves, but it was in a good cause. In the midst of one of the meetings a woman became so excited that she jumped out of a window, a distance of about twenty-five feet from the ground. We thought she must be severely injured, but she soon returned apparently unhurt. Forty-seven persons professed conversion in connection with the meeting. A white Methodist minister, named Forestine, did not like to have me hold meetings in that vicinity, as it was on his circuit, and he said I took away his hearers. He even went so far as to prefer charges against me in the church of which I was a member. The principal point of the charges was that I had broken the rules of the church in preaching in his circuit without authority. The case was brought to trial. I was asked if I knew it was Mr. Forestine's circuit. I replied that I did, but as I had been invited there by the plantation owners I felt that I had a right to go. The presiding officer inquired how long I had been accustomed to go there. I told him I had been there more or less for three years. At the close of the examination the charges were declared to have been improperly preferred, and Mr. Forestine was informed that he must go to the plantation owners if he wished to stop my preaching there, as the church could do nothing about the matter. At the conclusion of the trial many of my friends came forward and expressed their great pleasure in seeing me exonerated from all blame. I replied to their congratulations by telling them the Good Book commanded us to "Go into all the world and preach the Gospel to every creature," and I should go at least as far as Cape Fear river. I did go many times afterwards, and the Lord blessed my labors.

Another place of meeting was at a Mr. Mayer's plantation. Many were converted at this place, among whom was one man only a short time from Africa. In company with a number of others, he had been smuggled into America and sold to Mr. Mayers. Notwithstanding he could not speak a word of English correctly, he could and did receive the Lord Jesus into his heart. I also held meetings occasionally at a Mr. Duncan Moore's plantation. At the close of one of my meetings at Mr. Moore's, he made me a present of a ten dollar bill. I mention this fact to show that all slaveholders were not the hard-hearted characters that they are sometimes supposed to have been. On the contrary, many of them were as kindly in their feelings as human beings could well be. In this connection I will refer to Mr. Mall Bryant's as another place where I sometimes held meetings. The first time I ever visited this plantation was by invitation of Mr. Bryant. He invited me to come and conduct the funeral service of one of his slaves. On my way there I was met by the patrol. The leader asked me where I was going. I replied, "To Mr. Mall Bryant's, to preach a funeral sermon." He called for my pass, but I had forgotten to take it with me. He then ordered me to take off my clothes and prepare for a whipping. I did so, and he tied me to a tree. Just at that moment a carriage drove in sight. It proved to be Mr. Duncan Moore. He inquired of the patrol what they were going to do with me. "Give him the law," they replied. "No, you are not going to give him the law, either," said Mr. Moore; "you are not going to touch him." "But the law says we must whip every negro we find off his plantation without a pass." "I don't care anything about the law, and besides I am pass enough for Uncle Peter; he is on my land." Mr. Moore then ordered them to let me go. They did so, and he wrote me a pass for the remainder of the journey. I thanked him for his kindness, and started on towards Mr. Bryant's. I had gone but a short distance when I overtook an aged colored woman with whom I was somewhat acquainted, having met her at one of my meetings. Besides being very lame she was nearly blind, and could not get on very fast. She was then on the way to the funeral, thinking it might be the last opportunity she would ever have of hearing me preach. As I passed her she held up her two walking-sticks, and said, "I shall let go of these by-and-by, and fly away to Jesus." On arriving at Mr. Bryant's, I found between eight and nine hundred persons assembled to pay their last respects to the memory of a Christian brother. As the services proceeded, there was much weeping on the part of the audience. Mr. Bryant and his wife seemed as much affected as any of the company. At the close of the sermon I requested all who would try and meet our departed brother in the better land to manifest it. The invitation met with an almost universal response. It was indeed a blessed season, and one long to be remembered by us all. While bidding Mr. Bryant and his family good day, he remarked that he would call at my master's office in a few days, and leave something for me. I told him he need not do that, for I did not charge anything for my services. "Oh, never mind that," he continued; "I will call and leave something, all the same." He was as good as his word. In a few days my master gave me fifteen dollars Mr. Bryant had left with him. Thus you will see that there were some good men even among slaveholders. Another place of meeting was at Mr. Arthur Hill's plantation. One Sunday, as I was on my way to attend a meeting at Mr. Hill's, I was met by the patrol. As usual, they demanded my pass; I had forgotten to take it. "Well," said they, "we have got one for you." I was ordered to take off all my clothing except my pants, after which they tied me to a tree and gave me the fifteen lashes allowed by law. Every stroke of the whip drew blood. The whipping done, they let me go, telling me that if they ever caught me that way again they would repeat the dose. As I started on my journey I commenced singing the hymn beginning,

"Hard trials, tribulations, Lord,
  I feel I'm on my journey home." [23]

On arriving at Mr. Hill's I met two colored brethren, who said they had heard the patrol whipping me, and had turned aside into the woods to avoid a similar fate. We had a good meeting that day. In the afternoon I held a second service at a place known as Crowen's Brick Yard, and in the evening still another at Mr. John Sanders' plantation. These meetings were all productive of good, both to saints and sinners. At a funeral service held a few weeks later, we were again visited by the dreaded patrol. There were nearly three hundred persons present. All who were without passes were tied up and whipped, and we were ordered to disperse at once when the service closed. In dismissing the congregation, I remarked that it was useless to resist the powers that were, but we might still hold fast to Christ; there was nothing that need separate our souls from him. Many other meetings were held in different places, of which I cannot here speak in detail. I mention these as illustrations of the life I lived, and the labor I performed, in the cause of Christ. With a brief reference to one other, I will conclude my narrative of meetings held at the South during the old days of slavery. It was held at a place known as Blayden Camp Ground. A similar meeting was held annually, at the conclusion of the regular camp-meeting of the whites. I had to walk a distance of fifty-three miles in order to attend this meeting. I started about four o'clock in the afternoon, and reached the grounds about two o'clock next morning. There was a large number of persons engaged in worship even at that early hour. At ten o'clock in the forenoon there was preaching by a Mr. John Bosworth, on the "Prodigal Son." More than two hundred came forward for prayer at the close of the service, many of whom were hopefully converted. In the evening there was preaching again by the presiding elder, at which time about one hundred more requested prayers. A large proportion of these also came out into the light. Next morning the meeting broke up, and many of the company set out for home on board the steamer Henrietta Gleamer, Captain Rush commander. On the way down the river we held a religious service on the forward deck. About one hundred persons were present. As I was giving out a hymn a white man came up to me and said the meeting must stop; the other passengers did not want so much noise. We stopped for the moment, while one of the deck hands went to the captain about it. The captain came forward very soon and told us to go on with our meeting; he was captain of that boat, and we might sing and pray as much as we liked. We began singing again, and made the woods that lined the river-bank fairly ring with the music of our song. Captain Rush, though not a professing Christian, was a most excellent man. If his eye should ever fall on this little book, I wish him to know that I have never forgotten him. I hope I may one day meet him in the better land. In the evening of the same day we all met in the vestry of the Methodist church and held a grand thanksgiving service, in view of the many blessings God had bestowed upon us.

I must now return to my flight to the British provinces, and rehearse some of the experiences that befel me there. I traveled almost constantly, preaching and lecturing in churches and town halls to large congregations. The first place visited was at St. John's, New Brunswick, where I spoke in the Methodist, Baptist, Presbyterian, Congregational, and Catholic churches. I then visited Fredericton, and preached in all the churches in that place. Next I went to Rankinsville and preached in the Episcopal church. Notwithstanding it rained very hard, I found the church crowded. The minister was a noble Christian brother, and I shall never forget his kindness. I received from the good people of this place a present of fifty dollars. At Bay River I preached three nights in succession in the Baptist church. Eleven souls were converted, and I received a present of forty-one dollars. At Halifax [24] I spent three months, laboring with the different churches. I also held protracted meetings at Liverpool, with most blessed results. At Post Jolie I preached once in the Methodist church, and received a present of fifteen dollars. At Shelburn I spent one Sabbath. It was a day never to be forgotten. The Lord was indeed in the midst. Next morning a brother presented me twelve dollars, and on shaking hands with the minister he left with me a one-pound note. At Birch-town there was a colored settlement. I remained a week at this place, and preached every night. Thirty-eight were converted.

The morning of my departure a colored brother put in my hand a purse containing nineteen dollars, with the remark, "We are all very poor, but here is a little to help you on your way." At Causeway I preached two nights in the Methodist church, and received a present of ten dollars. At Bowshead I remained a week, lecturing on slavery and attending missionary meetings. At Great Island I preached three nights for the Freewill Baptists. I never saw people more eager to hear the word than at this place. At the close of my labors with them I received a generous collection. Returning again to the main land I visited Brass Hill, where I remained one week preaching in the Baptist church. Many were brought to Christ as the result of these meetings. There was a man over eighty years of age converted at this place, which of itself was ample reward for my weeks of toil. From Brass Hill I went to Salmon River, where I remained five weeks engaged in protracted services. It was a most glorious season. At Yarmouth I preached one Sunday in the Methodist church, of which a Bro. Wilson was pastor. If people shouted and made as much noise now as they did then, they would be called crazy. That was a Sabbath-day long to be remembered. The day following I attended a conference of Congregational ministers, and was very cordially entertained. At that meeting I was introduced to a Mr. Galaway, from England. He invited me to visit England, and promised if I would do so to introduce me to the public there. Later in the week I lectured on slavery in the Congregational church. The Sabbath following I lectured in the academy at Gebogue Point. At this place I met a Mr. Hilton, who had known me as a slave. At the close of my remarks he arose and spoke of his previous acquaintance with me, and proposed raising a sum of money for my benefit. The boxes were passed, and nearly fifty dollars contributed at that place.

Next day I returned to Yarmouth.[25] Mr. Hilton accompanied me, and procured a hall in which I delivered a course of lectures on slavery. The lectures were very largely attended, and netted me one hundred and eighty dollars. The following Sunday I preached in a school-house, at a place called Cranberry Head. At the close of the service a collection was taken, amounting to fourteen dollars. On returning again to Yarmouth, I received a letter from a Christian lady containing ten dollars. Thus the good hand of the Lord led me from place to place during my stay in the provinces, and thus were kind friends raised up to minister to my wants. I shall never cease to pray that God will abundantly reward them for their generous sympathy and kindly assistance in my time of need. Everywhere I went the same cordial welcome was extended to me, and the churches of all denominations, both Protestant and Catholic, were ever at my service. I have even been aided by those with whose language I was not at all acquainted, and who could not understand my speech. I will mention a single incident in illustration of this point. It occurred in a French settlement in Nova Scotia. Passing through the settlement one day, and being very weary, I paused at one of the houses and knocked for admission. A gentleman came to the door and addressed me in French. I indicated by signs that I wanted some water. He immediately grasped my hand and shook it heartily, at the same time motioning me to come in the house. I did so. He and his wife conversed together for a few moments in their native tongue, after which she went and procured some water, of which I drank freely, for I was very thirsty. I then thanked them as best I could for their kindness and took up my bundle to go, but the gentleman prevented me, and indicated by signs that they would like to have me stop and eat with them. I put down my bundle in token of my willingness to do so, and watched the preparation of their noon-day meal. First a large dish of potatoes was brought in and placed on the table. Then a quantity of fried pork was brought in and placed beside the potatoes. Next a plate, knife and fork, and a tin cup for each of us were set in order on the table, after which we all seated ourselves in readiness to partake of the repast. To my great surprise I observed that my host first bowed his head and reverently said grace before eating. I then knew that I was among friends. After we had done eating I waited a few moments to see what would come next. The gentleman immediately went to the stable, harnessed his horse and brought him to the door. He then made signs that he would carry me some distance on my journey. I bade his good wife good-bye, and took a seat beside him in the carriage. After proceeding about a mile we stopped at a house, and my companion went in. A few minutes later he returned, bringing a gentleman with him. The new-comer inquired of me where I wished to go. I gave the name of a village about ten miles distant. He spoke to my companion in French, telling him what I had said. He immediately resumed his place in the carriage and drove on. We did not stop again until we arrived at my destination. I offered to pay him for his trouble, but he refused to accept any pay. I thanked him, and bade him a kind good-bye. I have mentioned this little incident in order to show how God cares for a poor wanderer who puts his trust in him.

In the year 1854 I returned to the States. Words cannot express my joy in being once more on American soil, and in the company of the dear friends from whom I had been so long separated. On arriving in Boston, I went first to the office of my old friend Wm. Lloyd Garrison. He greeted me with all his old-time cordiality, and formally bade me welcome back to America.

He also expressed the hope that I would go forward in the good work of interesting the public in my down-trodden and oppressed brethren. I replied that with the help of God I would never cease to labor in that way so long as I lived. He informed me farther of an anti-slavery convention soon to be held in Cummington, Mass., in Rev. T. A. Stockman's church, and that Samuel May and Wendell Phillips[26] were to speak, and invited me to be present if possible. Accordingly, I took the cars and rode as far as Northampton, and then walked the rest of the way, a distance of eighteen miles. It was after dark when I reached Cummington, and I proceeded at once to the church. I found it crowded. Mr. Phillips was speaking when I entered the door. Mr. Stockman saw me and came and escorted me to the platform. After Mr. Phillips ceased speaking, I was formally introduced to the audience. A perfect storm of applause followed, which lasted for several minutes. I took a little time to rest, and then spoke briefly of my great pleasure in meeting my old friends again, and of my purpose to continue my labors in behalf of my brethren and sisters yet in bondage. I continued thus to labor in the cause of God and humanity down to the opening of the war of the Rebellion. Everywhere I went I proclaimed my belief that I should some day witness the downfall of slavery. When John Brown[27] was hung at Harper's Ferry for his so-called treason, in attempting to free the slaves, I felt that I could discern the beginning of the end. Praise God that end is now accomplished. He to whom vengeance belongeth has answered the prayers of his suffering ones. Many years have now passed since I began my life as a little slave boy away down in North Carolina. I have nearly run my race. Soon the summons will come for me to go hence and be here no more. I desire, in closing these brief sketches of my life's experience, to return my heartfelt thanks to the many kind friends who have contributed so much to my well-being and happiness. And I desire still further to testify to my unwavering confidence in the great truths of the Christian religion. They have been a never-failing support to me my whole life through, and I am persuaded they will uphold me to the end.

I would say here, God has dealt bountifully with me, and has blessed me beyond measure; for after I was sold from my dear mother, going to Wilmington, N.C., and while living there, three years afterwards, I providentially met my dear old father. I went to a cart to buy a watermelon, of which he had a load to sell. He came to the side of the cart where I was standing, and asked me how much money I had to buy a melon with. I answered, "Six cents." He said that was not enough to buy one, adding, "Is that all the money you have?" I answered, "This is all I have." He asked, "Whose boy are you?" I said, "I belong to Mr. Jones." He then asked me who my mother was. I told him my mother's name was Grace. He asked, "Where is your mother?" I told him she was up country, at Mr. Hawes' plantation. He asked, "What Hawes?" I replied, "Mr. John Hawes." He then laid the melon on the cart and took me in his arms, hugged and kissed me, and said, "You are my own child!" He asked me where I was living, and I pointed to the house. He said, "When I sell my load I will come up there and bring you a melon; you go home." I went home and attended to my business as usual. During the day I told my mistress, Miss Anna, that I had seen my father. She asked me where I saw him, and I replied, "Down to the market." She inquired what he was doing there, and I told her he was selling melons for his master, Mr. Hambleton. She said, "You go and tell him to come up to the house." I told her he said he would come up after he had sold his load, and that he would bring me a melon. She said. "Hurry and get your work done, so you can visit with him when he comes." I will assure you I worked as fast as possible, and finished my task before my father arrived. I watched for him anxiously. I suppose I went to the gate fifty times before he came. Late in the afternoon I saw him driving down Main street, coming towards my master's house. I ran into the house and said to Miss Anna, "My father is coming." She went to the window in the front room and sat down, waiting for him to come. I stood at one side of the window with her, watching every step of the horse. He soon arrived in front of the house. Miss Anna said, "Run out and tell him to drive his horse into the yard." I ran with all my might, threw the big gate wide open, and said, "My mistress says come in." Miss Anna came out on the back stoop, spoke to him very kindly, and said, "My boy says you are his father." "Yes, ma'am, he is my child; I have been sold away from him over three years." "Oh, uncle, that is too bad; I wish something could be done about this selling business. I cannot help it, uncle. I will try and treat your child kindly. He has been a good boy since he has been with me. If he behaves well, I will treat him well." My father turned to me, placed his hand on my head, and said, "My boy, hear what your mistress says? Now I want you to be a good boy. Mind and not tell your mistress any wrong stories; and when she tells you to do anything, do it just as quick as you can. I will come and see you as often as I can. Do you say your prayers at night, now?" I said, "Yes, sir." "Now don't you neglect them. I must go now, as it is getting late. I have got a melon in the cart for you, and will go and get it. Good-bye, my son. I will be in town soon, and will come and see you." Miss Anna said, "How far is it, uncle, to your master's plantation?" "Twenty miles, missus. I will get there in three hours." "Now, Uncle Tony, when you come to town, always come and see your son. I shall be glad to have you come. If you are hungry any time, come in and I will give you something to eat." "Thank you, missus, for your kindness. I must be going now. Good-bye, ma'am." "Good-bye, uncle." Miss Anna said to me, "Now you must be a good boy. You heard what your father said. Now you can go about your work, and set the table for supper." I returned to my work as usual.

I wish to say here to my dear readers, that my life was a checkered one from boyhood up to forty-three years of age, but I see now the hand of God in it all. Like Joseph, I was sold into bondage; but God has never forsaken me. I have seen father and mother again, and had the privilege of taking them by the hand and welcoming them under my own roof. I had the privilege of buying my father's time from the task-master, after he became old and decrepit, paying $50 annually. I could not do this myself, but was obliged to employ Mr. Owen Fennel, a Baptist deacon, to hire him for me. In this way I secured his liberty. While he was twenty miles from me I could not take care of him when he was sick, but after he was removed to my house I could attend to his wants.

My mother was old and broken down with hard labor, and through the blessing of God I succeeded in getting her from her master. I walked eighty-five miles, and found her on Enoch Hawes' plantation, all broken down with hard labor and sickness. I called on Mr. Hawes and asked him if he would let me have my mother and take care of her. After much persuasion he concluded to let me have her. His wife was bitterly opposed to it, but Mr. Hawes overruled her and persuaded her to consent to let me have her, after which I returned to my old mother and informed her that she was to go with me, and her future home would be with her son. She burst into tears, and prayed that God would ever bless me her youngest child. I told her it was a pleasure and duty for me to do all in my power to make her last days happy. I immediately started for the woods, where the plantation hands were engaged in cutting timber, and told them the news of securing my mother's liberty. They shouted, "Glory to God! We have been praying that God would deliver your mother in some way." Many of them wept for joy. I then asked them if they could tell me of any one who was going to Wilmington. One man by the name of James replied, "I can tell you of one who is going there, Mr. William Ramsey [a Methodist class-leader.] Take this footpath through the woods; it will lead you to his house two and a half miles distant." This was a blind path, and I was sometimes in the road and sometimes out; but I found the way at last. I reached Mr. R.'s house about an hour before sundown, and found the door open. I rapped, and a medium-sized white lady came and very politely asked me to come in and take a seat, which I accepted. I asked if she was Mr. R.'s wife, and she replied in the affirmative. I then asked if he was at home. She inquired if I wished to see him, and I said "Yes." She asked me if I lived near there, and I answered, "No, ma'am, I am a son of Aunt Grace Hawes." She then asked, "When did you arrive?" I said, "About noon, to-day." She asked me if I had seen my mother, and I said, "Yes; I have got the consent of her master to take her home with me." She exclaimed, "Thank God! thank God! I will blow the horn and call my husband; he has gone to feed the pigs." He answered, and soon was at the house. After calling her husband she came and sat down by my side and began to converse about my mother, and how I succeeded in getting her from her master. I told her I believed it was in answer to prayer. She replied, "It must be so. My husband and I have been praying these years that God would deliver Aunt Grace, for she has been a great sufferer, and we have carried her food in the night, unknown to her master." At this time Mr. R. came in, and I arose and extended my hand and called him by name. Mrs. R. said, "This is Aunt Grace's son, and he has succeeded in getting her from her master." He shouted "Glory to God!" jumped for joy, and said, "This is what we have been praying for, wife." I then asked him if he was going to town, and if he would take my mother with him. He said, "Yes, yes, gladly." I asked him how soon he would be ready to go, and he replied, "Next week I will provide a comfortable way for her to go." I asked how much he would charge me. He said, "Nothing at all, sir. Old aunty is a Christian; I will gladly take her free of charge. I hope you, too, are a Christian." I replied, "I cannot say, sir, that I am a Christian, but I am trying to do the best I can in serving the dear Lord." He exclaimed, "Amen! amen! God bless you, my son." According to promise, my mother took passage on his boat the next week for Wilmington. He spared no pains to make her comfortable, and she arrived there in safety on Thursday of the same week. As soon as he arrived in town he inquired for me, and a brother in the church came to inform me of his arrival. I immediately left my work and made all possible haste to Market wharf, where his boat was lying, and found Mr. Ramsey standing on the wharf. Having shaken his hand, he said, "Uncle Peter, I have brought your mother." I replied, "Thank you, Massa William; may God bless you when I am gone." "Yes, Uncle Peter, God blesses me every day. You had better procure a team and a bed and send your mother to your home." "I am afraid, sir, I will detain you here." "Oh, no; I have not disposed of my shingles yet" [of which he had brought a load.] I called Bro. Billy Merack, who had a cart close by, and requested him to go to my house and get a bed. He said, "Oh, no, I will take one from my own house, it is nearer." He did so, and removed my old mother carefully and tenderly to my home. I offered to pay him for his trouble, but he would not accept any remuneration. On my way back to my work my friends, white and colored, congratulated me and rejoiced with me in the fact that my dear old slave mother had found a home where she could be tenderly cared for by her loving son. I called at Dr. James F. McCree's office and requested him to come and prescribe for my mother. He did so, prepared a remedy, and sent it to my house, for which I offered to pay him, but he would not take anything. My dear old mother survived three years after this, when God called her from a life of toil and suffering to her reward. She called me to her bedside a few hours before she breathed her last, and said, "My son, preach the gospel faithfully, and meet me in heaven." I promised her I would, by the help of God. There were several of my colored brothers and sisters present. She shook hands with all of them, and said, "Meet me in heaven." My dear father died in April, 1848. He left a testimony I shall never forget while here on earth I stay.

I do not regret the sleepless nights or the privations and toil I endured on their account. It is one of the greatest comforts of my life to know that I was permitted to minister to their needs in their last days. My friends often said to me, "Uncle Peter, you cannot care for your parents to the end; you have the additional burden of your mother-in-law." But I told them God would help me through; and all praise to his dear name, he did. I had many white friends who furnished me all the work I could do, and if I needed money at any time I could borrow any amount without security. I have many warm friends with noble hearts in New England to-day. I said when a slave I would never leave my old father and mother to suffer, and I kept my word.

TESTIMONIALS.

To the Friends of the hunted American Slave in England:

BOSTON, March 29, 1851.

In consequence of the passage of the Fugitive Slave Law, at the last session of Congress, a general flight from the country of all fugitive slaves in the Northern States has become necessary as a matter of personal safety. Among the number thus compelled to leave is the bearer of this, Thomas H. Jones, a Wesleyan preacher, and a pastor of a colored church in the neighboring city of Salem, who carries with him a narrative of his life for sale. My personal acquaintance with him is limited; but those among my friends who know him intimately speak of him as a most worthy man, and one peculiarly entitled to the sympathy and aid of those who love God and regard man. Though he is a man, "created a little lower than the angels"—exemplary in life—a servant and minister of Jesus Christ—in all the United States there is not a spot on which he can stand in safety from pursuing bloodhounds, and must flee to England to prevent being again reduced to the condition of a beast! May the God of the oppressed raise him up many friends abroad!

WM. LLOYD GARRISON.

LYNN, Jan. 16, 1859.

I have been for several years well acquainted with the bearer of this note, Rev. Thomas H. Jones, and it is a pleasure to me to recommend him cordially to all who love God, humanity and freedom. He was forty-three years a slave, but by great courage, industry and perseverance, has fought his way to freedom of body and spirit, and has devoted himself with fidelity and success to the spiritual salvation of men. He has a family, part free and part yet in bonds, whose wants roll heavy responsibilities on him as a husband and father, and is therefore obliged to toil hard for daily bread. I bespeak for him the sympathy and benevolence of the public as an earnest, honest Christian man, worthy of all confidence that he may claim, and of all assistance that he may solicit.

FALES H. NEWHALL,
Pastor of South Street M.E. church.

WILMINGTON, April 25, 1857.

I am personally acquainted with Rev. Thomas H. Jones, a fugitive from slavery. During the past two years have heard him preach and lecture to large congregations with much acceptance.

Bro. Jones is a warm-hearted Christian and a worthy minister of Jesus Christ.

It will do any people good to hear him tell the "Story of his wrongs."

ORIGEN SMITH,
Pastor of the Baptist church in Dover, Vt.

GREENWICH, March 9, 1857.

This may certify that Thomas H. Jones, a fugitive from Southern bondage, lectured to us last evening in a very acceptable manner, and enlisted the interest and sympathy of the people in no ordinary degree. He is a true man and a beloved brother and a fellow-laborer in the Lord. He leaves behind him in his departure a pleasant impression, both in the family and in public. He is hereby commended to the kind regards and friendly aid of all who love the Divine Redeemer, and have sympathy with the oppressed.

E. P. BLODGETT.

PORTLAND, April 1, 1857.

Dear Brother Garnet:

This will introduce you to the Rev. Thos. H. Jones, who has been a slave in North Carolina, and who like thousands of others has been obliged to flee, and seek an asylum on British soil. He is a good brother, and considering his advantages, few can go before him as a lecturer. He has been for the last year settled in Salem, Mass., and has also lectured in most of the New England states, and I believe generally with acceptance; he has lectured and preached in my church; and I trust that he may meet with as kind acceptance in old England as what he has in New England.

Yours, with respect,

A. N. FREEMAN.

ST. JOHN, New Brunswick, June, 1851.

My Dear Brother Gallaway:

Mr. Jones, an emancipated slave, is on his way to Great Britain. He has been here for a few weeks—has occupied your old pulpit in the basement story, and mine too, much to the pleasure and enjoyment of our people. He is a very interesting and excellent man. If you can do anything to promote his interest in the great metropolis, you will, for the sake of humanity, for the sake of an old friend; and above all, for Christ's sake "remember the slave." He is a free man in Christ. Aid him, take him by the hand and receive him as a brother, and may the Lord free the spiritually bound.

Ever your affectionate brother,

R. IRVIN, Presbyterian minister.
Rev. J. C. GALLAWAY, London.

ST. JOHN, New Brunswick, B.N.A, June 9th, 1851.

DEAR BROTHER,—Knowing that you have an interest in the slave, permit me to introduce a fugitive one to your notice. He has with him a published narrative of his own life and hardships, and testimonials as to character. He has been in our city some weeks, has delivered public lectures, attended prayer-meetings, and preached for ministers of different denominations. From what I have seen of Mr. Jones, I am favorably impressed, and commend him to your confidence and love.

Yours in Christ,

J. D. CASWELL.

Rev. Dr. HOBY, or HOWARD HINTON, London.

LIVERPOOL, Nova Scotia, Oct. 21, 1852.

Rev. Dr. Campbell:

MY DEAR SIR, — This letter will be handed you by the Rev. Thomas H. Jones, a Wesleyan Methodist minister, and a fugitive slave. Mr. Jones came to me about a twelvemonth ago, highly recommended by ministers and gentlemen in New Brunswick and the United States. I have found him to be a worthy, good, grateful man. I introduced Mr. Jones to Mr. Gallaway, when on his mission here. Mr. Jones bought his wife's freedom when he was a slave. He then made his own escape, God helping him. His wife has a son toiling in bondage in the swamps of North Carolina. The owner of this youth, a female human form, (I will not pollute the name of WOMAN by applying it to her,) has written the mother to say she may have her son for $800. Mr. Jones wants to beg the money. He has got something towards it. I know Mrs. Jones; she is a kind, well-behaved, motherly woman. She has sat at my table, and when I have looked at her my heart has been wrung at the thought of her son, being treated worse than a brute, employed in carrying railroad sleepers on his back out of the swamps at the back of Wilmington. I am doing all I can for the "Banner's Witness" and "Penny Magazine" in these regions. Last month a very aged man (85) applied for admission into our church here, his mind enlightened and convinced by reading the "Witness." Formerly a Methodist, he has been a wanderer for 26 years. You have my earnest prayers and sympathies. Gorham Cole is prospering; upwards of forty students, and more applications. I trust you may have heart and health and mind for your huge task.

Yours very truly,

FREDERICK TOMPKINS.

BENNINGTON, Feb. 1, 1855.

To all whom it may concern:

I take the liberty of introducing the bearer of this, Bro. Thomas H. Jones, for forty years and more a southern bondman, but a Christian man and a minister of the Wesleyan Methodist church. His letters are very satisfactory, and I believe him to be all that he professes to be, a true man and a warm-hearted lover of the Saviour. He has lectured to large audiences in our village with great acceptance, and to the entire satisfaction of all, so far as I have heard. We believe him to be a true-hearted and zealous servant of Jesus Christ, and truly deserving of the sympathy and aid of the Christian public. I have no hesitation in saying that I believe that every friend of Jesus and of humanity will be pleased and edified by his conversation and public labors.

ENSIGN STOOER,
Pastor of the Methodist E. church in Bennington, Vt.

WILBRAHAM, Jan. 1, 1856.

I cordially commend the bearer, Thomas H. Jones, to all Christian and humane people. I believe him to be a worthy man, and an excellent Christian.

J. D. BRIDGE.

I can heartily respond amen to the above testimonial in favor of Brother Jones, from a presiding elder in the Methodist church, and would furthermore add that the bearer is not only "a worthy man and an excellent Christian," but an interesting anti-slavery lecturer, or a very acceptable preacher of the gospel. Receive him as a brother beloved, and aid him for the sake of Christ, his Master, and the cause of suffering humanity.

WM. C. WHITCOMB.
Globe Village, Southbridge, Mass., March 10, 1856.

WARDSBORO', Vt., June 30, 1857.

Dear Bro. Eastman:

I am happy to introduce to you Rev. Bro. Thomas H. Jones, a fugitive from slavery. He has been lecturing and preaching in this town, to the great satisfaction of the people. You will aid the cause of God and suffering humanity by facilitating his labors. He has abundant credentials and testimonials, and the spirit of ardent piety that he breathes, and the "marks of the Lord Jesus" upon his person, will very soon endear him to your heart.

Yours affectionately,

K. HADLEY.

APRIL 25, 1859.

This certifies that I believe the bearer, Rev. Thomas H. Jones, to be a man of untarnished Christian character and worthy of the confidence of the public. Personal acquaintance, as well as the best of recommendations, has convinced me of his untiring devotion to the cause of God and human freedom. His history, made thrilling by cruelty, will increase our hatred of oppression, his genial society will cheer the fireside, and his piety will hallow the means of grace. Aid him and you will bless a worthy brother, honor God, and elevate the race.

J. H. MANSFIELD,
Pastor of Union Street church, Lynn.

CUSTOM HOUSE, Boston, Collector's Office, June 22, 1867.
DEAR SIR, — I have known Rev. Mr. Jones many years as an honest, upright and worthy man, and I have seen no reason for losing my confidence in his integrity.
Yours very truly,

THOMAS RUSSELL.
LUTHER WAGONER, Esq.

Rev. Thomas H. Jones was some years since introduced to me by clergymen in whom I put great confidence, in terms of high commendation. I was interested in the narrative of his life which he has published, and have since known him as an unusually intelligent laborer among his colored brethren, and an earnest advocate of Republican and Temperance principles.

ROBERT C. PITMAN.
New Bedford, Dec. 17, 1867.

NEW BEDFORD, October 20, 1869.
The bearer of this note, the Rev. Thomas H. Jones, I cordially recommend. My intercourse with him during the last two years, has shown him to be a true laborer in the cause of Jesus. He is a thorough temperance man, and is ready and anxious to labor. May be have the cordial greeting of Christians wherever he may go, is the desire of

GEO. B. RICHMOND,
President of the Young Men's Christian Association.

HAVERHILL, Mass., May 14, 1878.

To whom it may concern:
This is to certify that I have known for a number of years the bearer, Rev.

Thomas Jones. As an upright, Christian man, he has always inspired my respect. I cheerfully recommend him to any who may need his services.

J. M. DURRELL,

Pastor of the First M.E. church.

BEVERLY FARMS, June 23, 1879.

My Dear Brother:

The bearer, Rev. Thomas H. Jones, I have met recently and conversed with, with much pleasure. You will find him an intelligent, earnest Christian and temperance worker, I have no doubt. His history and labors are very interesting. It gives me pleasure to introduce him.

Fraternally yours,

D. P. MORGAN.

BEVERLY FARMS, May 16, 1879.

Dear Bro. Gorham:

I think I have already spoken to you or to some of your people favorably of Bro. Thomas H. Jones, who has been spending a fortnight in our village and in Centreville. He will now bear to you this note in person, as his introduction. He came to me well recommended by Bro. Morgan, and from all I have seen of him, in our meetings and in private intercourse, I feel free to indorse fully all Bro. M.'s ideas of the piety and intelligence of the man. He has spoken several times in our chapel to large and deeply interested audiences. He is poor, and will gratefully acknowledge any help you can render him in disposing of his little book, or in securing a collection.

Very truly yours,

C. W. REDING.

BOSTON, Mass., July 19, 1880.

23 School St.

To whom it may concern:

We are all one in Christ Jesus, and "God is no respecter of persons." Thirty years have passed since the first testimonial was written in recommendation of the brother whose experience is herein narrated, Rev. Thomas H. Jones. We can but say that we know that during those years passed he has fully lived up to all that has been said in them, fulfilling all the expectations of those who in those early years, when it was but to be stigmatized, so willingly outstretched their hands to help and protect him. The sufferings in mind and body endured by him should warm all hearts toward him, to lend him a helping hand. His recital of the wrongs borne by him and his at the hands of his fellowman is most interesting and affecting. No compensation in this world, given to him or to those who have suffered in like manner, will ever repay them for their bitter trials and anguish. So we can thank God that the time is soon coming when the oppressed of every nation who have sought Christ will through him receive eternal life in his kingdom where "there shall be no more sorrow nor crying, neither shall there be any more pain, for the former things are passed away."

May the God of the armies of Israel strengthen and guide him. When the general roll is called may he sit down with us, with Abraham, Isaac, and Jacob, in the Kingdom of God, to go no more out forever.

Yours in the blessed hope,

F. S. CLIFFORD.

NEWBURYPORT, Mass., September 13, 1879.

To whom it may concern:

This will certify that the bearer, Thomas H. Jones, is a Christian brother in whom the Christian public may have confidence. After an acquaintance of several years, I most cheerfully commend him as a Christian brother worthy of support and fellowship.

DANIEL P. PIKE,
Pastor of the Christian church, Newburyport, Mass.

BOSTON, June 22, 1880.

I have known Brother Thomas H. Jones for some eight or ten years. I have always regarded him as an honest and respectable person, and a zealous Christian man.

Very truly yours,

B. B. RUSSELL.

BOSTON, July 21, 1880.

I have known the Rev. Thomas H. Jones for thirty-one years, and have respected him as a faithful, honest, conscientious citizen. His story should win for him the sympathy of all good and generous people.

JOHN L. SWIFT.

BOSTON, Mass., July 23, 1880.

I have known the Rev. Thomas H. Jones for some years, and I believe him to be an honest, upright man, a good citizen, and one of the most earnest, energetic men in the gospel work, and as such I can recommend him to the public.

OZIAS GOODRICH,

Treasurer and Business Agent of the A.C.P. Society.

LYNN, Aug. 3, 1880.

Having been for many years acquainted with the bearer, Rev. Thomas H. Jones, I take great pleasure in commending him to the favorable consideration of the public, as a man of good Christian character, of courage and energy, as seen in his lifting himself from the condition of a slave to that of a freeman before emancipation day, and of kindly and courteous bearing. His history is one of those marvels of the days of slavery, and cannot be read by a free people without both shame and profit. To the rising generation it will be stranger than fiction.

D. SHERMAN,

Ed. N. Eng. Methodist.

THIRD EDITION[28]

Notes

1. David Smith Jr. (1791–1830), printer and editor of the *Cape Fear Recorder*, Wilmington.

2. See John 3:1–21.

3. A traditional religious ceremony involving a worship service and a communal meal.

4. From a hymn by Joseph Hart (1712–1768).

5. Owen Holmes (1795–1840), a Wilmington attorney.

6. "The Avenger," an anonymous poem previously published in Frederick Douglass's abolitionist newspaper the *North Star* on February 11, 1848.

7. New Bern is about ninety miles north of Wilmington.

8. Hartford, the capital of Connecticut, is about 100 miles north of New York.

9. Passed in 1850, the Fugitive Slave Act required northern states that had protected fugitive slaves with personal liberty laws to assist in the capture and return of all escaped slaves.

10. Apparently, a nickname for Jones, possibly alluding to the ministry of St. Peter.

11. William Lloyd Garrison (1805–79), a founder of the American Anti-Slavery Society and the publisher of the *Liberator*, an abolitionist newspaper.

12. Sampson County is about seventy miles northwest of Wilmington.

13. From a hymn by William Cowper (1731–1800).

14. Clinton is the seat of Sampson County.

15. From a hymn by Charles Wesley (1707–88).

16. Matthew 11:28: "Come to me all you who are weary and carrying heavy burdens, and I will give you rest."

17. A traditional hymn.

18. John Greenleaf Whittier (1807–92), abolitionist, poet, and editor.

19. A watch meeting is a traditional nightlong service held on Christmas Eve or New Year's Eve. The service culminates in a fellowship meal at dawn.

20. The Washington Temperance Society was founded in Baltimore in 1842.

21. Fort Fisher is a coastal village ten miles south of Wilmington.

22. A traditional hymn.

23. From a traditional hymn.

24. Halifax is the capital of the Canadian province of Nova Scotia.

25. Yarmouth is city in Nova Scotia 140 miles south of Halifax.

26. Samuel May (1810–99) and Wendell Phillips (1811–84), prominent abolitionists.

27. John Brown (1800–1859), the zealous abolitionist who led a fatal raid on the U.S. Army Armory at Harpers Ferry, Virginia.

28. A notation that signals that this is the third edition printed by E. A. Anthony and Sons.

Made in the USA
Middletown, DE
06 August 2021